SEND OUT YOUR SPIRIT

SEND OUT YOUR SPIRIT

A Confirmation Candidate's
Handbook for Faith

MICHAEL AMODEI

ave maria press   notre dame, indiana

Dedicated to: Notre Dame du Lac

© 2003, 2010 by Ave Maria Press, Inc.

All rights reserved. No part of this book may be used or reproduced in any manner whatsoever, except in the case of reprints in the context of reviews, without written permission from Ave Maria Press, Inc., P.O. Box 428, Notre Dame, IN 46556.

Founded in 1865, Ave Maria Press is a ministry of the Indiana Province of Holy Cross.

Engaging Minds, Hearts, and Hands for Faith® is a trademark of Ave Maria Press, Inc.

www.avemariapress.com

ISBN: 1-59471-225-5 ISBN-13: 978-1-59471-225-8

Cover image © Thinkstock.com

Cover and text design by Katherine Robinson Coleman.

Bill Wittman: p. x, 90, 118, 142, 147, 184, 195, 206, 213, 217.

iStockphoto.com: 3, 7, 15, 17, 21, 22, 25, 29, 32, 36, 44, 71, 73, 80, 82, 104, 115, 116, 150, 156, 160, 162, 172, 186, 191, 197.

Thinkstockphotos.com: 10, 40, 55, 58, 61, 63, 64, 67, 77, 88, 99, 102, 140, 141, 154, 163, 166, 175, 205, 211, 226.

Printed and bound in the United States of America.

CONTENTS

Introduction vii

one   Belonging 1

two   God 23

three   Jesus Christ 45

four   Scripture 65

five   Church 91

six   Morality 119

seven   Social Justice 143

eight   Liturgy and Sacraments 163

nine   Holy Spirit and Confirmation 185

ten   Your Christian Vocation 207

Appendix: Catholic Handbook for Faith 227

Glossary 238

Engaging Minds, Hearts, and Hands for Faith®

An education that is complete is the one in which the hands and heart are engaged as much as the mind. We want to let our students try their learning in the world and so make prayers of their education.

Blessed Basil Moreau
Founder of the Congregation of Holy Cross

Preparation for Confirmation and reception of the sacrament will lead you to a more intimate relationship with Jesus Christ and a greater familiarity with the Holy Spirit. It will also prepare you for a meaningful celebration of the liturgy and a deeper commitment to Christ and the Church. This book will help in the following ways:

By understanding the foundational elements of the faith through the study of Scripture, essential doctrine, vocabulary, and the deep richness of the liturgy and sacraments.

By careful reflection on the Truth of Jesus Christ through the guidance of the Holy Spirit.

By active participation in several works in service of others. These are accomplished on your own, with your sponsor, and together with the other candidates preparing for Confirmation.

INTRODUCTION

As you prepare for and receive the Sacrament of Confirmation, the name "Christian" becomes a more profound part of who you are.

Christian comes from the name of Christ which means "anointed." Christ was the anointed one of God, anointed by the Holy Spirit. An anointing with sacred oil called chrism is the essential rite of the Sacrament of Confirmation. An anointing is meaningful because it highlights the name "Christian."

What will this mean for you?

When you were an infant, your family came to the Catholic Church and were asked what they wanted for you. Acting for you, they answered, "Faith." At your Baptism, you received the gift of faith, the grace of God giving himself to you. You became a member of Christ's Body, the Church.

Your parents not only accepted this gift for you, but they promised to share it with you as you grew.

Now it is your turn to make a public statement accepting the gift of faith.

Remember: Baptism is the essential sacrament. It does not need to be ratified to make it effective. But, by preparing for and receiving the Sacrament of Confirmation, you will *confirm* the promises made at your Baptism and *strengthen* the gift of baptismal grace.

This preparation is intended to lead you to a deeper relationship with Christ and a greater knowledge of the Holy Spirit in order to be more capable of assuming the responsibilities of Christian life.

May God—Father, Son, and Holy Spirit—be with you now and forever.

About This Book

Send Out Your Spirit is intended to teach and remind you of the risks, challenges, and rewards of being a Christian. Hopefully you will be able to break open the chapters of this book with other teenagers preparing for Confirmation, with able parish catechists, with your pastor, with your Confirmation sponsor, and with your parents. These people have been and continue to be your teachers in the faith and your model of the Church.

Use this book for what it is, a chance to whet your appetite for a deeper relationship with Jesus and a stronger faith as you decide, with the help of the Holy Spirit, how you will uniquely take on and live the name Christian.

one

$\mathcal{B}$ELONGING

Are you unaware that we who were baptized into Christ Jesus were baptized into his death? We were indeed buried with him through baptism into death, so that, just as Christ was raised from the dead by the glory of the Father, we too might live in newness of life.

Romans 6:3–6

Being Catholic

Have you ever been asked to list your "religious preference" when filling out an application, maybe for a scholarship or award? If you are beginning this book about the Sacrament of Confirmation, it is a safe bet to assume that you are able to write down the words "Catholic" or "Roman Catholic" when asked that type of question.

If so, how do you think of yourself as *Catholic*? What are some things that come to mind that define you as Catholic? You might say things like:

My family is Catholic. (Or my mom's side of the family is Catholic.)

I was baptized and I made my First Communion in the Catholic Church.

I go to Mass on Sunday.

I believe in Jesus.

I hold the same strong views that the Church teaches (for example, that life begins at conception and that sex should be saved until after marriage).

I am preparing for Confirmation, aren't I?!

The list above and more things besides are certainly things that would define a person as Catholic. If you can agree to most of these things, you can certainly write down the word "Catholic" under any items about your religious preference. But are items on a checklist all that it really takes to make you or anyone else a Catholic? A further and deeper question might be: How do my *desire and attitude* in these areas affect the kind of Catholic that I am?

Francis Bernardone of Assisi was what might be called a "rote Catholic" until young adulthood. At age twenty, Francis, the son of a wealthy clothing merchant, Peter Bernardone, became a knight. His father had purchased for him the most expensive armor, shields, banners, and weapons. That didn't matter. When his troop suffered a defeat, Francis was captured and imprisoned for several months before being sent home. While convalescing, Francis sought out answers to the age-old questions: Who am I? Where do I come from? Where am I going? The answers Francis received came from the basic knowledge of his Catholic faith that he had always known but never clearly made a decision to embrace.

One night he had a dream that changed his life. In the dream, he could envision all the spoils of military victory: trophies, a palace to live in, and even a beautiful wife to be his companion. Francis woke up in a sweat. He could tell that he was destined for some kind of glory—the kind he really wanted.

After recovering, Francis headed off to Southern Italy to re-enlist. On the way there he camped along the road and heard the same voice that he had heard in his dream. The voice spoke: "Francis, who can do more for you, the servant or the master?" Francis answered: "Why the master, of course." The voice responded in a way that led to permanent implications both for Francis's life and the life of the Church: "Why, then, are you seeking the servant instead of the master, the vassal instead of the prince?"

Francis recognized the voice as the voice of Christ. "Lord," he asked, "what will you have me do?"

"Return home. Your vision will have its spiritual fulfillment through me."

Francis's life was never the same again. He was never again a "rote Catholic." Rather, he forsook his father and his father's inheritance, stripped the clothing off his own back, and went to live in a cave. He soon attracted a group of men and women followers to his life of simplicity and sincere practice of Christ's Gospel. In 1209, Francis wrote a *Rule of Life* for his followers that has been followed ever since. Composed of Gospel texts and some very few precepts, this Rule aims at guiding committed Catholics to walk in the footsteps of Christ.

Is such a life of conversion possible among Catholics today? Can *rote* Catholics become *committed* Catholics? What about you? What scares you about going beyond the simple definition for being a Catholic? How can you be called and inspired to do God's will in such an unglamorous (remember, Francis lived in a cave) but lasting way? What can you do in your own life to incorporate the Gospel of Jesus Christ and your Catholic faith to the very core of your being? What can you do to at least *want* that to occur?

If you're reading this, you may be beginning your preparation for the Sacrament of Confirmation. Or, you may be nearing the time when you will receive the Sacrament of Confirmation. In either case, you will know that Confirmation is a Sacrament of Initiation, and, if you have already been baptized and received the Sacrament of the Eucharist, that Confirmation "completes" your initiation into the Catholic Church.

But what does "completion" mean in this case? Does it only mean that you are "completed" with "Confirmation class" or "religious education?" Is the sacrament like a graduation from school where the graduate never sets foot in the school corridors again?

After all of the effort you may have expended in preparing for Confirmation, do you feel you might deserve a time to retreat from the Church, perhaps enjoy the high school years with your friends without thinking about God at all?

Or, do you think you will be drawn to a more grown-up practice of your faith?

Have you heard Jesus' personal call to you to put him—not the ways of the world—first? These are some of the questions you may ponder as the time of the Sacrament of Confirmation approaches.

Interestingly, the timing of Confirmation has quite a bit to do with whether you are willing and able to take on an adult-level commitment to the faith. As you may have already observed, the age where Catholics participate in the initiation process varies greatly in the Catholic Church. In fact, you may note that one of your buddies from another parish has only eight weeks of preparation or you may wonder why a grade-school friend of the family was confirmed at the same time she made her First Communion. In fact, these types of variations in Christian initiation have always existed.

Essential Elements of Christian Initiation

From the earliest times, becoming a Christian was viewed as a journey that could be long or short. The initiation of a new Christian took place in several stages. There were always essential elements in the journey:

✚ Baptism

The first Sacrament of Initiation. It is "the basis of the whole Christian life, the gateway to life in the Spirit, and the door which gives access to the other sacraments" (CCC, 1213).

✚ Confirmation

A Sacrament of Initiation, it is sometimes known as the Sacrament of the Holy Spirit. It completes Baptism and seals the recipient with the Holy Spirit and confers the seven gifts of the Holy Spirit.

✚ catechumenate

The process of study, prayer, and participation in community for the purpose of preparing for the Sacraments of Initiation.

⋯➔ the hearing and acceptance of the Good News of Christ

⋯➔ the making of a profession of faith

⋯➔ **Baptism**

⋯➔ **Confirmation**, which more perfectly binds the Christian to the Church and enriches him or her with a special strength of the Holy Spirit (CCC, 1285)

⋯➔ full welcome into the Church through receiving Holy Communion

At first, a long period of **catechumenate** ("period of instruction") pretty much proceeded in the order described above, with culmination being the reception of all three sacraments on the vigil of Easter. Confirmation was a rite of laying on of hands directly connected with Baptism. A key point in this process was that it was reserved for adults.

The process changed with the advent of more infant Baptisms. At that point, the elements were still part of the process, though done in a very abridged way, with the preparation directed not to the infant, of course, but to the parents and godparents.

At the Second Vatican Council in the 1960s, the Church restored the original catechumenate process for adults. It also continued baptizing infants, with the understanding that a catechesis for the infant would take place in the years following and would later include preparation for and reception of Eucharist and Confirmation.

That's where we are now. If you were baptized as a baby, you probably celebrated your First Communion (and the Sacrament of Penance) in the second grade. Confirmation preparation could have come at the same time, but more likely, because you are reading this book, was reserved for right now.

With all the different variations in practice, there is no doubt that questions and dilemmas within the processes will arise. The question is, how to settle them? To do so requires more understanding of the essential elements of the catechumenate process and of the Sacraments of Initiation themselves.

Only then can you attempt to answer the bigger questions: "How can I become a more committed disciple of Jesus Christ?" "How do I belong to the Church?" "How can I be more than a rote Catholic?"

Look up and write five interesting facts about the life of St. Francis of Assisi.

What have been the consistent elements of Christian initiation?

Where do you find yourself on the spectrum between a "rote Catholic" and a "committed Catholic"? Explain.

Christian Initiation: Back to the Beginning

If it is any solace to those who question the timing of Christian initiation, history and circumstances have always contributed to how great or how little difficulty there is to become a Christian.

For example, after the **Apostles** first received the Holy Spirit at **Pentecost**, Peter stepped out on the balcony of the Upper Room in Jerusalem (the place where Jesus had shared his Last Supper) and spoke convincingly to the Jewish crowds gathered in the street below.

✔ Apostles

The Apostles are those who are "sent" to be Christ's ambassadors, to continue his work. In its widest sense, the term refers to all of Christ's disciples whose mission is to preach his Gospel in word and deed. It also refers to the Twelve whom Jesus chose to help him in his earthly ministry. The successors of the Twelve Apostles are the bishops.

✔ Pentecost

The day when the Holy Spirit descended on the Apostles and gave them the power to preach with conviction the message that Jesus is risen and is Lord of the universe.

Jews from many different neighboring regions in Jerusalem were there to celebrate the Feast of the First Fruits. By the end of the day, the Scriptures report, about three thousand of those who listened to Peter accepted the message about Jesus Christ and were baptized.

This relatively easy road to the Church is contrasted with a more difficult challenge faced by other potential new Christians described in the very same book of the New Testament. At first, the "New Way," as the Church was described, was thought only to be an extension of Judaism. All of the Christians had been raised Jewish. Jesus himself was a Jew.

🖢 Gentiles

The name for anyone not of the Jewish faith; a Christian.

When **Gentiles** began to hear and accept the Good News, they too were baptized. St. Paul—known as the Apostle to the Gentiles—was the leader of this movement. But disagreements arose about this. Some of the converted Jews wanted any of the baptized Gentiles to observe all the laws of Judaism completely. This included, in their belief, the circumcision of the Gentile males as well as observance of all of the Jewish dietary laws. This debate became the subject of a gathering of Church leaders at the Council of Jerusalem. Both sides presented their cases. Finally, the Apostle James offered the final decision:

> It is my judgment, therefore, that we ought to stop troubling the Gentiles who turn to God, but tell them by letter to avoid pollution from idols, unlawful marriage, the meat of strangled animals, and blood. (Acts 15:19–20)

Gentile Christians were spared some of the more difficult requirements of Judaism (most significantly, circumcision), and Christianity left behind some of its Jewish roots. But the process of Christian initiation did not become significantly easier in the next two centuries.

Development of the Catechumenate

Until AD 313, it was illegal to be a Christian in the Roman Empire. So the undertaking of new converts seeking Baptism was both a courageous and difficult one. It was always an answer to God's call that spurred a person on his or her way.

🖢 martyrdom

The state of choosing to suffer and give up one's life for faith rather than renouncing it.

Besides the built-in dangers associated with illegal Christianity—including persecution and **martyrdom**—the catechumenate itself was difficult. First of all, it was a three-year process. The candidate—sponsored by a baptized Christian—studied Christianity, prayed, fasted, and proved to be up to the challenge of choosing a lifestyle that could bring death.

During Lent of the person's third year of the catechumenate, a more intense immediate preparation began. The catechumen studied the articles of the Apostle's Creed as well as the words of the Lord's Prayer. On Holy Thursday, a final flurry of activity began. The candidates bathed and then began two days of complete fasting until the Saturday night vigil of Easter.

On that night, they were brought by their sponsors to the church at dusk. The local bishop presided over the entire service. First, the candidates were asked to renounce Satan and tell of their desire for Christ. While doing this, they turned from the West and its oncoming darkness to the East, the place of the rising sun and hope for new life.

Next, the candidates were baptized by the bishop. This took place in a submerged pool with three steps leading in and three steps leading out, signifying the three days Christ spent in the tomb. Oil was poured over each candidate's head as they entered the waters. The bishop then plunged each candidate's head three times, baptizing them "in the name of the Father, and of the Son, and of the Holy Spirit." On their way out of the pool, their five senses were anointed with oil, and each was given a white robe to wear and a lighted candle to hold to signify their new life in Christ.

The bishop also laid his hands on the new Christians and prayed for the Holy Spirit to come to them. This is the part of the ceremony that is the Sacrament of Confirmation. Finally, the Mass continued. The new Christians were permitted to remain for the Liturgy of the Eucharist for the very first time. The culmination of the initiation process was their reception of their First Communion.

After Easter, while now full members of the Church, another special period began. The new Christians—now called **neophytes**—were not left alone to merely sink or swim with the other long-time Church members. Another time of study and intense prayer began, known as **mystagogia**, where the neophytes could gradually assume their new role in the community. This time lasted at least to Pentecost, and usually beyond.

✝ neophytes

Those newly received into the Church through the Sacraments of Initiation at the Easter Vigil.

✝ mystagogia

A period of intense prayer in which neophytes can gradually assume their role in the Church.

"I AM A CHRISTIAN: WITH US, NOTHING EVIL HAPPENS"

The words above were spoken by a teenage girl named Blandina as she hung by a stake in the Roman amphitheater in 177 while wild animals roamed near to her. It was the month of August, and to celebrate Rome and the emperor, Christians were being displayed and tortured to provide entertainment as part of the festival. It was much cheaper entertainment than paying for gladiators and other professionals.

Blandina had been captured in Lyons, Gaul, which is in present-day France. She was a slave girl, and she was converted to Christianity with the entire household of her master. Sometimes slaves would renounce the Christian faith of their masters in order to be set free. But Blandina did not. Lyons was a newly converted area, and many of the locals' suspicions of Christians translated to their being beaten, robbed, and turned over to the civil authorities.

The captured Christians were confined for hours, days, and weeks in cramped prison cells where many died. Others had their flesh burned. Still others were placed in stocks. The survivors were taken to the amphitheater where beasts like wild lions would be released to devour them.

The youthful girl hanging from a stake seemed to inspire the crowd as she clearly resembled the crucified Christ. None of the animals came near Blandina, and she was removed from the stake only to return for another day of torture. This time she was ready to face her death, a death for Christ. She was placed in a large net and thrown on the ground. The lion toyed with her for a while, lancing her until she eventually bled to death. A passage from the *Letter of Lyons* describes the final scene:

> They were astonished that she still breathed, her body torn and wounded. They admitted that a single one of their tortures was enough to take away life; how much more such great tortures and so many of them. On the contrary, Blandina, like a generous athlete was renewed in her confession. For her, it was a comfort, a rest, a pause in suffering to say only: "I am a Christian: with us nothing evil happens."

How can you proclaim to others, no matter the place or with whom, "I am a Christian"?

Baptism of Blood, Baptism of Desire

As mentioned, the first three centuries of Christianity were dangerous ones. Christians were viewed by the Roman government as subversives because of their refusal to recognize the divinity of the Roman emperor, serve in the Roman army, and in some cases pay taxes to the emperor. Christians were hunted down, jailed, persecuted, and often martyred in brutal ways, including being fed to ferocious animals.

Sometimes, as the catechumenate process stretched for three years, a candidate preparing for Baptism never made it to the Easter vigil ceremony before being put to death. The Church never hesitated in declaring that their martyrdom—called a **baptism of blood**—was the equivalent of a baptism of water. Tertullian called the baptism of blood "a baptism which takes the place of the baptism of water when it has not been received, and which restores it when it has been lost."

baptism of blood

A martyr for the Christian faith who died before he or she could receive the sacrament receives a baptism of blood. The effects are the complete remission of sin and immediate entrance into Heaven.

Salvation

The extension of God's forgiveness, grace, and healing to the world through Jesus Christ in the Holy Spirit.

In the same way, catechumens who died a natural death before being baptized are also assured of the **Salvation** that they were not able to receive through the sacrament, because of their "desire to receive it, together with repentance for their sins, and charity" (*CCC*, 1259).

 What is the meaning of the term "baptism of blood"?

 Why was the process of becoming a Christian a dangerous one in the first three centuries?

Why do you think Jewish Christians wanted Gentile Christians to follow Mosaic law?

 How can you support your parish catechumens preparing for initiation?

Two Rites of Initiation

Everything changed in 313 when the Emperor Constantine was won over by his Christian mother Helen and agreed to make Christianity the official religion of the empire. What an extreme difference this made!

Now Christians could come out of hiding and go public with their faith. Entire families (including those with young children) sought Baptism. Prior to this time it was the bishop's role to preside at every Baptism. The sheer number of Baptisms would now prohibit him from doing this, so it was determined that presbyters (priests) could be the official ministers of Baptism. However, the bishops wanted to retain some role in the Sacraments of Initiation. They decided to administer a post-baptismal rite of the laying on of hands (later known as Confirmation) together with a large contingent of newly baptized. Sometimes this ceremony would take place many years after the Baptism, usually whenever the bishop could make time to come to a particular local parish.

Infant Baptism was not a completely new phenomenon, however. From the time of the Apostles, young children had been baptized. In fact, when Peter spoke from the window of the Upper Room on Pentecost, he said, "Repent and be baptized, every one of you, in the name of Jesus Christ for the forgiveness of your sins; and you will receive the gift of the Holy Spirit" (Acts 2:38).

Note that Peter said, "*every* one of you." He also added, "For the promise is made to you and to your children and to . . . whomever the Lord our God will call" (Acts 2:39). The New Testament also cites other examples of entire households that were baptized. Of course it is assumed that children were a part of each household. Several examples apply (these examples are worth noting because the Catholic practice of infant Baptism is often negatively critiqued by Christian fundamentalists who claim that it has no scriptural basis):

> Referring to a convert named Lydia, "After she and her household had been baptized, she offered us an invitation . . ." (Acts 16:15).

> Referring to a Philippian jailer whom Paul and Silas had converted, "He took them in at that hour of the night and bathed their wounds; then he and all his family were baptized at once" (Acts 16:33).

In his greeting to the Corinthians, Paul said, "I baptized the household of Stephanas also . . ." (1 Cor 1:16).

The increase in infant Baptisms was not only due to the legalization of Christianity, however. In the fifth century, St. Augustine used the term **Original Sin** to explain how all humans are born with the sin of Adam on their souls. One of the graces of Baptism is that *all sins*, personal sins and Original Sin, are forgiven. Thus in a time with high infant mortality, Christian parents sought Baptism for their children in order to purify them from sin, make them children of God, and give them a share of God's life, called sanctifying grace.

At no time did the initiation of adults ever cease. But with the increase in infant Baptisms at that time, both of the Church's rites of initiation were in the forefront.

> ❦ **Original Sin**
>
> The fallen state of human nature into which all generations of people are born. Jesus Christ came to save us from Original Sin.

Rite of Christian Initiation of Adults (RCIA)

The Second Vatican Council restored the catechumenate for adults, with four distinct steps, much as it had been in the early Church. The four steps are:

> ❦ **evangelization**
>
> A period in the catechumenate when a person hears God's Word and responds to it.
>
> ❦ **faith**
>
> One of the theological virtues. Faith is an acknowledgment and allegiance to God.

1. *Evangelization.* A person hears God's Word and initially responds to it. **Evangelization** takes place in many ways. A Catholic models her **faith** in the workplace through word and example, and notice of this is taken by a co-worker who inquires more of her faith. Or, a marquee in front of a Catholic church says simply, "Visitors Always Welcome," encouraging a passerby to come and share in a Sunday liturgy. Prayer, reading, and questioning accompany this stage. At the end of this period, a rite of acceptance is celebrated at Mass. The new candidates are welcomed by the community and plan to take more instruction in the faith.

2. *Catechumenate.* This step may take a full year or longer. The candidates take instruction in a special class held at the parish, are accompanied by a sponsor who answers their questions, do service work in the community, and participate in the Mass through the time of the Liturgy of the Word.

The season of Lent begins their final time of preparation. On the first Sunday of Lent, the candidates travel to the diocesan cathedral where the local bishop enrolls them in the Book of the Elect, naming those who will receive the Sacraments of Initiation.

3. *Purification and Enlightenment.* This step also takes places during Lent. On the Sundays of Lent, rituals known as the scrutinies help the catechumens look deeply at—scrutinize—their lives and do penance for their sins. They are gifted with the Lord's Prayer and the Creed, and promise to make these central to their lives. As in earlier times, this period culminates with the reception of the Sacraments of Initiation—Baptism, Confirmation, and Eucharist—at the Easter Vigil Mass. This Mass begins in literal darkness, representing the darkness of Christ's Death. The Easter candle is then lighted preceding several readings tracing the entirety of Salvation.

4. *Mystagogia.* The newly baptized (neophytes) continue to meet with one another after Easter and at least up until Pentecost. Sometimes these new Church members are so charged with a passion of faith that they try to volunteer themselves in several parish ministries; for example, signing up as a religious education teacher or as part of a meal ministry to the homebound. While these are worthy goals, the Church asks for a type of reflective "cooling off" period so that the neophytes will not be overwhelmed or discouraged as they begin their long life in the Church.

🕊 **RCIA**

Acronym for Rite of Christian Initiation for Adults. The process by which anyone of catechetical age is initiated into the Catholic Church.

You may have noticed some teens your own age who participate in a form of the **RCIA**. Church law requires any person over the age of reason (seven years old) who approaches the Church for Baptism to be prepared for all three Sacraments of Initiation. You may know classmates, acquaintances, or friends initiated through RCIA who do not undergo the same process for Confirmation preparation as you do.

WHAT ARE THE REQUIREMENTS
FOR CONFIRMATION?

As Chapter 1 points out, initiation into the Catholic Church is based on two separate rites. The age when the Sacrament of Confirmation takes place may vary from diocese to diocese and often even among parishes in a dioceses. The *Catechism of the Catholic Church* recommends the "age of discretion" as the reference point for receiving Confirmation. The United States Catholic Bishops decreed that the sacrament should be conferred sometime between the "age of discretion and about sixteen years old."

The immediate preparation for the Sacrament of Confirmation also varies from place to place. Consider the preparation requirements at St. Malachy Catholic Church in the Archdiocese of Boston. Confirmation is celebrated in the high-school years. The preparation covers a two-year period. Most teens at St. Malachy's begin their preparation in ninth grade and are confirmed in tenth grade. The expectations or the Confirmation process involve liturgical, ministerial, spiritual, and educational experiences.

The liturgical requirement is the expectation that the candidates will be regular communicants at the Sunday Eucharist. The parish requirements at St. Malachy's state: "Participation at Eucharist is so fundamental to our understanding of Confirmation as Catholics that one who does not regularly assist at Sunday Eucharist should seriously question whether he or she is ready for this sacrament." The candidate's ministerial component involves participating in ongoing service to the Church and in the world. Put in an objective number, St. Malachy's requires each candidate to do at least fifteen hours of service ministry for each year of preparation. The candidates are also expected to pray daily; for example reading the Bible for fifteen minutes or engaging in a centering prayer in the morning and/or evening. Also, the candidates are expected to attend an extended retreat. The educational component at St. Malachy's is to receive at least two years of high-school-level theology, which may be received in a variety of settings including at the parish or in a Catholic high school. A summary of the Confirmation requirements for St. Malachy's is listed below:

Liturgical

 🔥 Attendance at Mass every Sunday during the course of preparing for Confirmation.

 🔥 Some Sundays candidates, sponsors, and parents are to meet together after the Sunday noon liturgy.

Ministerial

 🔥 At least fifteen hours of ministry/service during the course of the year.

Spiritual

 🔥 Growing in prayer and deepening awareness of God.

 🔥 Participation in a retreat.

Educational

 🔥 Participation in and successful completion of one of the four options outlined in the Confirmation brochure for theology: theology courses at a Catholic high school, liturgy-based catechesis, parish courses, or home study.

How do these requirements compare to those at your parish?

Rite of Baptism of Children (RBC)

The Rite of Baptism of Children is the process that most Catholics are initiated in, at least so-called "cradle Catholics" who are born and raised in Catholic families.

🔥 **godparent**

The sponsor of one who is baptized. The person takes on the role of helping the newly baptized child or adult in the Christian life.

From the time infant Baptisms first became prevalent, the baptismal ritual itself changed. A **godparent** who spoke for the infant replaced the role of the sponsor. Catechetical formation for the infant could definitely not take place before Baptism or even immediately after. (An infant, of course, can't read or even talk too well!) The Rite of Baptism of Children calls for Christian formation and catechesis taking place gradually as the person grows, so that the infant child, grown up, may eventually accept for himself or herself the faith in which they have been baptized.

Part of this acceptance involves the other two Sacraments of Initiation—Confirmation and Eucharist. Early on, Confirmation was held separately from Baptism in the Roman Church in order to preserve the visible role of the bishop, though the Eastern rite (and some Roman Catholic nations in Latin America) continues to confirm babies. First Eucharist was still administered to infants until the thirteenth century; after that it was delayed until the age of eleven or twelve so that the person could understand more about the sacrament. In those years it was likely the child received Confirmation before Eucharist. In the early twentieth century, Pope Pius X moved First Communion to about the age of seven because of his belief that there should be frequent reception of Eucharist by as many people as possible. This meant that Confirmation was then delayed in most cases to a time after First Communion, usually to the junior high or high school years.

Today, many dioceses have moved to restore the original order of reception of the Sacraments of Initiation—Baptism, Confirmation, and Eucharist—with Confirmation now being celebrated with First Eucharist in about the second grade. But more of the dioceses in the United States continue to allow for Confirmation at a later time, stressing commitment and Christian maturity to the teens who receive it. For these reasons, rules are usually set up to determine a candidate's level of commitment and maturity.

Regardless of the age a person is confirmed, it all begins with Baptism. As the *Catechism* describes,

> Holy Baptism is the basis of the whole Christian life, the gateway to life in the Spirit, and the door which gives access to the other sacraments. (1213)

How do we know that infant Baptisms were always performed in the Church?

What was a reason infant Baptisms increased in the fifth century?

Name and explain the four steps of the RCIA process.

Explain how Confirmation fell out of the original order of the Sacraments of Initiation.

What was the date of your Baptism? Why did your parents choose that date?

Name any criticisms you have heard about infant Baptism. How can you answer those criticisms?

Baptism: The Essential Sacrament

If we try to answer succinctly the basic question, "What does it take to be Catholic?" we might respond with one word, "Baptism." After Jesus' Resurrection, he charged his Apostles with this mission: "Go, therefore, and make disciples of all nations, baptizing them in the name of the Father, and of the Son, and of the holy Spirit, teaching them to observe all I have commanded you" (Mt 28:19–20).

As mentioned, the disciples did not refuse baptism of anyone who professed faith in Jesus; both the Jews and pagans who confessed in him received Baptism. Entire families were baptized, indicating that parents took on the responsibility of both accepting and nurturing the faith of their children.

Baptism is the essential sacrament for us because of what it brings: new life in Christ. St. Paul wrote that in Baptism we are "clothed" with Christ (Gal 3:27). Christ lives in us and permeates our entire selves. We share in the common priesthood of Christ with the task of participating in his mission of Salvation. Another way to describe a person baptized is to say he or she is "configured" to Christ. That means we can recognize and grow to know Christ in the baptized Christian. Others can do the same with us.

❦ Church

The Body of Christ on earth. The Church is the community of people who profess faith in Jesus Christ and who are guided by the Holy Spirit. The Roman Catholic Church is guided by the Pope and his bishops.

Baptism makes us part of Christ's Body which is the **Church**. Like the Church, Baptism is necessary for our Salvation. St. Irenaeus wrote that "Baptism indeed is the seal of eternal life." Baptism marks us with a spiritual character that will be with us until the day of our death. This spiritual mark will be with us as we prepare to meet God face to face.

Water: Sign of Life and Death

Certainly, if you play word association with the symbols and rite of Baptism, the first word that comes to mind is "water."

No living thing can survive without water. Water is a sign of life throughout the story of Salvation. The world was created from water;

from a stream welling up out of the earth God formed man (Gn 2: 6–7).

Water is also destructive. The waters of the Great Flood (Gn 7–8) destroyed the world and the closing waters of the Red Sea wiped out the Egyptian soldiers in pursuit of Moses and the Hebrews (Ex 14:23–31). We know this to be the case in floods today.

But, from the destruction, life regenerates again. In the blessing over water at the Easter vigil, the priest says,

> The waters of the great flood
> you made a sign of the waters of Baptism,
> that make an end of sin and a new beginning of all holiness.

The Great Flood initiated God's everlasting covenant with Noah that led to the formation of a Chosen People and ultimately a savior. The crossing of the Red Sea into the freedom of the desert prefigures the freedom we receive at Baptism.

Also, Jesus himself was baptized in the water of the Jordan River, the same river the Hebrews crossed into the Promised Land that would be their own, an image of God's eternal Kingdom. Jesus submitted to the Baptism of sinners voluntarily as a sign of his own self-emptying, which would be fully visible at his crucifixion.

In doing so, Christ established this Sacrament of Baptism, so that when we are baptized, we are baptized into both his life and Death.

What Happens at Baptism

The essential rite of Baptism consists of either immersing the candidate in water or pouring water on his or her head, calling the person by name, and pronouncing the words, "I baptize you in the name of the Father, and of the Son, and of the Holy Spirit." Many Catholic churches today have returned to Baptism by immersion, building small pools with three steps down and three steps up to symbolize the candidate's willingness to die and rise with Christ.

The candidate is also anointed with sacred chrism. This is perfumed oil that is blessed by the bishop of the diocese on Holy Thursday or a special Mass during Holy Week. It signifies to the baptized the gift of the Holy Spirit and the incorporation into Christ. This post-baptismal anointing with chrism announces that a second anointing will be conferred later by the bishop at the Sacrament of Confirmation, the completion of the baptismal anointing.

The newly baptized puts on a white garment to symbolize that the person has put on Christ and is risen with Christ. A candle lit from the Easter candle signifies that, in Jesus, the baptized are "the light of the world."

Baptisms of both adults and infants usually take place at Mass in the presence of the faithful community, the Body of Christ to which the person will belong. Whereas the Baptism of adults is reserved for the Easter vigil and is followed by Confirmation and Eucharist, the Baptism of an infant may take place on any Sunday. In the Roman rite, the child will return for First Communion at the age of reason. To show Baptism's connection with Eucharist, the infant may be brought to the altar for the praying of the Our Father.

For you and others in your Confirmation class, the completion of the Sacraments of Initiation comes with Confirmation some time after First Communion. One way to describe Confirmation is "a celebration of faith." In Baptism we receive the gift of faith. In Confirmation we reaffirm that faith in a way we could not do as infants. We do this through our

⋯→ personal commitment,

⋯→ understanding,

⋯→ freedom,

⋯→ active participation.

It is prudent and wise to pray over your decision to be confirmed and to think about how each of these aspects of your faith impacts your decision to be confirmed either now or in the future.

 What is the essential rite of Baptism?

 How do you understand what it means to be "configured to Christ?"

 Share a recent example from the news of how water is destructive. Share a second example of how water is life-giving.

Catholic 🐟Apologetics

Who can baptize?
✚ The normal ministers of the Sacrament of Baptism are the bishop, priest, or deacon. However, in an emergency (like the imminent death of a newborn) any person—even a nonbaptized person—can baptize another as long as he or she has the right intention, uses water, and recites the Trinitarian formula: "I baptize you in the name of the Father, and of the Son, and of the Holy Spirit."

Who can receive Baptism?
✚ Any person who has not yet been baptized can receive Baptism. This means that when the Church welcomes a convert from another Christian denomination, that person's Baptism in his or her original church will usually be accepted. The Church confesses in its creed that it believes "in one Baptism for the forgiveness of sins."

Can a non-Catholic be a godparent at Baptism?
✚ A Catholic, who has been confirmed and received the Eucharist, must be the baptismal sponsor. A baptized person who is not Catholic may serve as a witness with the Catholic sponsor.

What happens to children who die without Baptism?
✚ The Church trusts these children to God's mercy and recalls Jesus' words, "Let the children come to me" as a sign of hope that children who have died without Baptism will be saved. Still, the Church recognizes the urgency to welcome children to Christ through Baptism.

Someone told me I have to be "born again" in order to be saved. Is that true?
✚ The phrase "born again" comes from a translation of John 3:3–5 where Jesus tells the Pharisee Nicodemus that "No one can enter the kingdom of God without being born of water and Spirit." Some Christians believe that the phrase "born again" refers to a personal conversion experience that guarantees the person Salvation. Catholics understand "born again" to mean the spiritual rebirth that takes place at Baptism. So, if you have been baptized, you can respond that you have already been "born again."

Shouldn't a person be able to choose whether or not he or she wants to be baptized?

✛ This brings up the issue of infant Baptism. Remember, no person chooses his or her Salvation. This is an event of God's initiative, of God's unconditional love, and God's election. God chooses the time and place to bring a person to Salvation.

 # For **You** to **Do**

The Importance of Name

At Baptism you are given the name "Christian" when you are anointed with chrism. This name charged you to live as a disciple of Jesus Christ and a committed Catholic.

You also received your own name. At the beginning of the liturgy, the celebrant asks the parents, "What name do you give your child?" In most cases, parents name their children for a Christian saint. In this way the saint's example serves as a lifetime guide for the newly baptized.

Assignment

Name and research the following information about your name.

✛ What does your name mean?

✛ If you were named (first or middle name) for a saint, write some facts about the saint's life. If you weren't named for a saint, share some information about one of your favorite saints.

✛ What were some of the qualities of your saint that you admire?

For extra credit, write a detailed account of your saint's life. Incorporate what you wrote into a PowerPoint presentation that you can share with others.

Prayers and **Reflections**

Conclusion of the Baptism Rite

> You have put on Christ,
> in him you have been baptized.
> Alleluia, alleluia.

God Be in My Head

God be in my head and in my understanding.
God be in my eyes and in my looking.
God be in my mouth and in my speaking.
God be in my heart and in my thinking.
God be at my end and my departing.

—*Sarum Primer* (1527)

For Our Children

Lord, help our children
to know the road you have chosen for them:
may they give you glory and attain salvation.
Sustain them with your strength,
and let them not be satisfied with easy goals.
Enlighten us, their parents,
that we may help them to recognize their calling in life
and respond to it generously.
May we put no obstacle in the way of your inner guidance.

—*The Pope's Family Prayer Book*

two

GOD

Searching for God

In the famous words of St. Augustine, God has "made us for him-self, and our hearts are restless until they rest in him."

The search for God is a universal one. Consider Rabindranath Tagore, a Bengali mystic and poet who lived in the latter half of the nineteenth and first half of the twentieth century. He won the Nobel Prize for literature in 1913. Though raised in a Hindu family and culture, Tagore made it a point to write and tell others of his rejection of formal religion. He once described his own spiritual vision as the "religion of an artist." Yet, Tagore never abandoned his search for God and often wrote essays and poems describing his quest. In *Gitanjali*, Tagore wrote:

> I have been seeking and searching God for as long as I can remember, for many many lives, from the very beginning of existence. Once in a while, I have seen him by the side of a faraway star, and I have rejoiced and danced that the distance, although great, is not impossible to reach. And I have traveled and reached to the star; but by the time I reached the star, God has moved to another star. And it has been going on for centuries.

> The challenge is so great that I go on hoping against hope. . . . I have to find him, I am so absorbed in the search. The very search is so intriguing, so mysterious, so enchanting, that God has become almost an excuse—the search has become itself the goal.

And to my surprise, one day I reached a house in a faraway star with a small sign in front of it, saying, "This is the house of God." My joy knew no bounds—so finally I have arrived! I rushed up the steps, many steps, that led to the door of the house. But as I was coming closer and closer to the door, a fear suddenly appeared in my heart. As I was going to knock, I became paralyzed with a fear that I had never known, never thought of, never dreamt of. The fear was: If this house is certainly the house of God, then what will I do after I have found him?

Now searching for God has become my very life; to have found him will be equivalent to committing suicide. And what am I going to do with him? I had never thought of all these things before. I should have thought before I started the search: What am I going to do with God?

I took my shoes in my hands, and silently and very slowly stepped back, afraid that God may hear the noise and may open the door and say, "Where are you going? I am here, come in!" And as I reached the steps, I ran away as I have never run before; and since then I have been again searching for God, looking for him in every direction—and avoiding the house where he really lives. Now I know that house has to be avoided. And I continue the search, enjoy the very journey, the pilgrimage. (*Gitanjali*, Filiquarian Press, November 7, 2007)

What do you think about the resolution of Tagore's story? After he found God, he did not know what to do next. For Tagore, restless life was preferred. It was better to seek out God than to find God and not to know what to do next.

As part of your human makeup, you are searching for the Lord, God, your Creator. And what will you do when you find him? Is there another response different than Tagore's? Consider the answer proposed in the prayer of St. Anselm, an Archbishop of Canterbury from the early twelfth century. He wrote:

O Lord my God,
Teach my heart this day where and how to see you,
Where and how to find you.
You have made me and remade me,
And you have bestowed on me
All the good things I possess,
And still I do not know you.
I have not yet done that
For which I was made.

Teach me to seek you,
For I cannot seek you
Unless you teach me,
Or find you
Unless you show yourself to me.
Let me seek you in my desire,
Let me desire you in my seeking.
Let me find you by loving you,
Let me love you when I find you.

Left to our own reason, we can know that there is a God—a higher and supreme power—with complete certainty. Yet, God has also freely revealed himself and given himself to us. Through this gift of **Divine Revelation** we come to know God. In Jesus Christ, the fullness of God's Revelation, we can see God face to face. Jesus said: "And whoever loves me will be loved by my Father, and I will love him and reveal myself to him" (Jn 14:21). As St. Anselm realized, when we reach out to God it will be in love.

✔ **Divine Revelation**

The way God communicates knowledge of himself to humankind, a self-communication realized by his actions and words over time, most fully by his sending us his divine Son, Jesus Christ.

Your faith, first affirmed at Baptism and now to be confirmed in the Sacrament of Confirmation, is an acknowledgment of and allegiance to God. Through an exploration of Divine Revelation—past and present—this chapter calls you to continue your search for God and to love him when you find him.

 What will *you* do when you find God?

Who Is God?

First, a working definition from the *Catholic Encyclopedia*:

God, a word with Anglo-Saxon roots, is "the proper name of the one Supreme and Infinite Personal Being, the Creator and Ruler of the Universe, to whom we owe our obedience and worship."

There are many different understandings of God. All of the major religions believe in some invisible, higher reality, though it may be named differently. For example, Hindus name this deity as Brahman. Buddhism does not name a personal God, but does acknowledge an

Ultimate Reality of the universe. Muslims call
God "Allah." Many theologians ("those who
study God") have presented arguments to
"prove" the existence of God and to expound on
God's nature. Our Catholic **creed** begins with
our central beliefs about God:

⤳ There is one God.

⤳ God is Creator, not created.

⤳ God is almighty.

⤳ God is Trinitarian (Three Persons in the one God).

❦ **creed**

A statement of our
beliefs, a summary of our
faith. Catholics recite the
Nicene Creed at Mass.
The Apostles' Creed is
another summary of our
faith.

The Church has also taken up questions more specifically tied to
God's existence and nature, especially in answer to the continually
growing tide of atheism, overt or not, that seems to ignore the existence of a Supreme Being altogether.

These next sections look at these efforts to "prove" God's existence
and "name" God's nature, from God's Revelation, from Church teaching, and from our own human experience.

The Existence of God

Of the several "proofs" of God's existence, St. Thomas Aquinas
advanced some of the most popular arguments. Here are brief summaries of these proofs:

1. *Motion.* That there is movement and motion in the universe,
   implies an unmoved Mover who is God.

2. *The First Cause.* Related to the first argument, this supposes
   that there is a cause for everything that exists. That is, everything can be traced back to a cause (e.g., you to your parents). Working back through this argument to the beginning,
   there must be a "first cause," something that was always in
   existence and was not caused by anything else. You may
   have heard of the "big bang" theory of creation in which a
   cosmic explosion resulted in the creation of the universe.
   Still, even using this theory, there must be some way to name
   the force that was present to cause the "big bang." If you
   question where this force came from, you are really arguing
   for the existence of God as the First Cause.

3. *Scientific Discoveries.* Recent discoveries, for example related
   to human DNA, only support a God of vast intelligence who
   has concocted the universe and all of creation in its most
   minute detail. The scientific process has only cast more light

on a God who is able to uniquely configure human persons, each with their own unique makeup. Certainly, there has been an evolution of life including human life. But this evolution only makes God's creation even more remarkable. In 1996, Pope John Paul II called the theory of evolution "more than a hypothesis," while declaring that science and Catholicism couldn't clash because "truth cannot contradict truth."

4. *The Supreme Moral Ruler.* All humans have a built-in conscience or sense of moral responsibility that allows them to know basic principles of right from wrong. For example, every human society recognizes that murder, stealing, or lying is wrong. Where do these ingrained laws come from? Just as in the case of the First Cause, they can be traced to a superior Lawgiver whom humans are bound to obey.

5. *The Existence of Humankind.* The very existence of human beings and their development through history lead us to believe that there is a Higher Being who has made humans and led us on the journey from the beginning to now.

Additionally, our own Sacred Scriptures lay out cogent arguments for God's existence. For example, a passage from Wisdom 8:1–9 explains that

- things that are seen require a cause ("And if riches be a desirable possession in life, what is more rich than Wisdom, who produces all things" vs. 5).
- the cause of all things is God, who is knowable (Wisdom is the instructress in the understanding of God).
- God's existence can be known by the right exercise of human reason.

St. Paul's Letter to the Romans expounds on this final point in more detail: "Ever since the creation of the world, his invisible attributes . . . have been able to be understood and perceived in what he has made" (Rom 1:20).

Ways We Can Know God

The **Ecumenical Councils** for years have also pointed out "proofs" of God's existence and the ability of humans to know of God. Consider some of the ways that you can come to know of God through your own personal experience:

✔ Ecumenical Councils

Worldwide, official assemblies of the bishops under the direction of the Pope. There have been twenty-one Ecumenical Councils, the most recent being the Second Vatican Council (1962–1965).

Hopes and Dreams. We are built to look outward to a positive future. School children (including teens!) live in hope for the end of a term, summer vacation, graduation, and life after school. Our dreams are positive ones as we imagine better and better futures for ourselves and our families than we have now. Ultimately, we strive for a presence before God where what we hope and dream for, and more besides, will come true.

Beauty and Awe. No matter what region of the world you live in, or if you live in the country or city, God's beauty as expressed in nature cannot be dismissed. Consider a scene where young children (beautiful in themselves) frolic on a lake or ocean shore at sunset. Or, less naturally, but also beautiful, think about the lit skyline of a major city on a snowy winter night before Christmas. How can scenes like these, and many more that you can yet imagine, not lead you to God?

Death and Rebirth. Life is so fragile. Think about situations of loss that don't even include physical death. A broken relationship with a friend. A failed grade on a test. Then also imagine how rebirth occurs. The friendship is healed or a new friendship to replace the old is found. A better grade is gained on the next test.

Justice and Compassion. How often have you heard it said that "life isn't fair"? Cheaters get away with their crimes. Bullies and mean people still seem to get the best dates and keep their place in the pyramid of popularity. But the "life isn't fair" lament doesn't hold up when we give or receive compassion. Also, we seem to know instinctively that finally those who are guilty but unpunished in this life will receive what is coming to them after they have died.

In the end, we can know of God because of *love*. Love is the greatest reality of all. Most of us experience love in several places—in our family and with our friends. We marvel at the unconditional dimension of love (e.g., why a parent can still love a child who has been convicted of murder). We rack our brains to understand where love came from and where it will take us. That there is no concrete answer leads us to name a God who is love.

FINDING GOD

Blessed Mother Teresa of Calcutta is known for her service to the "poorest of the poor." Originally a Sister of Loreto, in 1948 she heard a "call within a call" to leave the convent and minister to the poor in Calcutta. In 1950 she founded a congregation that would become the Missionaries of Charity, whose task was, in Mother Teresa's words, to care for "the hungry, the naked, the homeless, the crippled, the blind, the lepers, those people who feel unwanted, unloved, uncared for throughout society, people that have become a burden to the society and are shunned by everyone."

One wouldn't imagine that a person of such conviction as Mother Teresa would have ever been plagued by her doubts about God and his existence, but she was. The dryness and darkness of faith came periodically over a span of nearly fifty years. She once confessed in a letter to her spiritual director:

Where is my faith? Even deep down . . . there is nothing but emptiness and darkness. . . . If there be God—please forgive me. When I try to raise my thoughts to Heaven, there is such convicting emptiness that those very thoughts return like sharp knives and hurt my very soul. . . . How painful is this unknown pain—I have no Faith. Repulsed, empty, no faith, no love, no zeal. . . . What do I labor for? If there be no God, there can be no soul. If there be no soul then, Jesus, you also are not true.

Atheists and other skeptics scoffed at Mother Teresa's admittance, saying things like "If a person with her reputation as a Catholic is unsure of the existence of God, then how can anyone be sure?" Rather, her experience of religious doubt is typical of saints, mystics, and any person who seeks God. St. Thérèse of Lisieux described such times as a "night of nothingness."

Mother Teresa's life should not be known only or primarily for these dark times of crisis. Rather, she was one who witnessed the face of God in the poor and uncovered more about God in her prayer. In a short book called *Words to Love By* Mother Teresa wrote:

> The beginning of prayer is silence . . . God speaking in the silence of the heart. And then we start talking to God from the fullness of the heart. And he listens.
>
> The beginning of prayer is scripture . . . we listen to God speaking. And then we begin to speak to him again from the fullness of our heart. And he listens.
>
> That is really prayer. Both sides listening and both sides speaking.
>
> To be able to pray, we need a pure heart.
> With a pure heart, we can see God.
> We need prayer to understand God's love for us.

What is one doubt you have about God? Draw yourself to prayer to lessen that doubt.

Write a brief argument for God's existence citing the summaries above.

What is unconditional love?

Describe a scene from nature that has helped lead you to God.

Spend twenty minutes listening to someone who is rarely heard from. How do you recognize God in that experience?

The Nature of God

One of the central beliefs most people have about God is that "God is good." If this wasn't so, theologians or students like yourself would not spend time trying to figure out and analyze his nature. If our God was evil and vindictive, we'd all be more likely to simply run for cover and hide!

We know from our personal experience, from the words of Scripture, and from other Divine Revelation passed on to us in the Church, that God is indeed good and, not only that, but he loves each person even more than the person loves himself or herself. Also, God is capable of receiving love in return and hopes that we will offer our love to him freely.

Different from many people who lived years ago—both collectively and individually—we also believe that there is but one God. This belief seems natural for us now, but it wasn't always so. Prior to the self-revelation of God and his covenant with the Israelites from the Old Testament, **monotheism**—the belief that there is only one supreme God—was not developed. For example, Hinduism, though it proclaims one supreme God, also permits and worships lesser gods. Zoroastrianism believes in the triumph of a good god, but also acknowledges an equally powerful evil force. This makes its beliefs essentially dualistic. Buddhism, in some forms, considers Siddhartha Gautama as the supreme god, but he is also considered essentially a man who achieved enlightenment and Salvation.

✦ monotheism

Describes religions that believe there is only one God. Christianity, Judaism, and Islam are three great monotheistic religions.

Monotheism contradicts not only atheism (the belief in no God), but also polytheism (belief in many gods) and pantheism (belief that God and nature are the same). Accurately, of the major religions, only Judaism, Christianity, and Islam are purely monotheistic.

These monotheistic religions believe in a God who is not only good, but also almighty—above all others—and the creator of all that exists. These major characteristics of God help to fill in more of the details of God's nature.

Attributes of God

St. Thomas Aquinas named nine attributes that seem to tell us some things about God's nature. They are:

1. *God is eternal.* He has no beginning and no end. Or, to put it another way, God always was, always is, and always will be.

2. *God is unique.* God is the designer of a one and only world. Even the people he creates are one of a kind.

3. *God is infinite and omnipotent.* This reminds us of a lesson we learned early in life: God sees everything. There are no limits to God. Omnipotence is a word that refers to God's supreme power and authority over all of creation.

4. *God is omnipresent.* God is not limited to space. He is everywhere. You can never be away from God.

5. *God contains all things.* All of creation is under God's care and jurisdiction.

6. *God is immutable.* God does not evolve. God does not change. God is the same God now as he always was and always will be.

7. *God is pure spirit.* Though God has been described with human attributes (e.g., a wise old man with a long beard), God is not a material creation. God's image cannot be made. God is a pure spirit who cannot be divided into parts. God is simple, but complex.

8. *God is alive.* We believe in a living God, a God who acts in the lives of people. Most concretely, he came to this world in the incarnate form of Jesus Christ.

9. *God is holy.* God is pure goodness. God is pure love.

Of all the attributes of God, only his omnipotence is named in our Creed. Our belief in an almighty God affects how we live our lives. In an almighty God, we believe that not only does God rule everything, but he can *do* everything and anything. When the angel visits Mary and tells her that she will bear a Son without conceiving it with a man, this is believable to us because of God's almighty power. The angel reinforces this and says, "For nothing will be impossible for God" (Lk 1:37).

God's almighty power is not coercive. Oppositely, it is loving. God is a loving Father who takes care of our needs. He says, "I will be a father to you, and you shall be sons and daughters to me" (2 Cor 6:18). Jesus teaches that our heavenly Father "knows all that we need" and will grant these things to us when we accept him first.

Finally, God's almighty power sustains even the evidence of weakness when we witness evil and suffering in our world. This is part of another of God's attributes—his mystery. Still, though we might not fully understand why there is evil, suffering, and death, we do witness how the Almighty God is even able to conquer these too— through the Resurrection of his Son, Jesus, and through the ultimate end of all sin and death.

Creator of Heaven and Earth

In our Catholic creeds, we confess that God the Father is "Creator of heaven and earth," of "all that is, seen and unseen." The first words of the Scriptures say that "In the beginning . . . God created the heavens and the earth" (Gn 1:1).

Through our examination of creation, we learn several things about God.

First, we know that God created from nothing. God did not use any preexistent thing nor did he need any help to create. As St. Theophilus of Antioch put it:

> If God had drawn from preexistent matter, what would be so extraordinary in that? A human artisan makes from a given material whatever he wants, while God shows his power by starting from nothing to make all he wants.

Second, God intends to create what he wants. Creation is not left to blind fate or chance. God made his creatures because he wanted to share his being, goodness, and wisdom.

Third, what God has made is good. As humans, because we are created in God's goodness, we share in his goodness. All creation—including the physical world—is a product of God's goodness.

Fourth, God is greater than his works of creation. God is outside of his creation, yet at the same time he is present to it. As the Acts of the Apostles puts it, "In [God] we live and move and have our being" (Acts 17:28).

❦ **providence**

God's leading and guiding us to our final end, Salvation and union with him.

Fifth, God supports his creation. This means that we are not created and then abandoned by God. Rather God's **providence** leads and guides us to our final end, Salvation and union with God.

God's act of creation was the first witness to his love and wisdom. In creation, we get the first glimpse of God's saving plan of love, one that culminates in Jesus Christ. This plan of God's is one in which we, his creations, take an active involvement. God intended for people to share not only in the saving work of the world, but also in creation itself. That is why humans are made as male and female. God created man and woman to be procreators, to share in the divine activity of bringing life to the world.

Creation itself is the work of the Holy Trinity—Father, Son, and Holy Spirit. God the Father has traditionally been given the role of Creator, that he made everything by himself—or with the Son and the Spirit who are, according to St. Irenaeus, "his hands."

Ultimately, the work of creation was the common work of the Holy Trinity.

Define *monotheism, polytheism,* and *pantheism.*

Which is the only attribute of God mentioned in the creeds?

Name and explain two things we can learn about God from creation.

Do you find the fact that God is almighty more scary or comforting? Explain.

When God was at the drawing board planning your creation, what were three unique characteristics he infused in you?

Create something from preexistent matter (e.g., an essay, artwork, song). Keep it as a remembrance of your preparation for Confirmation.

The Holy Trinity

From their Jewish roots, the early Christians easily understood that there was one God. Yet, through the teaching of Jesus, as well as their experience of him—God in human form—it was gradually

revealed to them that there is one God who acts in Three Persons—
Father, Son, and Holy Spirit.

Actually, there was one experience at the beginning of Jesus' ministry when the Trinitarian nature of God was clearly revealed. It was at Jesus' baptism by John in the River Jordan.

Jesus, God incarnate, was there. John the Baptist recognized that he was the chosen one of the Scriptures. "I need to be baptized by you, and yet you are coming to me?" (Mt 3:14), John wondered aloud.

After Jesus was baptized, God the Holy Spirit was visible in the form of a dove. "He came up from the water and behold, the heavens were opened, and he saw the Spirit of God descending like a dove, coming upon him" (Mt 3:16).

Finally, the voice of God the Father was heard from Heaven: "This is my beloved Son, with whom I am well pleased" (Mt 3:17).

From this revelation and others connected with Jesus and his teaching, the Church's understanding of Three Persons in one God originated and grew. This central mystery of the Christian faith is known as the **Holy Trinity**.

🕊 **Holy Trinity**

The central mystery of the Christian faith. It teaches that there are Three Persons in one God: Father, Son, and Holy Spirit.

The mystery of the Holy Trinity is a difficult one to understand and explain. Some of the Church's dogmas—beliefs—about the Trinity can help. For example,

> *The Trinity is One.* The Trinity does not mean there are three Gods, but one God in Three Persons. The Three Persons do not share their divinity among themselves, but each one of them—Father, Son, and Holy Spirit—is God whole and entire. There are not three separate consciousnesses, intelligences, or wills in God. There is one God.

> *The Three Persons are distinct from one another.* This means that the Father is not the Son, nor is the Son the Holy Spirit. Rather, the Father is Creator, the Son is begotten of the Father, and the Holy Spirit proceeds from the Father and Son.

> *The Divine Persons are related to one another.* The Father is wholly in the Son and wholly in the Holy Spirit; the Son is wholly in the Father and wholly in the Holy Spirit; the Holy Spirit is wholly in the Father and wholly in the Son. Though they are intimately related to one another, the Three Persons have one nature or substance.

Theology of the Holy Trinity

The theology of the Holy Trinity is a very difficult concept to grasp. Suffice to say that "person" cannot be thought of in the way we imagine distinct human persons. There is only one God. When one person of the Trinity acts, the other two persons also act. Though the persons—Father, Son, and Holy Spirit—are distinct, they do not act apart from each other.

In this understanding, the first person of the Trinity is God the Source. In Greek, the name for source is *Arché*, which means "first." God is the first Source of all being, all knowledge, all love.

God the Source knows himself perfectly. When he speaks this perfect knowledge of himself it is known as *Logos*, or the Divine Word. The Word of God is the second person of the Trinity.

The first and second persons of the Trinity communicate with one another in love. This love is "breathed out" between the two as a third person, the Divine Spirit or *Pneuma* in Greek. As our creeds describe, the love *proceeds* from the Father and Son.

❦ **Salvific Trinity or Economic Trinity**

The active and inseparable work of the Triune God—Father, Son, and Holy Spirit—in Salvation History.

These human attempts to understand how God understands himself are of course incomplete, for it is an impossible task. A second way of understanding the Trinity is known as the **Salvific Trinity or Economic Trinity**. In this second approach, we know God by what he does, how he acts in our lives and in the world. We begin with a knowledge of Jesus and our faith in him as the Son of God. He was sent by the Father to reveal the Father to us. Yet he and the Father are one. And after his earthly life was ended and he had returned to the Father, he fulfilled his promise by sending, in union with the Father, the Holy Spirit.

Thus it is that the work of our Salvation reveals to us the Trinitarian nature of God. We know God by the way he has acted, as Father, Son, and Holy Spirit. The ultimate work of the Trinity is to bring all of creation into unity with God in Three Persons. As Jesus told his disciples, "Whoever loves me will keep my word, and my Father will love him, and we will come to him and make our dwelling with him" (Jn 14:23).

More on God the Father

Just before he was arrested, Jesus prayed, "I revealed your name to those whom you gave me" (Jn 17:6).

The "name" referred to in this prayer is **Abba**, which in the commonly spoken Aramaic means "Daddy." That Jesus would refer to God as Daddy or Father exclusively when he could have used a number of other words and titles from the Hebrew Scriptures for God (e.g.,

ᔍ Abba

The Aramaic word for "Daddy." This was the way Jesus addressed God, his Father.

Lord, shepherd, rock, etc.) is significant. As the word of his prayer communicates, Jesus came to earth to tell us about his Father. He came to tell us the name of God is Father. Church father Tertullian reported it this way:

> The expression God the Father had never been revealed to anyone. When Moses himself asked God who he was, he heard another name. The Father's name has been revealed to us in the Son, for the name "Son" implies the new name "Father."

In recent years, there has been some movement to avoid addressing God as Father because of the implication that God is distinctly male. This implication is not accurate. God is pure spirit who is beyond biological distinction. God has both feminine and masculine characteristics, as evidenced by the fact that both men and women are created "in the image and likeness of God."

This all said, we are called by Jesus himself to address God as Father, and to turn to him as the children he loves. What is God the Father like? Even in the Old Testament, where *YHWH* (the name used for God, meaning Lord) is often depicted more in his power, the image of fatherhood is used several times, and YHWH's compassion comes through. The book of Hosea describes YHWH's relationship with the people of Israel:

> I drew them with human cords,
> with bands of love;
> I fostered them like one
> who raises an infant to his cheeks. (Hos 11:4)

Yet, it is Jesus who not only names the intimate form of Father, Abba, but also allows us to really know God as Father. Jesus spoke over and over of his Father. He calls on his disciples to also address and know God as Abba. St. Paul wrote to the Romans:

> For those who are led by the Spirit of God are children of God. For you did not receive a spirit of slavery to fall back into fear, but you received a spirit of adoption, through which we cry, "*Abba*, Father!" (Rom 8:14)

What God the Father is like is perhaps best summed up by Jesus' parable of the Prodigal Son (Lk 15:11–32) in which a father shows unconditional love for a son who has wasted his inheritance. Jesus tells us that Abba's love for us is the same, he will never abandon us, and will always rejoice in our returning to him.

Finally, Jesus tells us to address God as Father in our prayer. In doing so, we learn to depend on God's providence for us, that his will, not ours be done.

Read and comment on the other accounts of Jesus' baptism from Mark 1:9–11, Luke 3:21–22, and John 1:32–33.

Explain the meaning of Salvific Trinity or Economic Trinity.

What are some qualities of human fatherhood that can be likened to qualities of God?

Interview two parents (but not your own), one younger and one older. From the interviews create a list of essential characteristics of parenthood.

Catholic 🔥Apologetics

Does God have a body?
+ No. As Jesus explained, "God is Spirit, and those who worship him must worship in spirit and truth" (Jn 4:24).

If God is good, why is there evil, suffering, and death?
+ This is one of the most challenging and perplexing questions that humans have ever faced. With Job who wondered as much, we are ultimately resigned to the fact that God's ways are much higher than our own and that we will never have a complete answer to this question while on earth. However, we do know that God is in no way, directly or indirectly, the cause of any moral evil. God permits evil, suffering, and death, because he respects human freedom and, mysteriously, knows how to derive good from them. From our human experience, we know that pain often brings perfection and satisfaction. Consider the athlete who puts in months and months of painful weightlifting and running in order to achieve a satisfying season. Ultimately, we only have to look to the greatest moral evil ever committed—the Passion and Death of

God's only Son—and the subsequent good (Christ's Resurrection and our Redemption) that came from it. However, even for all that, evil itself never becomes a good.

What is a soul?

✝ The soul refers to the innermost part of a person. It is the spiritual part of the person. Every soul is created immediately by God. It is not produced by parents. The soul is immortal. It does not perish with the body at death. At the final resurrection, it will be reunited with the body.

Does God know all things?

✝ Yes. God is *omniscient*, meaning "all knowing." God knows even our most secret thoughts, words, and actions.

If God knows everything about us, how can we really be free?

✝ God gives us the gifts of intellect and free will, allowing us to make choices. Also, God created a world with natural laws (e.g., the law of gravity) with which he rarely interferes. To God, everything about your life—beginning to end—is happening now. It's something like standing over and watching an ant trail from the ant's hole in the ground to a source of water. You can see an individual ant's past, present, and future. But you don't interfere with the ant's freedom to choose the route from point A to point B.

Since we can't see God, how do we know God exists?

✝ We know God exists because he reveals himself, most perfectly in Jesus Christ. We see the effects of God's existence. In the same way, we would not know that there was wind unless we saw and felt its effects.

For **You** to **Do**

Called to be Contemplative

Contemplative prayer is a special kind of prayer. A Trappist monk, Basil Pennington, said that in this kind of prayer, "We go beyond thought and image, beyond the senses and the rational mind, to the center of our being where God is working in a wonderful work."

Think of people who are deeply in love. There are times when they can simply *be* with each other. They are silent together, enjoying each other's company, whether sitting in the same room, taking a walk together, or enjoying a moonlit sky in each other's presence. This kind of comfortable "being together" usually comes only after the friends have spent considerable time sharing and growing closer. Contemplative prayer can be compared to this special human experience.

All Christians are called to contemplative prayer, to a close relationship of love with God. Contemplative prayer is sometimes called passive because we don't have to do anything except be ourselves and put ourselves in God's presence. St. John Vianney, a parish priest in a small village in France, knew of an old peasant who spent hours and hours sitting motionless in the chapel before the Blessed Sacrament, apparently doing nothing. When the saint asked him what he was doing all those hours, the old peasant said, "I look at God, God looks at me, and we are happy."

Today, many Catholics are turning to contemplative prayer. One way to begin is through a "centering" prayer, an active prayer that can lead to the passive prayer of contemplation. An example of centering prayer is the Jesus Prayer, an ancient prayer that was first developed by the Desert Fathers in response to the words of St. Paul: "Rejoice always. Pray without ceasing. In all circumstances give thanks, for this is the will of God for you in Christ Jesus" (1 Thes 5:16–18).

There are many variations of the Jesus Prayer, but the most common one is: "Lord Jesus Christ, Son of God, have mercy on me a sinner." This is a centering prayer than can be said in preparation for contemplation, or at anytime, anywhere. Try it:

Inhale as you say "Lord Jesus Christ."
Exhale as you say "Son of God."
Inhale as you say "have mercy on me."
Exhale as you say "a sinner."

Assignment

Contemplate the attributes of God described by St. Thomas Aquinas. Read and reflect on the passages from the Old Testament that help to support the descriptions:

✢ *God is eternal.* (Read Isaiah 40:28)

✢ *God is unique.* (Read Isaiah 45:18)

✢ *God is infinite and omnipotent.* (Read Psalm 135:5–6)

✢ *God is omnipresent.* (Read 1 Kings 8:27)

✢ *God contains all things.* (Read Wisdom 11:24–12:1)

✢ *God is immutable.* (Read Psalm 102:26–28)

✢ *God is pure spirit.* (Read Exodus 20:4)

✢ *God is alive.* (Read Jeremiah 31:1–3)

✢ *God is holy.* (Read Isaiah 55:8–9)

Prayers and **Reflections**

The Trinity

Think of the Father as a root,
of the Son as a branch,
and of the Spirit as a fruit,
for the substance of these is one.
The Father is a sun
with the Son as rays
and the Holy Spirit as heat.

—St. John of Damascus

Word of God

But when the fullness of time had come, God sent his Son, born of a woman, born under the law, to ransom those under the law, so that we might receive adoption. As proof that you are children, God sent the spirit of his Son into our hearts, crying out, "Abba, Father!" So you are no longer a slave but a child, and if a child then also an heir, through God.

—Galatians 4:4–7

Lord, you have probed me,
you know me,
you know when I sit and
stand;
you understand my thoughts from
afar.

—Psalm 139:1–2

Prayer before the Gospel

May the word of God be in my mind, on my lips, and in my heart.

Prayer of Blessed Elizabeth of the Trinity

O my God, Trinity whom I adore, help me forget myself entirely so to establish myself in you, unmovable and peaceful as if my soul were already in eternity. May nothing be able to trouble my peace or make me leave you, O my unchanging God, but may each minute bring me more deeply into your mystery! Grant my soul peace. Make it your heaven, your beloved dwelling and the place of your rest. May I never abandon you there, but may I be there, whole and entire, completely vigilant in my faith, entirely adoring, and wholly given over to your creative action.

A Spirit to Know You

Gracious and holy Father,
please give me:
intellect to understand you,
reason to discern you,
diligence to seek you,
wisdom to find you,
a spirit to know you,
a heart to meditate upon you,
ears to hear you,
eyes to see you,
a tongue to proclaim you,
a way of life pleasing to you,
patience to wait for you
and perseverance to look for you.
Grant me a perfect end—
your holy presence,
a blessed resurrection
and life everlasting.

—attributed to St. Benedict of Nursia

*J*ESUS CHRIST

Catholics Are Christians

"Are you a Christian?"

"No, I am Catholic."

Have you ever heard an exchange like that? If so, the confusion probably comes from a Catholic who thinks the questioner is referring only to a religious denomination, not a belief.

Of course there are many "Christians" who do not think of Catholics as Christians either. These people are mostly ill-informed. Sometimes they are prejudiced, making false claims that Catholics worship Mary or the Pope.

Let's set the record straight. Catholics *are* Christians. We believe in Jesus Christ. One of our Catholic creeds says so:

> I believe in Jesus Christ, his only Son, our Lord.
> He was conceived by the power of the Holy Spirit
> and born of the Virgin Mary.
>
> —from the Apostles' Creed

Without Jesus, none of the other aspects of our faith would even exist. As St. Joan of Arc once said, "About Jesus Christ and the Church, I simply know they're just one thing, and we shouldn't complicate the matter." When Joan of Arc died—burned at the stake as a martyr—she had just one word on her lips: "Jesus."

This chapter will look at what we as Catholics believe about Jesus. It will also address some of what we are called to when we say, "I believe in Jesus Christ," in other words, the meaning of discipleship.

How do you answer the question "How are you Christian?"

How do you answer the question "How are you Catholic?"

Who Is Jesus?

The titles and names for Jesus confessed in the creed provide answers to his identity.

In Hebrew, the name Jesus means "God saves." Jesus' name is also his mission. Jesus saves all of humanity from sin. This task was expressed even before his birth. The angel Gabriel told Joseph that Mary "will bear a son and you are to name him Jesus, because he will save his people from their sins" (Mt 1:21).

The Redemption of the entire human race—for all times and all places—was the work of Jesus. Only God can save people from sins. The name Jesus shows that God's name is present in his Son. The Acts of the Apostles reports of the name Jesus, "There is no salvation through anyone else, nor is there any other name under heaven given to the human race by which we are to be saved" (Acts 4:12).

🐦 **Christh**

The Greek term for "Messiah." It means "the anointed one."

Christ is not Jesus' family name. The word "Christ" is the Greek translation of the Hebrew *Messiah*, which means "anointed." Jesus could be called "the Christ" only because he perfectly accomplished what he had come for.

And, what was it that he came for?

Peter, Jesus' chosen disciple, correctly understood that Jesus was the Messiah (see, for example, Mk 8:29). But Peter's understanding of what the Messiah stood for and accomplished was different than Jesus' understanding. Perhaps Peter felt that God's anointed one would be a powerful earthly king who would remove the Romans from power and restore Israel as the ruling people of the time. Jesus told Peter and the others it wasn't to be like that. Instead, the Messiah would suffer, be rejected, be killed, and then rise after three days. As Jesus put it, "For the Son of Man did not come to be served but to serve and to give his life as a ransom for many" (Mk 10:45).

Jesus is also called the "Son of God." Depending on how this title was used, those who said it did not necessarily mean that Jesus was more than human. In the Old Testament, "son of God" is used as a title for angels, kings, and others among the Israelites who had a particularly intimate relationship with God. However, the title takes on new meaning at certain times in the New Testament. For example, there are two times—at Jesus' baptism and his transfiguration—when a voice from Heaven is heard to say "this is my beloved Son." In Matthew's Gospel, when Peter confesses Jesus' identity, he says to Jesus: "You are the Messiah, the Son of the living God." Jesus calls Peter blessed because "flesh and blood has not revealed this to you, but my heavenly Father" (Mt 16:17). It was through his teachings and his actions that Jesus revealed himself to be the only **Son of God**.

❧ Son of God

A title that refers to Jesus. He is the unique Son of God the Father, the Second Person of the Holy Trinity. Jesus Christ is the natural son of the Father who shares God's very nature.

The title **Lord**—used often to address Jesus—also has various meanings. For example, a king or ruler could be addressed as "Lord." However, as with Son of God, the title Lord means something more regarding Jesus. In the Greek translation of the Old Testament, the Hebrew name for God, YHWH, is translated as *Kyrios*, "Lord." From that point on, the use of Lord indicates divinity. From the time of the early Church on, to address Jesus as Lord implies that all power, honor, and glory due God are also due Jesus.

❧ Lord

When referring to Jesus, the title "Lord" proclaims his divinity. The Greek translation of the Old Testament used the word *Kyrios* ("Lord") to render the most sacred named YHWH ("I am"), which God revealed to Moses.

Explain the meaning of these names and titles: Jesus, Christ, Son of God, and Lord.

Jesus' names and titles revealed several things about him. Which title do you use when you speak with him in prayer? Why?

What is the significance of your name?

What are some nicknames people have for you? What do they tell about you?

"Offering up" something for God is a traditional practice of sharing in Christ's suffering by giving over the challenges of your day to him. Make a promise to offer up three challenges you face today to Jesus.

St. Thérèse of Lisieux: For the Love of Jesus

As a model for following Christ, there are few examples greater than St. Thérèse of Lisieux. This is ironic because as St. Thérèse would likely have admitted, there was nothing remarkable about her life that would make anyone notice her. And that was exactly as she intended.

Thérèse Martin was born in Alençon, France, on January 2, 1873. With her family, Thérèse moved to Lisieux in 1877. She entered the Carmelite convent there when she was fifteen years old and only lived for another nine years. She died of tuberculosis in 1898. Her story may never have been known if not for the publishing of her biography, *The Story of a Soul*.

Love was what Thérèse Martin was all about. From her earliest days she was fascinated by love and determined to plumb its depths regardless of personal cost. She was driven by a ferocious desire to unlock nothing else but the mystery of life itself. "How can a soul as imperfect as mine aspire to the possession of love?" she wondered. It was through her determination that she was determined to reach out and possess love.

The well-known symbol Thérèse chose for her life was the "little flower." The symbol was deceptive. Her purpose in using it was to explain that, like a tiny wild flower in the forest, she survived and indeed flourished through all the seasons of the year—through the warmth of spring and summer as well as the winds and snows of fall and winter. It was her way of saying: "I am a lot stronger than I look. Don't let appearances fool you."

Jesus was the source of her strength. She interpreted her whole life and all its events as Jesus teaching and revealing himself to her. Jesus taught her the sure path to follow—abandonment to God's will. He did not require great deeds, only her love.

Thérèse was also moved by the Suffering Servant passages from the Book of Isaiah. The prophet said the servant would be crushed with suffering, but through this innocent man's wounds we would be healed. The Gospels developed Isaiah's teaching and described Christ himself as the Suffering Servant. It is through Christ and his sufferings that God brings healing to us all.

It was one particular passage from Isaiah 53 that Thérèse took to heart:

He was spurned and avoided by men,
a man of suffering accustomed to infirmity,
One of those from whom men hide their faces,
spurned, and we held him in no esteem. (Is 53:3)

Thérèse wrote "I desire that, like the face of Jesus, my face be truly hidden, that no one on earth would know me. I thirsted after suffering and longed to be forgotten." In the Carmelite community, she took for her name "Sister Thérèse of the Child Jesus and the Holy Face."

Abandonment to Christ

Thérèse felt that Jesus was calling her to participate in the continuation of his redemptive suffering and Death. Like Jesus, she recognized that souls were to be won through the mystery of suffering, and it was to this that she dedicated her life. She wanted to love people the way Christ loved them, but she knew this was impossible. And yet this was the command Jesus had given. So, the only way for her to fulfill the commandment would be to let Jesus take possession of her and then to have him love others through her.

Thus she had to abandon herself to Christ. She came before him with all of her faults and failings. She was not shamed by her failings, knowing that Jesus was merciful and would quickly forgive them.

Thérèse remained aware of her smallness:

It is impossible for me to grow up, so I must bear with myself
such as I am with all my imperfections. But I want to see out
a means of going to heaven by a little way, a way that is very
straight, very short, and totally new.

Thérèse went on to describe how she imagined herself reaching up to Jesus by riding an elevator to him (much easier than climbing stairs):

I wanted to find an elevator which would raise me to Jesus,
for I am too small to climb the rough stairway of perfection.
I searched then in the Scriptures for some sign of this elevator, the object of my desires and I read these words coming
from the mouth of Eternal Wisdom: "Whoever is a little one
let him come to me." The elevator which must raise me to
heaven is your arms, O Jesus, and for this I have no need to
grow up, but rather I have to remain little and become this
more and more.

And so she abandoned herself to Jesus and her life became a continual acceptance of the will of the Lord.

The Lord, it seems, did not demand great things of her. But she felt incapable of the tiniest charity, the smallest expression of concern and patience and understanding. So she surrendered her life to Christ with the hope that he would act through her. She again mirrored perfectly the words of St. Paul who wrote, "I can do all things in him who strengthens me." "All things" consisted of almost everything she was called upon to do in the daily grind of life.

Jesus, True God and True Man

One of the most significant questions the early Church had to answer about Jesus' identity was this one: Is Jesus Christ God? In answering the question, the Church also needed to explain that Jesus was also human.

The New Testament authors only moderately addressed the question. Most clearly in the Gospel of John—the final Gospel written—is the divinity of Jesus covered. John's Gospel focuses on seven "signs" of Jesus, beginning with the changing of the water to wine at the wedding of Cana. "Sign" is an important choice of words for John. These events are viewed as more than miracles or displays of power, but evidence that Jesus is the Great Sign of God the Father. John's Gospel puts more emphasis on Jesus' divinity by showing him always in command of the various situations he faces. This focus on Jesus' divinity is present from the very opening of the Gospel:

In the beginning was the Word,
and the Word was with God,
and the Word was God.
He was in the beginning with God.
All things came to be through him,
and without him nothing came to be.

—John 1:1–3

This passage refers to Jesus as the ever-present Word of God (*Logos* in Greek) who was always one with the Father before the beginning of time.

After the apostolic era, the Church looked more deeply at the question, "Is Jesus Christ God?" along with the accompanying question, "Is Jesus true man?"

The answers to these questions developed mainly in response to several heresies, that is, false beliefs about Jesus' identity. The earliest heresies denied that Jesus was human. They said that Jesus only took the *appearance* of a man. The Christian faith had always insisted on Jesus' true **Incarnation**, the taking on of human flesh.

✔ Incarnation

The dogma that God's eternal son assumed a human nature and became man in Jesus Christ to save us from our sins. The term literally means "taking on human flesh."

An early bishop in the Church, Arius, taught that Jesus was not truly God. He said that Jesus "came to be from things that were not" and that he was "from another substance" than God the Father.

The Church answered these false teachings in several early gatherings of bishops and Church leaders called councils. After the first of these councils, at Nicaea in 325, a creed was composed called the Nicene Creed. This is the creed we recite at Sunday Mass. Many of the teachings about Jesus' divinity and humanity are answered in the statements of the Nicene Creed:

Jesus is eternally begotten of the Father. The Council of Nicaea confessed that Jesus is "begotten, not made, of the same substance as the Father." Begotten is different from "created." The Son always existed in relationship to the Father. God the Father did not make or create the Son in the same way that human fathers help to create their children.

Jesus is God from God, Light from Light, true God from true God. Jesus is truly God. Just as the light that comes from a source is the same light, Jesus is truly God as he comes from the Father and is "one in Being with the Father."

Through Jesus all things were made. Because the Son was present from the beginning, he shared in the Father's creative action.

There were likewise many debates about Jesus' humanity. How could the all-powerful God take human form? But that is exactly what happened so that God could save the world from sin. Years and years of sacrifice by the Jewish people—including prayer, fasting, and Temple sacrifice of animals—were not enough to bring Salvation. As the Letter to the Hebrews points out, "it is impossible that the blood of bulls and goats take away sins." Continuing, Hebrews quotes Jesus praying the words of the Psalms:

Sacrifice and offering you did not desire,
but a body you prepared for me;
holocausts and sin offerings you took no delight in (Heb 10:4–6).

By becoming fully human, God has united himself to us. Unlike the early heresies that supposed that Jesus only "appeared" to be human, the Church believes that Jesus is truly human—in body, mind, and soul.

As both true God and true man, Christ had two intellects and wills, divine and human, which cooperated with one another. As a human, Jesus was like us in all things but sin. In his humanity, Jesus models what it is to be a person. While Jesus' human will and intellect developed in a completely human way, it never lost touch with his divine will and the mission the Son of God took on a human body in order to accomplish.

What does it mean to say that Jesus is "eternally begotten of the Father"?

Why did God take human form?

Summarize three statements of Jesus' humanity and divinity from the Nicene Creed.

How would your faith be affected if Jesus Christ was not God, but only God's greatest prophet?

The Life of Christ

The Creed speaks only of the beginning and end of Jesus' earthly life:

For us men and for our salvation
he came down from heaven:
by the power of the Holy Spirit
he was born of the Virgin Mary, and became man.
For our sake he was crucified under Pontius Pilate;
he suffered, died, and was buried.
On the third day he rose again
in fulfillment of the Scriptures;
he ascended into heaven
and is seated at the right hand of the Father.
He will come again in glory to judge the living and the dead,
and his kingdom will have no end.

These events are part of the mystery of our faith; likewise Christ's whole life is a mystery: his hidden life in his early years in Nazareth living with Mary and Joseph, as well as his public life beginning with his baptism in the Jordan River, and including his proclamation of the coming of the Kingdom of God. A summary of several of these important events follows:

The Incarnation. On the first Christmas, Jesus Christ was born of the Virgin Mary. Incarnation literally translates to "in the flesh." Only the Gospels of Matthew and Luke mention Jesus' birth. Jesus was born in Bethlehem, the city of King David of the Old Testament, and laid in a manger, because there was no room for him in the inn. Jesus' humble birth reminds us to also be humble ourselves. The Incarnation reminds us that we must make ourselves like little children and be dependent on God for all our needs.

Jesus' Infancy. The Scriptures also tell of Jesus' circumcision on the eighth day after his birth. Jesus was Jewish. He was raised in a Jewish family. To be circumcised was to incorporate himself into the Jewish faith and a sign that he would submit himself to Jewish Law and worship the God of his ancestors. At the **Epiphany**, the foreign magi from the east come bearing gifts. This is a fore-shadowing of the far-reaching benefits of the Incarnation: God's Salvation will be offered to people of all nations. When he was forty days old, Jesus was presented in the Temple according to Jewish law and recognized by Simeon and Anna as the long-awaited Messiah, but also one who will bring sorrow on his mother. As King Herod ordered the execution of infant boys, Joseph fled with his family to Egypt to recall the emergence of Moses in Egypt and the exodus of the Israelites into the freedom of the Sinai desert.

> **Epiphany**
>
> The name for the feast that celebrates the mystery of Christ's manifestation as Savior of the world.

Jesus' Hidden Life. The majority of Jesus' life was spent without fanfare. From the time of Jesus' infancy until the beginning of his public ministry at about the age of thirty, there is little known about Jesus. Rather, he lived a life of obedience to his parents, performed manual labor, and studied Jewish teaching and the Law. He "advanced in wisdom and age, and favor before God and man" (Lk 2:52). The only event from those years mentioned in the Gospels is the finding of Jesus in the

Temple by his parents. Jesus answers his worried parents by saying, "Did you not know that I must be in my Father's house?" (Lk 2:49).

Jesus' Baptism. The public ministry of Jesus began with his baptism by John in the Jordan River. As he received his baptism, the Holy Spirit came upon Jesus in the form of a dove, and a voice proclaimed, "This is my beloved Son." From the beginning of his ministry, Jesus associated with sinners, and was the "Lamb of God who takes away the sins of the world." His baptism is a sign for us to do the same. To be baptized in Christ is to share, not only his Passion and Death, but also his Resurrection.

Ushering in the Kingdom of God. Jesus said: "This is the time of fulfillment. The kingdom of God is at hand. Repent, and believe in the gospel" (Mk 1:15). The Kingdom of God means the rule of God over all people. In the understanding of the Kingdom ushered in by Christ, it is established in stages, beginning with Jesus' public ministry and ending, finally, at the end of time when he comes again. Through powerful signs (miracles) worked by Jesus and his teachings, we know that

⤑ the Kingdom of God is for everyone.

⤑ the Kingdom of God belongs to the poor and lowly.

⤑ sinners are welcome in the Kingdom.

⤑ Jesus' invitation to enter the Kingdom comes in the form of parables.

⤑ the coming of God's Kingdom means the defeat of Satan.

⤑ certain authority—the keys of the Kingdom—were given by Jesus to his Twelve Apostles, particularly Peter.

❦ **Transfiguration**

An occasion when Jesus revealed his divine glory before Peter, James, and John on a high mountain, where his face "shone like the sun and his clothes became white as light" (Mt 17:2).

Jesus' Transfiguration. Jesus appears, his face and clothes a dazzling white, with Moses and Elijah from the Old Testament to three witnesses, Peter, James, and John. For these disciples, the **Transfiguration** is a foretaste of the Kingdom and of Jesus' divine glory. It is at this time that Jesus also informs his followers that he must go to Jerusalem, be handed over to the authorities, suffer many things, and be killed, in order to "enter his glory."

Why is it important to become like "little children" in order to enter God's Kingdom?

What are the characteristics of God's Kingdom?

Develop a profile for Jesus when he was your current age.

Be more like little children. Serve children by volunteering your time teaching a religious education class, visiting children confined to a hospital, coaching a youth sports team, or offering free babysitting for children in your neighborhood.

Jesus' Passion, Death, and Resurrection

Why did the Messiah have to suffer and die? Did Jesus really rise from the dead? These questions not only puzzle us today, they puzzled the first-century followers of Jesus too. There was no common understanding among Jews that the Messiah would suffer and die. In fact, the Jews of Jesus' era mostly believed that the Messiah would be a military leader who would defeat the occupying enemies and restore Israel to its greatness as a nation. While the Old Testament did call for a messiah who would deliver the people from their sinfulness and bring everlasting life, this understanding was directed more to the people of Israel as a whole, not to individuals. It was believed that the people of Israel would live on in their ancestors. Not many Jews in Jesus' time had any notion of personal salvation or resurrection for the individual person.

Jesus told his disciples what would happen to him. In Jerusalem, Jesus would be handed over by some Jewish leaders to the Romans who would mock him, spit upon him, scourge him, and put him to death. Why *did* this have to happen? Jesus had to die to redeem humankind from sin. Because of the disobedience of Adam, all of his descendents were wounded by this Original Sin.

In their fallen condition, all men and women, from Adam and Eve until today, have committed personal sins as well. By freely giving his life on the cross, in complete obedience to his Father, Jesus atoned for both Original Sin and personal sins. His Death was an expiation—a purging or cleansing—of sin. The Apostle John wrote: "In this is love: not that we have loved God, but that he loved us and sent his Son as expiation for our sins" (1 Jn 4:10).

It was in this way that God's saving plan was accomplished "once for all" (Heb 9:26). There would be no more need for animal sacrifices. As Jesus pointed out, "The Son of man did not come to be served but to serve and to give his life as ransom for many" (Mk 10:45). This was the plan of God the Father. Jesus also said: "I am the good shepherd. A good shepherd lays down his life for his sheep. . . . No one takes [my life] from me, but I lay it down on my own. I have power to lay it down, and power to take it up again. This command I have received from my Father" (Jn 10:11, 18). The events of our Salvation unfolded in this way:

Jesus' Entry into Jerusalem. Jesus was greeted and hailed in Jerusalem as a prophet by the crowds as he entered the city gates at the time of the Passover. They waved leafy branches and called out "Hosanna! Blessed is he who comes in the name of the Lord!" Jesus entered the Temple area, then because it was late in the day, retreated back outside the city walls to the small town of Bethany for the night.

Hostility toward Jesus. The mood in Jerusalem changed over the next two days. First, Jesus reacted strongly against the commerce taking place in the Temple courtyard. This was really business as usual. Jews coming from throughout Palestine had to exchange their secular money for the Jewish coin to be given as an offering. Jesus' driving out of the moneychangers and those buying and selling was really a statement against the leaders of the Temple—the elders and priests—and their lack of attention to authentic religious matters, especially at the time of the **Passover**. These were the people who later tried Jesus in the Jewish court and handed him over to the Romans. Besides these Jewish officials, Jesus was also challenged by others within Judaism—the Pharisees, Herodians, and Sadducees—about where he received his authority, his beliefs in the resurrection of

❦ **Passover**

The most important Jewish feast; it celebrates the Exodus, YHWH's deliverance of the Chosen People from Egypt.

the dead, and whether or not it was necessary to pay taxes to the government.

The Last Supper. At this Passover meal, Jesus gathered with his disciples. He broke bread and said, "This is my body." He shared a cup of wine and said, "This cup is the new covenant in my blood, which will be shed for you." This meal was in anticipation of the giving of Jesus' Body and Blood in his Passion and Death.

The Agony in the Garden and Arrest of Jesus. After the Last Supper, Jesus retreated to the garden at Gethsemane. He prayed, "Abba, Father, all things are possible to you. Take this cup away from me, but not what I will but what you will" (Mk 14:36). His disciples were unable to stay awake with him. Jesus was betrayed by Judas, one of his Apostles, and arrested in the garden by a crowd with swords and clubs who came from the chief priests and elders.

Jesus before the Sanhedrin. The Sanhedrin was the formal assembly of chief priests, elders, and scribes. When the high priest asked Jesus, "Are you the Messiah, the son of the Blessed One?" Jesus answers, "I am" (Mk 14:61–62). The high priest then tore his own garments. Others spat on Jesus. He was convicted of **blasphemy**, that is, claiming to be God. The next day, in another council gathering, the Sanhedrin bound Jesus and took him to the Roman governor Pontius Pilate, because they had no authority to carry out his conviction.

> ✆ **blasphemy**
> Any thought, word, or act that expresses hatred or contempt for God, Christ, the Church, saints, or holy things.

Jesus before Pilate. The details of the actual trial before the Roman governor vary between the Gospel accounts. Pilate is portrayed as one who has very little interest in the religious squabble between Jesus and the Jewish authorities. Yet it is clear that he knows Jesus is innocent, and still sentenced him to death under the charge that he claimed to be a king. Hung on the cross were the words, "Jesus of Nazareth, King of the Jews."

The Death of Jesus. Jesus' entire life was an act of love. His final, greatest act of love was that he gave up his very life. This was also a perfect act of obedience to God the Father. Jesus' final words as he hung on the cross were, "Father, into your hands

I commend my spirit" (Lk 23:46). Crucifixion was a form of capital punishment used in the Roman Empire until it was banned by the emperor Constantine in AD 315 for being too cruel. It was usually reserved for slaves and criminals convicted of the worst types of crimes.

◣ **Resurrection**

Three days after Jesus was buried in a tomb, he rose from the dead. Belief in the Resurrection is central to our Christian faith.

The Resurrection. Three days after he died and was buried in a tomb cut out of a rock, Jesus rose from the dead. There were no witnesses to the actual **Resurrection**, but to the empty tomb and to the Risen Jesus. This was verified by many witnesses, including Mary Magdalene and the women who discovered the empty tomb; Peter and the other disciples to whom Jesus appeared in the Upper Room (the place of the Last Supper); the disciples on the road to Emmaus; and to more than five hundred disciples gathered in one place (see 1 Cor 15:5–8). Belief in Jesus' Resurrection is central to our Christian faith. Christ, "the first-born from the dead" (Col 1:18), makes our own resurrection someday possible.

Ascension to Heaven and Return in Glory. After his Resurrection, Christ's Body was glorified. It operated with new and supernatural properties. For example, he appeared in rooms with locked doors. Yet, while he remained on earth and appeared to his disciples and many others, his glorified body was recognizable.

Jesus also was hungry; he ate fish. He invited the Apostle Thomas to probe his wounds by touch. Mary Magdalene, who first mistook him for a gardener, embraced him. For forty days, Jesus remained on earth. Then, the Scriptures report, he was taken back to Heaven where he is seated at the Father's right hand, signifying the start of the Messiah's Kingdom, one that will have no end.

How is Jesus the Good Shepherd?

What bothered Jesus' enemies about him?

Catholic Apologetics

Is Jesus God?

✝ Yes. Jesus Christ is true God and true man. He became truly man while remaining truly God. Jesus is one person, the Second Person of the Trinity, with two natures, human and divine. He is the "Word made flesh."

Was Jesus really human in the same way I am human?

✝ Jesus was a real person who lived and walked on this earth. He lived in Nazareth, a town in Israel nearly two thousand years ago. Jesus is like us in everything but sin. He was able to grow in "wisdom, age, and grace."

Did Jesus know he was God?

✝ The union of the human and divine is a mystery that is hard to comprehend. Most theologians recognize that because Jesus had a human nature, he came to understand his divine nature in that context. This means the three-year-old toddler did not likely tell his mother all there is to know about God or predict the future. Rather, as he developed as a human, he was able to express more clearly his identity and mission as God.

Did Jesus have brothers and sisters?

✝ The New Testament does mention "brothers and sisters" of Jesus (e.g., Mk 3:31–35). The Church understands these references to be to children of another Mary, a disciple of Christ. The words brother and sister may also refer to close relations like cousins. The

Church holds that Jesus was Mary's only child and that she was ever-virgin, though she is the spiritual mother of all.

Who is responsible for the Death of Jesus?

✤ Throughout history, the Jews have taken unfair blame for the Death of Jesus. The Jews, collectively, must not be held responsible for the Death of Jesus. As to the personal sin of participants like Judas, members of the Sanhedrin, and Pilate, it is known to God alone. Rather, the answer to the question is more accurately "all sinners are responsible for the Death of Jesus" as our sins affected Christ himself.

Why did Jesus descend into hell?

✤ In Scripture, the place where the dead go was called hell—*Sheol* in Hebrew or *Hades* in Greek. When the Apostles' Creed says that Jesus descended into hell, it is teaching that Jesus really died and through his Death conquered death. He did not descend into hell to free the unjust or to destroy hell, but to lead the dead who were just to Heaven. As the first letter of Peter says: "The gospel was preached even to the dead" (1 Pt 4:6).

When will Jesus come again?

✤ Since the Ascension of Jesus to Heaven, Jesus' Second Coming is imminent, though we do not know the day or hour. We are to live each moment as if Jesus may come. Before Christ's Second Coming, the Church will pass through a final test that will severely challenge the faith of many. At the end of time, all creatures in the universe will acknowledge Christ as Lord.

 For **You** to **Do**

The Lord at the Center of Your Life

To St. Thérèse of Lisieux, Christ was the center of her life. In a poem titled *A Lily Among Thorns* she wrote:

> When my youthful heart was afire
> with the flame we call love,
> You came and claimed it for Yourself.
> And You alone, O Jesus, could satisfy my soul,
> For boundless was my need of loving You.

How has Jesus claimed *you* for his own? Look back over your life and name ways that Jesus as been at the center of your life. What are some memories you have that involve your relationship with Jesus. Examples might be:

+ at the birth of a younger sibling
+ when a family member was ill
+ the time around your First Communion
+ the occasion of joy: a birthday celebration, acing a test, reuniting with a friend
+ at a special Mass

Next, consider your future. What are some concrete actions you can take to show that you are willing to put Jesus at the center of your life? Answer questions like these:

+ Will you attend a Catholic college or join a Catholic club while in college?
+ Will you continue to attend and participate in Sunday Mass?
+ Will you continue your study of the Bible and other faith issues?
+ Will you take an active adult role in your parish?
+ Will you reach out to the poor and help them to meet their needs?
+ Will you support the right to life from conception until natural death?
+ Will you consider a vocation to either the priesthood or consecrated life?
+ Will you look for a marriage partner who shares your commitment to faith?
+ Will you raise your children to be Catholic?
+ Will you speak up on the job for your Catholic values?

Assignment

Choose an age for yourself some time in the future (e.g., five, ten, fifteen, or twenty years from now). Prepare a three- to five-minute talk that you might give to introduce yourself to a potential employer on a job interview, to the parents of your prospective spouse, or to reacquaint yourself with a friend you have not seen since high school. Tell about your life, including your career and vocational plans. Reserve at least half of your talk to tell about the commitment you have to Jesus at that age and what the commitment entails. Plan to share your talk with your Confirmation class and/or with your sponsor.

Prayers and Reflections 🏃

One Solitary Life

He was born in an obscure village, the child of a peasant woman.
He grew up in another village, where he worked in a carpenter
shop till he was thirty. Then for three years he was a traveling
preacher. He never wrote a book. He never held an office. He never
traveled two hundred miles from the place where he was born. He
did none of the things one usually associates with greatness.

He was only thirty-three when the tide of public opinion turned
against him. He was turned over to his enemies and went through
the mockery of a trial. He was nailed to a cross between two
thieves. When he was dead, he was laid in a borrowed grave.

Twenty centuries have come and gone, and today he is the central figure of the human race and the leader of humanity's progress.
All the armies that ever marched, all the navies that ever sailed, all
the kings that ever reigned have not affected the life of human persons as that One Solitary Life.

—Anonymous

Logos

The Logos of God was made flesh . . . to destroy death and to give
life to man, for we were in the chains of sin and destined to be born
through the state of sin and to fall under the empire of death.

—St. Irenaeus

Word of God

The Lord is my shepherd; there is nothing I lack.

—Psalm 23

Prayer of the Criminal

Jesus, remember me when you come into your kingdom.

The Lord's Prayer

Our Father
who art in heaven,
hallowed be thy name.
Thy kingdom come;
thy will be done on earth as it is in heaven.

Give us this day our daily bread
and forgive us our trespasses
as we forgive those who trespass against us.
And lead us not into temptation,
but deliver us from evil.
For the kingdom, the power, and the glory are yours,
now and forever.
Amen.

four

SCRIPTURE

Sacred Book

For Catholics, the Bible is the Book of the Church.

This is a significant statement because for many other Christians the opposite is true: they belong to a church of the Book.

Think about the differences in these two statements.

Catholics believe that Sacred Scripture is "the speech of God as it is put down in writing under the breath of the Holy Spirit" (*Constitution on Divine Revelation*). It was the Church—real people—who were inspired by God to write the words God intended. The Scriptures ("writings") are one of the ways that God communicates to humankind.

The inspired text of the Bible contains the fullness of God's Revelation. In the first century, following the apostolic Tradition, the Church determined which writings were to be included in the Bible. The complete list is called the canon of Scripture. While these books contain the fullness of God's Revelation, the Church continues to guide the People of God through its integration and application of the truths of Scripture. God continues to guide the successors of the Apostles—the Pope and bishops—in every generation to preserve, expound on, and spread God's Word to all. This ongoing teaching is known as the Church's **Sacred Tradition**.

Both Scripture and Tradition are accepted by Catholics as equal means for transmitting God's Word.

❦ Sacred Tradition

The living transmission of the Church's Gospel message found in the Church's teaching, life, and worship. It is faithfully preserved, handed on, and interpreted by the Church's Magisterium.

65

What about the phrase "church of the Book"? Honestly, there are several Christian denominations that do not assign equal weight to Scripture and Tradition. For some Christians, the Bible is God's final Revelation to the world. Answers to every human concern can be answered in the pages of the Scriptures according to this view. In these denominations, the Bible is the primary focus for instruction, worship, and prayer.

The Bible is a rich and varied work that tells the story of our Salvation—truly the greatest story ever told. For years, Catholics did not spend much time individually reading the Bible, relying instead on bishops and priests to interpret the text. Things have changed now. You probably own your own Bible, and you may study the Bible whether you are in Catholic or public school.

It's important to know not only what is in the Bible, but how it was written, and how the Bible continues to have a place in the Church today. It is, after all, the Book of the Church.

 In what ways has the Bible been a vital part of your life?

Truth and Inspiration

You may have fielded questions from friends and acquaintances alike who like to rattle your cage and challenge your faith. Regarding the Bible, they may ask things like:

···→ How could God make the world in only seven days?

···→ If God didn't make the sun and the moon till the fourth day, how could he have created light on the first day?

···→ Did Moses really live to be 120 years old?

···→ If Mary was ever-virgin, why does the Bible say that Jesus had brothers?

You yourself may have wondered at different times and in various ways "Is the Bible true?"

Answering that question demands expanding our understanding of truth. A dictionary defines truth as "conformity to fact or actuality." This definition works well when speaking of mathematical or scientific truth, two kinds of truth we are most used to today. Mathematical truth is well defined through calculation, the citation of laws of arithmetic, and is verifiable through the use of calculators or computers. Scientific truth operates in much the same way: a hypothesis is drawn, it is proven by experiments and observations, and is verified by others through many other occasions of testing.

Is the Bible true in those same ways? Hardly. There is little mathematical truth in the Bible, though weights, measurements, and currencies are occasionally mentioned. The same is true of modern scientific truth. The Bible reflects the scientific understanding of the day, which by our standards is very primitive.

But there are other kinds of truth besides mathematical and scientific truth.

For example, what about the statement: "My mom loves me." Wouldn't most people consider that to be true for them? This type of truth—call it relational truth—cannot be verified by experiment or calculation. Rather, *you know it is true from your experience and from the testimony of others.*

Or, consider the comment on the weather "It's raining cats and dogs." How is this true? Certainly we know that animals are not falling from the sky. We also know that the statement probably describes a torrential downpour. This type of truth may be described as *symbolic truth.*

The Bible has examples of both relational truth and symbolic truth. The people described in the Bible are relational in all the ways we know: they are sons and daughters, husbands and wives, friends and enemies. Within all of the different types of relationships are the normal give-and-take elements that are part of human life. Symbolic truth is also common in the Bible. Think of one of the ways that Jesus taught. For example, the Gospels recount many times Jesus taught through the use of parables—a story using easily understood symbols that ends with a surprising moral lesson.

There are two other areas of truth that must be mentioned here. The first is *moral truth*: the Bible contains many laws and standards for living (most obviously, the Ten Commandments). The other type of truth is *religious truth*. This type of truth describes God's relationship with humankind, both the old covenant between YHWH and the Jews and the New Covenant established by Jesus between all who come to believe in him and the Father who sent him.

God Is the Author of the Scriptures

Over and above the examples of *kinds* of truth and the different *ways* the Bible is true, the Bible is true because God is the author.

What does this mean? Did God magically pen the Sacred Scriptures and then rain it down from the sky so that it suddenly appeared in places of worship? Hardly. Rather, God inspired the human authors of the sacred books. Again, be careful as to how you envision the **inspiration** occurring.

✌ **inspiration**

The guidance given to the human authors of the Sacred Scripture so that they wrote what God wanted written for our benefit.

Very few scholars would hold that God spoke each word of the Bible into the ears of the human authors and they simply transcribed what they were told, word for word, punctuation and all.

More accurately God, as the Second Vatican Council explains, "chose certain men who, all the while he employed them in this task, made full use of their own faculties and powers so that, though he acted in them and by them, it was as true authors that they consigned to writing whatever he wanted written, and no more" (*Constitution on Divine Revelation*). This is a good summary of the Catholic understanding of inspiration.

Under this understanding, the human authors not only had the freedom to choose the words they wrote, but also the arrangement and discretion of stories and incidents that they would include in their texts. For example, the Gospel of Matthew was the only Gospel to include the story of Joseph taking Mary and Jesus to Egypt. Why did Matthew include this story? Probably because he wanted to associate Jesus with Moses, who was also called from Egypt, as he was writing for Jewish converts to Christianity. This connection between Jesus and Moses is what God intended—it is inspired.

Catholics call for an examination of the author's intention to analyze the Bible. Other Christians—those who believe in a literal interpretation—would disagree. They would argue that whatever is written in the Bible actually happened. That's the way it is. Hence, those who interpret the Bible literally may hold that God did make the world in six twenty-four-hour days. Or that Moses really did live to be 120.

How Do We Understand the Scriptures?

The Scriptures were written by human authors using human language. To understand the Scriptures, we must try to figure out what the authors wanted to say and what God wanted to reveal in those writings. This means paying special attention to the historical time and the culture in which the writing took place and to the literary styles the author used.

The study or explanation of a biblical book or passage is known as *exegesis*. This is a Greek word that means "leading out." The goal of exegesis is to lead out or bring out the biblical author's intentions, purpose, and meaning related to the writings. Biblical exegesis takes into account the original language in which the book was written (the Old Testament was mostly written in Hebrew, the New Testament in Greek), the cultural and social background of the author and the audience, the geographical setting of the text, Church doctrines related to the Bible and biblical studies, the quality of the translations of the biblical texts, and the literary forms or styles of writing used.

For example, consider two of the criteria for biblical exegesis: cultural and social background and analysis of literary forms or styles of writing used.

It is easy to note how cultural and social differences in the author and the author's intended audiences play a part in differences between the Gospels. Mark's Gospel, likely the first written, was intended for a Gentile (non-Jewish) audience. Matthew's Gospel was written for Christians with Jewish ancestry. Matthew's Gospel includes about 600 of Mark's 661 verses, including an incident when the Pharisees question Jesus about why his disciples do not follow Mosaic Law and wash their hands before eating a meal. The text of the question in Matthew goes like this:

> Then the Pharisees and scribes came to Jesus from Jerusalem and said, "Why do your disciples break the tradition of the elders? They do not wash their hands when they eat a meal." (Mt 15:1–2)

The same incident in Mark's Gospel is described as follows:

> Now when the Pharisees with some scribes who had come from Jerusalem gathered around him, they observed that some of his disciples ate their meals with unclean, that is, unwashed hands. (For the Pharisees and, in fact, all Jews, do not eat without carefully washing their hands, keeping the tradition of the elders. And on coming from the marketplace they do not eat without purifying

themselves. And there are many other things that they have traditionally observed, the purification of cups and jugs and kettles and
beds.) So the Pharisees and scribes questioned him, "Why do your
disciples not follow the tradition of the elders but instead eat a
meal with unclean hands?" (Mk 7:1–5)

It is easy to determine the reason for the longer text in Mark. Writing for Gentiles who were not familiar with Jewish law, the author
needed to put into context the question of the Pharisees and scribes by
explaining more about the law they were violating. The author of
Matthew, on the other hand, did not need to go to such lengths. His
Jewish audience would be well familiar with the law Jesus' disciples
were accused of breaking.

As to literary genres and types of writing used in the Scriptures,
you are probably already aware of many of the different kinds. A sam-
pling of some of the kinds includes:

> *Parables.* These are short stories with a moral lesson that fea-
> ture commonly understood people and things. The moral les-
> son is usually told around a surprising ending. Most of the
> parables are in the Gospels and are told by Jesus.
>
> *Proverbs (wise sayings).* These short, often famous sayings are
> contained in the books of Proverbs, Ecclesiastes, Wisdom, and
> Sirach.
>
> *History.* These are accounts of important events told from the
> perspective of religious experience. Many books in both the
> Old and New Testaments contain histories that are verifiable by
> parallel historical accounts from other sources of the period.
>
> *Hymns.* The Book of Psalms is made up completely of songs of
> praise to God. Hymns can be found elsewhere too, for exam-
> ple in Paul's letters.
>
> *Letters.* All of the Epistles of the New Testament are written in
> letter style.
>
> *Genealogies.* A list of ancestors of Moses occurs in Exodus 1,
> and Matthew's and Luke's Gospels both have genealogies of
> Jesus. Interestingly, Matthew's genealogy traces to Abraham,
> the first Jew. Luke's genealogy begins with Adam, the first
> man. Recall that the author of Matthew wrote for Jews and the
> author of Luke wrote for Gentiles.

Prayers. The Psalms are prayers. Also, Jesus teaches his disciples to pray the Lord's Prayer, included in Matthew 6:9–13 and Luke 11:2–4.

Of course, understanding the Bible is different than understanding any other written text. Besides just delving into the text, the Scriptures must be interpreted with the help of the Holy Spirit, who inspired the texts in the first place. To do so, you must be attentive to the content and unity of the entire Bible, not only focusing on one book. The Scriptures must be read from the perspective of the living Tradition of the Church rather than individualistically—that is, you must consider what the Church says about their meaning. Also, the Scriptures must be understood within the whole plan of God's Revelation.

Finally, there is an additional point to consider for understanding Scripture. It is Jesus Christ, the Incarnate Word of God, who is present throughout the Bible. The Old Testament sets the stage, if you will, for Christ's coming. The New Testament completes the story and tells how Jesus brought Salvation to all who believed in him. Jesus, the Word of God, is the one unique word of Sacred Scripture. As St. Augustine (at right) explained:

> You recall that one and the same Word of God extends throughout the Scripture, that it is one and the same Utterance that resounds in the mouths of all the sacred writers, since he who was in the beginning God with God has no need for separate syllables; for he is not subject to time.

"George Washington never told a lie" is an example of which kind of truth?

Explain how the Bible is inspired.

Read Mark 10:35–45. Compare it with Matthew 20:20–28. What are the differences? What is one possible reason for the differences?

Name and explain three styles of writing in the Bible.

Name an occasion when you were inspired to do something. How did this experience help you to understand the meaning of inspiration?

Read the Gospel of Mark in its entirety. List at least three insights you gleaned about the Gospel from the commentary in the page margins.

The Canon of Scriptures

As you probably know, the word *bible* is from a Greek word *biblion* that means "book." You also likely know that the Bible is different from other typical books that you are used to. Most easily recognized, the Bible is not actually one book at all, but is made up of seventy-three books divided into the Old Testament and the New Testament.

There are other anomalies about the Bible as compared to other compendiums of modern writings. For example, the books in the Bible are not organized chronologically by the order they were written. The Book of Genesis comes first because it deals with topics of creation and beginnings, not because it was the first book written. In the same way, the Book of Revelation is placed at the very end of the New Testament because it deals with the end times and final judgment. It was most likely *not* the last book of the Bible to be written.

Also, interestingly, very few of the biblical books were written by a single author. The writings developed from years of oral sharing and when finally written down were considered more a production of a community than of a single author. In fact, a commonly accepted practice was to put the name of a famous member of the community or a famous ancestor of faith on the book rather than the actual author or, at least, to attribute authorship to him.

❧ **covenant**

A sacred and unbreakable agreement that God made first with the Israelites and renewed in Jesus with the Church.

The biblical writers also have a different way of recording history than we do today. The biblical writers began with a central theme or teaching—Salvation offered by God through his **covenant** with humankind—and worked backwards to illustrate this theme with historical evidence. For example, Mark's Gospel begins by announcing to the reader that "Jesus is the Son of God." The author then arranges events in Jesus' life and ministry that help to reveal this mystery to his disciples and explain it to the reader.

The "canon" of the Scriptures comes from the Greek word *kanon* which means "measuring rod" or "norm." The canon refers to the twenty-seven New Testament books and forty-six Old Testament books that are accepted as inspired books by the Church.

The Old Testament

The Old Testament canon took many years to develop. The law found in the book of Deuteronomy was discovered in 621 BC and attributed to Moses. Over the next two hundred years other writings

of the Law and the stories about creation were also credited to Moses. Eventually these first five books of the Bible—Genesis, Exodus, Leviticus, Numbers, and Deuteronomy—became known as the Pentateuch (Greek for "five books") or Torah.

Later other historical accounts of Joshua, the Judges, Samuel, and Kings were recorded and also well-read and accepted. Also writings of prophets (e.g., Isaiah, Jeremiah, Ezekiel, and the minor prophets) were being circulated. These became part of the Bible known as the "Prophets." The writings from after the Jews returned from exile became known as the "Writings," a category that basically covered anything not part of the Torah or Prophets. There were some disputes over the authenticity of some of these later books. The results of these disputes are still present today.

In the third century BC the Hebrew scriptures were translated to Greek. This translation is called the Septuagint, Greek for "seventy." According to tradition, seventy translators, working independently of one another, came up with exactly the same translated text from the original Hebrew Scriptures. Catholics accept this translation as inspired. However, when a group of Jewish rabbis met around AD 90, they decided to consolidate the scriptures and only include those they found written in Hebrew.

The seven books dropped by the rabbis—1 and 2 Maccabees, Judith, Tobit, Baruch, Sirach, and Wisdom—are also not included in most

**⚘ Protestant
Reformation**

An effort to reform the
Catholic Church in the sixteenth century that led to
the separation of large
numbers of Christians
from the communion with
Rome and with each
other.

Protestant Bibles. At the time of the **Protestant Reformation**, Martin Luther decided to include only the books approved by the Jewish rabbis. Most Protestant Bibles do print a separate section in the back with these books, referring to them as *apocrypha*, which means "hidden." Catholic Bibles include the seven books but refer to them as *deuterocanonical*—"second canon"—to show that these are not accepted in the Jewish canon.

The Church has always held that the Old Testament is the true Word of God and rejected any claim that the New Testament has voided the Old. Rather, the Old Testament is oriented toward and bears witness to the coming of Christ. All its books are inspired by God and contain a great store of teaching about God, wisdom on human life, a treasury of prayers, and a glimpse at the mystery of Salvation.

As an old saying, quoted by St. Augustine, puts it, "The New Testament lies hidden in the Old and the Old Testament is unveiled in the New."

The New Testament

The accepted books of the New Testament canon came relatively quickly by comparison to the Old Testament. By the second century AD, several Church leaders—including St. Clement of Rome, St. Ignatius of Antioch, and Tertullian—were using the term "New Testament" and referring to the accepted books for teaching and praying the faith. By the year 367, St. Athanasius fixed the canon at twenty-seven books. Finally, the Council of Trent in the sixteenth century confirmed that the canon was the inspired Word of God, using the following criteria: (1) the book had origins with the Apostles; (2) it was widely circulated and accepted by more than one local Christian community; and (3) the doctrine it taught was essential to the Christian faith.

The books of the New Testament are divided into three categories: the Gospels, letters written to local Christian communities or individuals, and letters intended for the entire Church. Many of the letters, or epistles, either are attributed to, or were actually written by, St. Paul. The heart of the New Testament, and in fact of all of the Scriptures, are the Gospels, a word that means "Good News." They are the principal source of the life and teachings of Jesus Christ.

The Gospels were formed in three stages. The first stage was the life and teaching of Jesus Christ. While he lived, Jesus preached and taught like all of the rabbis of his time, with the spoken word. In the years after his Resurrection, his followers did the same: by spreading the Good News in the oral tradition of their ancestors. This was the second stage of Gospel formation. The only difference was that their understanding of Jesus and his message was even fuller than before as they had received and were inspired by the promised Holy Spirit. These first disciples had no need to write down the Gospel as long as they were alive to share it and clarify it. Besides, they expected Jesus' return to be imminent.

Finally, in the third stage, the Gospels were written, beginning with Mark's Gospel (in about AD 65 to 70) and concluding with the writing of the Gospel of John near the end of the first century. Why the need to *write* the life and teachings of Jesus after so many years of the oral tradition? There were several reasons, for example:

> *The Apostles were dying.* As the years went on and the eyewitnesses to Jesus realized that he might not soon return, it became imperative that the Gospel be recorded.

> *There were weaknesses in the oral tradition.* The stories needed consistency in their telling and transitions between one story and the next. The stories themselves needed to be arranged in chronological order.

> *A catechetical manual and worship aid was needed.* So many new Christians were being instructed, a written document was necessary as the Apostles could not be in all places at once. Christians also needed worship aids for the same reason. The written Gospels would help to bring unity to the liturgy.

❦ catechetical

Having to do with a process of "education in the faith" for young people and adults with the goal of making them disciples of Jesus Christ.

It's important to remember that the four Gospels were written for different Christian communities. The Gospels of Mark, Matthew, and Luke are very alike, so much so that they are known as the Synoptic Gospels. *Synoptic* is Greek for "one-eye." The Gospel of John is different from the Synoptic Gospels and reflects a fuller understanding of Jesus' divinity.

The Acts of the Apostles is really in a special category all its own. It was written by the author of Luke's Gospel, almost as a sequel to the Gospel in order to fill in the details following Jesus' Resurrection through the early days of the Church. Acts details how the Gospel message spread through the Roman Empire, with much of the credit going to the missionary efforts of St. Paul, a Jewish convert who persecuted Christians before his conversion.

Paul is the writer of many of the letters of the New Testament. Other members of local churches may actually have written some of the letters ascribed to him, with Paul writing only the introductory or concluding remarks and signing the letter. Paul's letters are addressed both to whole communities—for example, those in Corinth, Philippi, or Rome—and to individual people like Titus, Philemon, and Timothy.

Letters that don't have a specific audience are called *catholic* or *universal* letters. They were credited to various Apostles like John, Peter, and Jude.

The Book of Revelation is written in a particular style of writing known as **apocalyptic literature**. The Book of Revelation centers around visions of events that are to come using veiled language that is difficult to decipher. It speaks primarily of the persecutions faced by the early Christians and their faith in the saving power of Christ.

🕊 apocalyptic literature

The word *apocalypse* means "revelation" or "unveiling." Apocalyptic literature, usually written in times of crisis, uses highly symbolic language to bolster faith by reassuring believers that the current age, subject to the forces of evil, will end when God intervenes and establishes a divine rule of goodness and peace.

NEW HOLY WORDS

Today there are many different translations of the Bible; your ears may immediately pick out a translation different than the one you are used to.

This was also the case in the fourth century when Christians first heard the Scriptures in Latin as translated by a young priest named Jerome. For years, Greek had been the common language spoken in the Roman Empire and, of course, the Christian Bible was in Greek, the New Testament was composed in Greek, and Christians used the Greek translation of the Hebrew Scriptures, the Septuagint.

But near the end of the century, much of the Empire, especially in the western half, spoke and read only Latin. Many books of the Bible had already been translated into Latin, but these were unauthorized and mostly inadequate translations. Pope

Damasus wanted a usable, accurate Latin translation. He assigned Jerome, one of his assistants, to the task.

Jerome was certainly qualified. He had studied rhetoric and Latin grammar in Rome beginning at the age of twelve. He could also speak and write Greek and Hebrew. As a devout Christian and priest, Jerome was also committed to doing a prayerful study of the Bible with his translation.

The Gospels were translated by Jerome prior to Pope Damasus's death in 384. When Jerome himself was bypassed as Pope, he moved eventually to Bethlehem where he lived the life of a hermit. He took it upon himself to move from the Gospels to the Old Testament, which he also hoped to translate to Latin.

Jerome (at right) took a con-troversial approach with the Old Testament. Not only did he draw from the popular Greek Septuagint, he referred to the Hebrew texts and relied on the help of Jewish rabbis as well. Jerome did not translate the Scriptures word for word either. Rather, often faced with no Latin word to substitute for the Greek, he translated more by what he called "sense by sense." What resulted was that Roman Christians mildly protested what they heard. Most simply had not had enough time to get used to the new language for the holy words.

St. Augustine was one of Jerome's harshest critics, and he even claimed that the new translation was capable of touching off riots by Christians who heard it. He cited an incident in Tripoli when the people protested strongly to the local bishop about Jerome's translation of the Jonah story from the Old Testament.

Eventually the protests died down, and Jerome's Latin translations became well-accepted. Interestingly, though, Jerome is technically not the author of the *Vulgate*, a name associated with the Latin translation that literally means "commonly known." Jerome only worked on the Gospels in the New Testament. The Latin translations of the epistles were included from other translators.

St. Jerome's legacy, however, rests in his work as a translator, commentator, and scholar. His final place of settlement in Bethlehem was a cave, thought to be the place where Jesus was born. Jerome died on September 30, 420, now his feast day.

How did the biblical authors record history?

Name the five books of the Torah.

Why were the Gospels written?

Detail the three stages of Gospel formation.

What is a Gospel story you find particularly meaningful?

Scripture in the Life of the Church

Scripture now has a much more accessible role in the life of the Church than it did just a hundred years ago. At that time, the Scripture readings at Mass were all in Latin. It was rare for Catholic high schools or colleges to offer any courses specifically devoted to the study of the Scriptures. When the Scriptures were covered, students usually read only summaries of the stories and did not read directly from the Bible. Catholic biblical scholarship—for example, studying the literary forms of the Scriptures—was also relatively limited prior to the 1900s.

The Second Vatican Council of the 1960s contributed greatly to the Church's renewed interest in the Scriptures. Prior to the Council, only a few selections of Old Testament and New Testament passages were read at Mass. Now the Church has a three-year cycle of Sunday readings and a two-year cycle of weekday readings so that Catholics are able to hear a good selection of the Old Testament and samples from virtually all of the books of the New Testament over that period at Mass. And all of the readings are now done in the vernacular, the common language of the people.

Besides hearing the Scriptures read at Mass, the Church also encourages Catholics to study and pray with the Bible as part of a life-long effort, always keeping in mind that the Sacred Scriptures along with Sacred Tradition form together the Word of God. As the Second Vatican *Council's Constitution on Divine Revelation* reminds us:

> Easy access to Sacred Scripture should be provided for all the Christian faithful. . . .
>
> This sacred Synod earnestly and specifically urges all the Christian faithful, too, especially religious, to learn by frequent reading of the divine Scriptures the "excelling knowledge of Jesus Christ" (Phil 3:8). "For ignorance of the Scriptures is ignorance of Christ" (St. Jerome).

In addition, the Bible is a great bridge for unity with other Christians who are separated from the Church. The healing words of Scripture can help to bind the wounds of disunity.

The Bible in Liturgy

For most Catholics, Mass is their greatest exposure to the Scriptures. At each Mass there are two or three readings from Scripture— always one Gospel reading—as well as a Psalm response, Gospel acclamation, communion antiphon, and several songs that are based in Scripture. The Scriptures are a vital part of the liturgy, for just as Christ is truly present in the person of the priest and especially in the consecrated bread and wine, he is also present in the Scriptures. As the Second Vatican Council taught: "He is present in his word, since it is he himself who speaks when the holy Scriptures are read in Church" (*Constitution on the Sacred Liturgy*, 7).

The Scripture readings for Mass are gathered in the *Lectionary* ("book of readings"). The Lectionary is organized around the cycle of the Church year with the primary focus being the **Paschal Mystery**—the life, Death, Resurrection, and Ascension of Jesus.

The texts of the readings are limited in length so that people can listen attentively more easily. Gospel readings are sometimes longer because they contain parables and stories of Jesus that are more likely to hold a person's attention. One of the three Synoptic Gospels—Matthew (Year A), Mark (Year B), or Luke (Year C)—is read throughout a particular liturgical year. The Gospel of John is read during the Lent and Easter seasons and in five Sundays of Year B to make up for the shortness of Mark's Gospel.

Prior to the Gospel, a first reading is chosen from the Old Testament that has been selected especially to relate to the theme of the day's Gospel. Oftentimes the Old Testament reading foreshadows

✔ Paschal Mystery

The way our Salvation is made known through the life, Death, Resurrection, and Ascension of Jesus. The Paschal Mystery is made present in the sacraments, especially the Eucharist.

something that will occur in the Gospel. For example for Year B, the Ninth Sunday of the Year, the first reading from Deuteronomy 5:12–15 is the Lord's command to keep holy the Sabbath day. The Gospel for that day, Mark 2:23–28, details the Pharisees' question to Jesus about why his disciples disregard some of the Sabbath laws. (Jesus goes on to explain, "The Sabbath was made for man, not man for the Sabbath.")

A Psalm response follows the first reading. On Sundays and holy days, a selection from one of the New Testament letters is read. This reading does not usually have a thematic connection to the first reading or the Gospel. During the homily, the bishop, priest, or deacon explains the meaning of the Scripture readings. His primary focus is on the main theme from the first reading and Gospel and how it applies to our lives. He may also touch briefly on the teaching found in the second reading.

Studying the Bible

The Church exhorts all Christians to faithfully study the Bible. Again, since the Second Vatican Council there are many more organized efforts to help Catholics do just that. For example, for Catholics your age, Catholic high schools typically offer a one- or two-semester course in the Old and New Testament, which will include opportunities to explore the ways  that God is speaking to you through the Scriptures. Even though your study may be personalized, you join your study with the teachings of the universal Church, especially through the teaching authority of the Magisterium. This can be done by consulting with many sanctioned biblical handbooks or study editions of the Bible as you read a specific book or passage.

As to the questions of where, how, and with which biblical passage to begin, there are really no pat answers. Some people have attempted to read the Bible from cover to cover (usually without much success). Others use the Sunday readings to guide their study, but there are many passages that never appear there, even over the three-year cycle. Some choose Bible study courses offered through youth ministry and parish religious education programs.

You are also encouraged to do individual Bible study. This can be a daunting assignment because of the size of the Bible, the number of books, and the perceived difficulty in deciphering material that is thousands of years old. You may have considered studying the Bible on your own only to be turned back by not being able to answer the question "Where do I begin?"

Here are two hints for getting started: First, remember the Bible is different than any other book in the world. It is the inspired Word of God. You may choose to read specific Bible readings for a particular Sunday liturgy. Or, you may begin by focusing on one part of the Bible, for example the Gospels. You may wish to use the following strategy:

1. *Choose a passage.* Let's say you've chosen the parable of the Good Samaritan from Luke 10:29–37.

2. *Read the passage all the way through, paying special attention to the people and setting.* In the parable of the Good Samaritan, the setting is a steep road and the characters are the man victimized by robbers and those who pass his way, including the Samaritan.

3. *Read the passage again, this time writing down any questions you have about the passage or anything else that drew your attention.* Example: "Who are priests and Levites?" or "Why is it so surprising that the Samaritan helped the man?"

4. *Seek answers to your questions as well as more background on the passage from biblical commentaries either within or separate from your Bible.* Example: Priests and Levites are representatives of Jewish leadership and would have been expected to come to the aid of the man. Samaritans and Jews were enemies going back to the time of the Babylonian exile. (This step helps you to keep your study connected to the larger teaching Tradition of the universal.)

5. *Pray over the passage. Listen for a special message God is giving you regarding this passage.*

Step Five reminds us of the most important way to use the Bible, as a book of prayer.

Praying with the Bible

You can't treat the Bible like your favorite novel or simply as a school textbook. The Bible is *primarily* a book of prayer. As St. Ambrose put it: "We speak to God when we pray; we hear God when we read the divine sayings." The Bible's central importance in the liturgy and sacraments reinforces its place as a book of prayer. But Catholics must also use the Bible for personal prayer. As God truly

speaks through the words of Scripture, reading and praying these words allows us a very intimate way of communicating with God.

There are many different ways you can pray with the Bible on your own. One common form of prayer is called by its Latin name *lectio divina*, which literally means "divine reading." You can also think of lectio divina as "prayerful reading." To pray this way with the Bible, choose a passage. Your choice may be the Gospel reading of the day or of a nearby Sunday, or another familiar passage, or it may be chosen through a random paging through the Scriptures. (St. Augustine once randomly opened the pages of the Bible to a passage from Romans 13:12 where he read that it was time to "throw off the works of darkness and put on the armor of light." This was the catapult for Augustine to reform his own life and seek Baptism.) Call on the Holy Spirit to be with you when you pray with the Bible. Read through the passage slowly. Don't rush through in an effort to see what comes next. Let each of the verses speak to you. If you do hear God speaking in your heart, pause and listen to the message. Take some more time to mull over what the Scriptures and their message may mean for you. Use the reading as a springboard for further prayer.

Other tips for praying with the Scriptures are:

⟶ Choose a quiet place for prayer. This may simply mean throwing a soft pillow in the corner of your room or finding a peaceful place under a backyard tree.

⟶ Reserve a regular time each day (or week) to pray with the Bible. Try to keep to your schedule.

⟶ Don't always expect to feel inspired or that God has spoken directly to you. Occasions of spiritual dryness are to be expected, learned from, and eventually cherished along with the "high" moments.

⤍ Always conclude with a prayer in your own words, sharing with God your gratefulness for your time spent together.

How did students typically study the Bible prior to the Second Vatican Council?

When is the Gospel of John read at Sunday Mass?

How often do you read, study, and pray with the Bible?

Using the past Sunday's readings, name a common theme between the first reading and the Gospel.

Randomly open the bible. Name a passage on the open page that speaks especially to you.

Catholic  Apologetics

How is God the author of the Sacred Scripture?

✝ God is the author of the Sacred Scriptures because all of the divinely revealed truths contained in the Bible have been written under the inspiration of the Holy Spirit. God inspired the human authors of the Bible. It was as true authors that they wrote whatever God wanted written, and no more.

Who wrote the Bible?

✝ Several human authors wrote the words of the Bible. Both the Old and New Testaments developed from an oral tradition in which stories were passed by word of mouth over generations. Much of the Hebrew scriptures was recorded during the Babylonian captivity. Originally the first five books of the Old Testament were attributed to Moses. More accurately, entire communities, under God's inspiration, helped to record the Scriptures. A similar process for the New Testament writings also took place. The Gospels were written thirty to sixty years after Jesus' Death and Resurrection.

Why should Christians bother reading the Old Testament?

✝ The Old Testament is important to Christians for several reasons. The books are divinely inspired. They are heard in liturgy and contain many beautiful prayers. The books of the Old Testament are a testimony to the entire story of our Salvation, including a prophecy of the coming of Jesus Christ, our Redeemer.

Is the Bible true?

✝ Yes. While there are scientific and historical errors in the Bible according to today's understanding, the Bible teaches primarily religious truth. The Bible teaches the truth God wants to communicate to humankind. As the Second Vatican Council taught, the Bible teaches "firmly, faithfully, and without error that truth which God wanted put into the sacred writings for the sake of our salvation" (*Constitution on Divine Revelation*, 11).

How should we read the Bible?

✝ Catholics read the Bible contextually. That is, they understand the Sacred Scriptures in the broad historical, cultural, and geographical context in which they were written. They also examine the styles of literature present. Catholics rely on the Magisterium (Pope and bishops) to help them interpret the meaning of the Bible. Oppositely, a fundamentalist approach at reading the Bible involves taking all the words literally. For example, a fundamentalist would believe that God created the world in six twenty-four-hour days.

What is the most important message of the Bible?

✝ As the *Catechism of the Catholic Church* points out, Christ is the unique Word of the Scriptures. The most important message of the Scriptures is that Christ—the Word of God—became man and brought Salvation to humankind through his life, Death, and Resurrection.

 For **You** to **Do**

The Catholic Letters

There are seven letters known as the "catholic" letters or epistles because it was presumed that they were written to address issues that were of importance to the entire universal Church.

The catholic letters address several wide-ranging and timeless issues, including the necessity of combining good works with faith, of living as good citizens despite being treated as society's outcasts, and of loving enemies and neighbors alike.

The letters have been given the names of Apostles, as happened with other New Testament writings, but exact authorship and dates of composition are uncertain. More background information on each of the seven catholic letters is given below.

The Letter of James

The author is probably the James who is called a relative of Jesus in Matthew 13:55 and Mark 6:3. He was a leader of the Jerusalem Jewish Christian church and spoke out at the Council of Jerusalem (see Acts 12). The letter was written approximately AD 65, though it may have been later if published by a disciple of James.

MAIN THEMES

✦ How to handle temptations

✦ How to control your speech and speak only the truth

✦ Why Christians do good work because of their faith

✦ The need for the rich to care for the poor

✦ The power of prayer, especially involving illness

The First Letter of Peter

Early Church tradition considered St. Peter to have written this letter from Rome shortly before his death somewhere between AD 60–67. Because the letter includes use of very developed Greek, a doubtful skill of the Apostle Peter, recent scholarship has attributed the letter to a later Christian disciple.

MAIN THEMES

✦ How to remain Christian in a world that doesn't like Christians

✦ Why Baptism is important

✦ How to stand firm against those who belittle your faith

The Second Letter of Peter

The author of this letter is unknown. He does incorporate much from the Letter of Jude that wasn't written until the last part of the first century. The letter also refers to a collection of letters by St. Paul that were not collected until the late 90s. The Second Letter of Peter is likely the latest document of the New Testament, written early in the first century.

MAIN THEMES

✦ The meaning of Jesus' Second Coming

✦ A reminder not to fall back into bad habits

The First Letter of John

The author is likely the same (or of the same school of authors) as that of the Gospel of John. It was written after the Gospel of John in the late first century.

MAIN THEMES

+ That Jesus, besides being divine, was truly human
+ To be a "child of light" you must refrain from sin
+ The antichrist is anyone who denies that Jesus is the Messiah

The Second Letter of John

The author is the same person who wrote the First Letter of John. In the Second and Third Letters of John the author introduces himself as the presbyter, a title that likely indicated his close relationship with one of the first disciples.

MAIN THEMES

+ Follow the great commandment: love one another
+ Jesus was a historical figure who lived on earth

The Third Letter of John

The same author who wrote the other two letters and the Gospel of John likely wrote this letter. It was written at the end of the first century, likely at Ephesus.

MAIN THEMES

+ The flexibility of Church leadership
+ The importance of imitating the good, not evil

The Letter of Jude

The Jude associated with this letter is probably the brother of James who is identified as the author of the Letter of James. He was not the Apostle Jude or Judas but was more likely among those relatives of Jesus listed in Matthew 13:55 and Mark 6:3.

MAIN THEMES

+ Be careful of false teachers who seek to destroy your faith
+ Continue to persevere in leading a Christian life

Assignment

1. Read the synopses of the catholic letters above. Focus especially on the main themes in each letter. Then choose one of the following letters or sets of letters to read completely:

   ✝ The Letter of James

   ✝ The First Letter of Peter

   ✝ The Second Letter of Peter and the Letter of Jude

   ✝ The First, Second, and Third Letters of John

2. Write down any questions that occur to you related to the main themes in the letter(s).

3. Go back and answer the questions.

4. Note personal thoughts and insights you gleaned from the passage.

Prayers and Reflections

Take Holy Scripture

Sometimes, when I read spiritual treatises . . . my poor little mind soon grows weary, I close the learned book which leaves my head splitting and my heart parched, and I take the Holy Scriptures. Then all seems luminous, a single word opens up infinite horizons to my soul.

—St. Thérèse of Lisieux

Knowing Scripture

Ignorance of the Scriptures is ignorance of Christ.

—St. Jerome

Word of God

Rejoice!

Rejoice in the Lord always. I shall say it again: rejoice! Your kindness should be known to all. The Lord is near. Have no anxiety at all, but in everything, by prayer and petition, with thanksgiving, make your requests known to God. Then the peace of God that surpasses all understanding will guard your hearts and minds in Christ Jesus. Finally, brothers and sisters, whatever is true, whatever is honorable, whatever is just, whatever is pure, whatever is lovely, whatever is gracious, if there is any excellence and if there is anything worthy of praise, think about these things.

—Philippians 4:4–8

Responses at Liturgy

The word of the Lord.
Thanks be to God.
The gospel of the Lord.
Praise to you, Lord Jesus Christ.

five

Church

"Where the Spirit Flourishes"

The Church Fathers once described the Church as being like the moon, all its light reflected from the sun. Echoing the words of St. Joan of Arc, we might say Jesus is the light that allows the Church to shine.

Just as we cannot consider the Church without Jesus, in the same way, we cannot discuss the Church without the Holy Spirit. Indeed, in the Nicene Creed, the article "We believe in one, holy, catholic, and apostolic church" is preceded by "We believe in the Holy Spirit." St. Hippolytus wrote that the Church is the place "where the Spirit flourishes."

The Church has both a human and divine dimension. It has a definite history, but, at the same time, it transcends history and can only be understood with the eyes of faith. The article of the Creed concerning the Church uses four characteristics, or marks, to help us understand more about what the Church is, who it includes, and what its mission is. These marks of the Church—one, holy, catholic, and apostolic—stand for the ways in which Christ and the Holy Spirit work in and among the Church. Yet, the marks also point out the weaknesses of the Church as its members often fall short of what they stand for.

Your commitment to the Church is at an important milepost. Will this Church remain for you one of rote obedience, where you belong and participate only to the extent that family members expect of you? Will you keep only marginal membership in order to secure a place for a wedding sometime down the road? Or, as you ready for and receive the Sacrament of Confirmation, will you let the light of Christ shine brightly on your face and let the reflection help others to uncover in you what it means to be a member of the Church?

 How will you answer the questions in the paragraph above?

The Church Is One

There are definite bonds within the Church that help to define and maintain its unity.

The Church remains one first and foremost because of its source: the unity in the Trinity of the Father, Son, and Spirit in one God. The Church's unity can never be broken and lost because this foundation is itself unbreakable. Also, Christ, the founder of the Church, died on the cross to restore the unity of all in one people and one body. Christ's gift of the Holy Spirit continues to join all believers together in Christ.

It is the gift of love given by the Holy Spirit to Christians that is the "bond of perfection" (Col 3:14). Other visible signs of the Church's unity include:

···→ The same creed. The Church professes one faith as received from the Apostles.

···→ A common celebration of divine worship, especially the sacraments. The Church respects diversity in this area. For example, the Mass is celebrated in many different languages, incorporating the traditions of several cultures.

🖋 **Sacrament of Holy Orders**

A Sacrament of vocation in which the Church ordains baptized men to the orders of deacon, priest, and bishop.

···→ A recognition of the bishops ordained in the **Sacrament of Holy Orders** as successors to the Apostles.

Admittedly, there are divisions among various Christian churches. You may have wondered, for example, why you can't receive communion at your friend's Lutheran service, nor she at our Catholic Mass. There are even divisions within the Catholic Church herself. These human failings and divisions are not the whole story in any way. There is a unity in Christ that is the Church's foundation and calling.

It's important to understand that from the beginning the Church has been diverse within its unity. Consider that the Church is represented by people of countless races, cultures, and nations. These people have different gifts, traditions, and ways of life. As to the differences in beliefs and practice of many denominational churches as represented above, the Second Vatican Council pointed out that several of these "particular churches that hold their own traditions" hold a rightful place at home in the one, true Church (*Dogmatic Constitution on the Church,* 13). The Catholic Church, the one, true Church, proclaims the fullness of faith and possesses the fullness of the means of Salvation. It is governed by the Pope, the successor of Peter, and the bishops who are in communion with him.

In discussing the Church's unity, there are several questions that need to be addressed. For example: How do such denominational churches fall under the one Church founded by Christ? What is the history of some of the divisions within the Church that have taken place? How can these wounds be repaired? The succeeding sections trace some of these issues.

Ruptures in Christian Unity

From the very beginning of the Church's history, there were rifts in its unity. St. Paul spoke of it when some of the local Corinthian church began to exclusively align themselves with different Christian leaders and consider some people to be superior to others. Jealousy was at the root of most of these early disagreements.

In later centuries, the divisions were more severe and lasting. Large communities became separated from the Catholic Church. Sinfulness on both sides contributed to these divisions, but the primary causes were heresy (denying essential truths of the faith), apostasy (abandoning the faith), and **schism** (breaking of the Church's unity).

For about the first thousand years, Christians belonged to one Church. This was the Church that took its moral and spiritual direction from the bishop of Rome, believing that he was given this role of primacy because St. Peter had been the first bishop of Rome and Jesus had personally commissioned Peter to be the leader of the Apostles and the Church.

A major schism in 1054 took place between the churches of the West (centered in Rome)

✮ **schism**

A break in Church unity that takes place when a group of Christians separates itself from the Church. This happens historically when the group breaks in union with the Pope, for example, when the Eastern Orthodox Church broke from the Roman Catholic Church in 1054.

and the East (centered in the Greek city of Constantinople). The Roman Church had added the expression "and the Son" to the article of the Nicene Creed referring to the Holy Spirit ("he proceeds from the Father and the Son") without seeking approval for such a change from a Church-wide council of bishops. Though there were other issues involved, this controversy led to a split that lasts to this day between what is now known as the eastern Orthodox Churches and the Roman Catholic Church. These eastern churches have many of the same doctrines, sacraments, Mass, and devotions as the Roman Catholic Church, but they do not accept the Pope as the universal leader of the Church. Still, great strides have been made in recent years to repair this rift.

A second major rupture in the Church's unity occurred in the Protestant Reformation of the sixteenth century. The root word of Protestant is *protest* and several Church leaders protested against perceived abuses in the Church. Several of these issues involved the mixing of the spiritual and political realms. Martin Luther, a Catholic priest from Germany, was the first to protest. Other protestors were John Calvin in Switzerland and John Knox in Scotland. These individuals and their followers broke from the Roman Catholic Church and formed their own branches or denominations of Christianity that came to be known as Lutherans, Calvinists, Presbyterians, Anglicans, Baptists, and more. From that time on, Christians who continued to accept the authority of the Pope were known as Roman Catholics, those who did not were called Protestants. While the authority of the Pope was a focal point of the disagreements, there were many other important issues as well, including the way in which God's **grace** works in our lives, the celebration of the sacraments, and the nature of the priesthood, to name only a few.

✔ grace

The supernatural gift of God's friendship and life. Grace allows us to respond to God and share in his nature and eternal life.

Nevertheless, the Catholic Church has a great deal in common with most Protestant churches, including belief in the Trinity, acceptance of the Bible as God's inspired word, a life of prayer, Baptism, a moral code, and service of the needy.

Christians in these churches are accepted by Catholics as brothers and sisters in faith. The Holy Spirit uses these churches as means of Salvation, "whose power derives from the fullness of grace and truth that Christ has entrusted to the Catholic Church" (*CCC*, 819). The Catholic Church is understood as being governed by the Pope—the successor to St. Peter—and the bishops who are in communion with him.

Repairing Christian Unity

Jesus prayed for the unity of his disciples on the night before he died "'so that they may all be one, as you, Father, are in me and I in you, that they also may be in us" (Jn 17:21). The Church will always be one because of its source (one God: Father, Son, and Holy Spirit), founder (Christ), and soul (the Holy Spirit). However, because of the ruptures (due in part to human sinfulness), the Church must continue to work toward unity and repair any damage to the unity that has taken place.

The *Catechism of the Catholic Church* lists seven things that are required of Catholics to help in this movement toward Christian unity:

1. A permanent renewal of the Church's vocation (e.g., especially toward charity).

2. The living of holier lives. This example counteracts the unfaithfulness of Church members that often play a part in divisions.

3. Common prayer with other Christians. We can pray for Christian unity and with Christians in other churches.

4. Fraternal knowledge of each other. This often takes place through participation together in social and service activities.

5. Formation of all the faithful—especially of priests—in this charge to develop greater unity. A first task is for us is to study our own faith so that we can comfortably share our knowledge of it with others.

6. Dialogue between the theologians and meetings among Christians of different churches.

7. Collaboration with other Christians in efforts of service to all people, for example to the poor.

Ecumenism is the name given to the efforts to build unity among all Christian denominations among themselves. It is an effort that encourages understanding among the various Christian churches and avoidance of needless opposition to one another. Interreligious dialogue is a related effort to foster religious understanding. These are dialogues between the Church and non-Christian religions in order to improve those relationships as well.

The ecumenical effort is one in which we can all participate. However, the reconciliation of all Christians to the one and only Church of Christ, the Catholic Church, is something that "transcends human powers and gifts." We place our hope "in the prayer of Christ for the Church, in the love of the Father for us, and in the power of the Holy Spirit" (*Decree on Ecumenism*, 24).

What have been some of the major causes of divisions within Christianity?

What does the Catholic Church have in common with most Protestant churches?

What do you think is the main cause of continued divisions within Christianity?

How can you participate in the Church's ecumenical efforts?

Attend an ecumenical prayer service around the Christmas or Easter seasons, or near a national holiday. Or, work on an ecumenical service project that brings together Catholics and other Christians.

The Church Is Holy

That the Church is holy might seem to be stating the obvious. Yet, *holiness*, a word that means "to be set apart" or "of God," does not come to the Church because of anything its members do. You cannot "make" yourself holy, for example, by sitting in church eight hours a day, by delivering three meals a day to the poor, or by being extra kind to the kid who sits next to you in math.

While those examples are worthy of themselves and can help you to grow in deeper holiness, the Church is *already* and *only* holy because Jesus, the founder of the Church, is holy and he joined the Church to himself as his body and gave the Church the gift of the Holy Spirit. Together, Christ and the Church make up the "whole Christ" (*Christus totus* in Latin). St. Gregory the Great wrote, "Our redeemer has shown himself to be one person with the holy Church whom he has taken to himself."

Together with Christ, everything we do as the Church has the intention of making ourselves and all the world holy in Christ and for the glory of God. Though our holiness is imperfect now, we are each called—through whatever course our lives take—to the perfect holiness by which God the Father himself is perfect.

What Is Holiness?

If someone described you as a "holy" person, how would you feel? You might think that being holy would not fly well among your peers. A holy person might be thought of as the one who never misses an assignment, is respectful of all adults, avoids situations where alcohol and drugs are present, and goes to church on Sunday. Actually, a person who acts in these ways *is* deeply respected by others, whether they admit it or not. And we would say that he or she is "holy."

The true test to determine holiness and the way to be holy is to love. Love is the visible evidence that shows us to be holy. St. John of the Cross wrote that "at the end of our life, we shall be judged by love." St. Thérèse of Lisieux called love "the vocation which includes all others; it's a universe of its own, comprising all time and space—it's eternal." According to St. Augustine:

> Love is itself the fulfillment of all our works. There is the goal; that is why we run: we run toward it, and once we reach it, in it we shall find rest.

Jesus gave us the most difficult criteria for love. We are to love others as we love ourselves. We are to have special love for children and the poor. We are to love even our most contemptible enemies. We do this because Jesus loved in these ways. Though we are sinners, Jesus loved us so much that he willingly died on the cross for us.

We are still a Church of sinners. One of the first characteristics of holiness is to acknowledge this fact, and also to know that the Church gathers us up in our sinfulness and carries us through the life of grace to holiness. As Pope Paul VI put it, "The Church is therefore holy, though having sinners in her midst, because she herself has no other life but the life of grace" (see *CCC*, 827).

Taking steps to overcome our sinfulness is part of the life plan to be holy. We do this through acts of penance and by seeking forgiveness for our sins. All the sacraments, and in this case the **Sacrament of Penance**, provide occasions for grace, for the absolution of sins, and the opportunity to be more loving.

❦ **Sacrament of Penance**

The name for the sacrament that allows a sinner to return to communion with Christ and the Church.

CALLED TO BE A SAINT

Thomas Merton, a famous writer and Cistercian, or Trappist, monk of the twentieth century, once had this conversation about holiness with his friend Bob Lax:

"What do you want to be, anyway?"

I could not say, "I want to be Thomas Merton, the well-known writer of all those book reviews in the back pages of the *Times Book Review*," or "Thomas Merton, the assistant instructor of Freshman English at the New Life Social Institute for Progress and Culture," so I put the thing on the spiritual plane where I knew it belonged and said:

"I don't know; I guess what I want is to be a good Catholic."

"What do you mean, you want to be a good Catholic?"

The explanation I gave was lame enough, and expressed my confusion, and betrayed how little I had really thought about it at all.

Lax did not accept it.

"What you should say," he told me, "what you should say is that you want to be a saint."

A saint! The thought struck me as a little weird. I said:

"How do you expect me to become a saint?"

"By wanting to," said Lax simply.

"I can't be a saint," I said. "I can't be a saint." And my mind darkened with a confusion of realities and unrealities . . .

The next day I told Mark Van Doren:

"Lax is going around saying that all a person needs to be a saint is to want to be one."

"Of course," said Mark.

All these people were much better Christians than I.

—from *The Seven Storey Mountain*

Increase your desire to be a saint. Take one small step toward that goal today.

A Communion of Saints

The Church is known as the "People of God," and its members are called "saints" or "holy ones" (see Acts 9:13). "Who me? A saint?" you may be questioning. A saint is simply a person who chooses to be holy. And all Christians are called to be holy.

The term *communion of saints* refers to the unity of all those living on earth (the pilgrim Church), those being purified in purgatory (the Church suffering), and those enjoying the blessings of Heaven (the Church in glory). In this sense, we are, in fact, all saints.

The Church also has a process of canonization in which it recognizes the particular examples of Christians who have led good and holy lives and died a death faithful to Jesus. The process includes careful study of the person's life and a sign from God (usually in the form of miracles) that this person is truly with God in Heaven. When completed, the Church can call these people saints and seek them out to intercede to God on our behalf and imitate their good examples.

Some non-Catholics criticize Catholics for "praying to saints." We *honor* saints for their holy lives, but we do not pray to them as if they were God. We ask the saints to pray with us and for us as part of the Church in glory. We can ask them to do this because we know that their lives have been spent in close communion with God. We also ask the saints for their friendship so that we can follow the example they have left for us.

Mary, the Mother of God, is the Queen of the Saints and the most worthy model of faith. What follows is a brief look at Mary and two other models of Christian holiness.

Mary was a young Jewish girl living in or around Nazareth when the angel of the Lord appeared to her with a monumental message. It was a call she was free to accept or reject: "Behold, you will conceive in your womb and bear a son, and you shall name him Jesus" (Lk 1:30). Mary's unwavering answer of "yes" to the angel's news was given in the obedience of her faith. St. Irenaeus later said of her decision, "Being obedient she became the cause of salvation for herself and the whole human race."

Mary, a virgin, was unmarried but engaged to Joseph at the time she conceived her Son. Jesus was conceived solely by the power of the Holy Spirit, fulfilling the prophecy of Isaiah: "Behold, a virgin shall conceive and bear a son" (Is 7:14). Mary's virginity was perpetual throughout her life; the Church holds that Jesus is Mary's only son, but her spiritual motherhood extends to all.

With her faithful husband Joseph, Mary raised Jesus in a loving home and taught him the Jewish faith of his ancestors. When Jesus began his ministry of preaching and healing, Mary supported him. When he was unfairly persecuted, tried, and hung on a cross to die, Mary was there. Finally, after Jesus' Resurrection, Mary remained with his disciples in the Upper Room of Jerusalem awaiting the coming of the Holy Spirit at Pentecost as her Son had promised.

The Church teaches several important truths about Mary. First, she was herself conceived immaculately, meaning from the first moment of her existence she was without sin and "full of grace." This belief is called the *Immaculate Conception*. At the time of her death she was assumed body and soul into Heaven, foreshadowing our own eventual glorious Resurrection. This belief is called the Assumption.

Finally, of all her titles (e.g., Our Lady, Queen of Heaven and Earth), the most significant is that Mary is the Mother of God. She is our Mother too, the Mother of the Church who fully cooperated with the Holy Spirit to bring Christ into the world.

St. Catherine of Siena was born in Siena, Italy, in 1347, during the time of the Black Death. She was the youngest of twenty-five children of Giacomo and Lapa Benincasa. Her father was a wool-dyer.

As a child, Catherine had a deep devotion to Mary and Jesus and experienced many visions. On one occasion, she was walking home with one of her brothers after a visit to the home of her married sister. Suddenly she stopped cold in the road, not even acknowledging the calls of her brother to come along. Catherine did not wake until he grabbed her hand. She then burst into tears and described her vision of Christ sitting in glory with the Apostles Peter, Paul, and John. At age seven, she consecrated her virginity to Christ.

Yet, around age twelve, Catherine's mother had dreams of seeing Catherine married and urged her to pay better attention to her appearance. For a time, Catherine agreed and even wore a bright dress and jewelry her parents had acquired for her and a sister. But soon after, Catherine would only dress simply. When her family continued to press marriage, Catherine cut off her hair. Her father realized that pressuring Catherine to marry was fruitless. He allowed her to retreat to a three-by-nine-foot cell where she prayed and fasted, scourged herself three times a day with an iron chain, and slept on a board. At age sixteen she became a lay member of the Third Order of St. Dominic. She also returned to live with her family and engaged in many charitable acts around her home.

Catherine's personal holiness attracted many followers, both men and women. Leaders sought her out to settle disputes. She dictated letters that were sent to many leaders around Europe to encourage them to reform. Catherine was also a great mystic. Her inspired *Dialogue* is a rich treatise on prayer. She believed that love of God is most dramatically shown in love of neighbor. Her famous letters to Pope Gregory XI helped to encourage him to return the papacy to Rome from Avignon, where he had been living in exile.

Pope Gregory's successor, Pope Urban VI, called Catherine to Rome to serve him as a counselor and advisor. She lived in Rome until her death in 1380, at the age of thirty-three.

St. Maximilian Kolbe is a saint of recent times. An activist Catholic priest at the time of the Nazi influence in Europe, he was held at Auschwitz as a prisoner in 1941. In July a prisoner escaped, and to punish the remaining prisoners, the Nazi guards lined the men up for the purpose of randomly choosing ten prisoners to execute. When Franciszek Gajowniczek, a husband and father, was chosen, Fr. Kolbe offered, "I want to die in place of this man." The guards were stunned and wondered why. "Because I am a Catholic priest," he told them. In the starvation cell, six of the ten prisoners died within two weeks. Maximilian Kolbe was fully conscious when he was killed by lethal injection on August 14, 1941, the eve of the feast of the Assumption.

We can all learn from the examples of these saints and countless others. We are to seek sainthood for ourselves. The Church assists us in our effort to be holy: through the holy Scriptures, the apostolic tradition, the teaching office of the Church, in the sacraments, and in the writings of the saints.

What is the true test of holiness?

What is Mary's most significant title?

Share a description of someone you consider to be holy.

Tell about one of your favorite saints.

Describe a basic "game plan" for becoming a saint.

The Church Is Catholic

The mark of the Church *catholic* (note the small "c") means "universal" or "for everyone." The Church is catholic in two ways. First, it is catholic because Christ is present in the Church in the fullness of his Body, with the fullness of the means of Salvation, the fullness of faith, sacraments, and the ordained ministry that comes from the Apostles. The Church is also universal because it takes the message of Salvation to all people.

All people are called to this catholic unity of Church. However, though the Church is for everyone, not everyone belongs to the Church in the same way. There is a certain ordering of people in the Church; full members are those who are baptized Catholics and who accept all the tenets of the Church, besides behaving in a loving way.

The Church also knows that other Christians, who for various reasons do not profess the Catholic faith in totality or have had their unity with the Pope severed, are still joined in many ways with the Church. Others who have not received the Good News of Jesus Christ are related to the Church in various ways.

For example, Jewish people are "the first to hear the Word of God" as we hear in the Good Friday liturgy. Both Jews and Christians await the coming of the Messiah, though the Jewish understanding of the Messiah remains hidden and mysterious while the Christians await the Second Coming of a Messiah they know to be the Risen Christ. With Muslims, the Church shares a belief in the one Creator God and the faith of Abraham, to whom God spoke. Finally, the Church shares a bond with people of all non-Christian religions because of our common humanity. The Church recognizes that all people are searching for the God who gives them life.

Why is the Church catholic? First and foremost it is because Christ is present in the Church. As St. Ignatius of Antioch wrote, "Where there is Christ Jesus, there is the Catholic Church." Because Christ is present in the Church as the Head while the Church is the Body, all Salvation comes through the Church. For this reason it is absolutely necessary for all Catholics to help lead others to Christ through the Church and to work to repair Christian unity.

To the Ends of the Earth

The Church's missionary mandate to share the Good News of Christ with *all people* began with Christ's own words at the time of his **Ascension** to Heaven: "Go, therefore and make disciples of all nations, baptizing them in the name of the Father, and of the Son, and of the holy Spirit, teaching them to observe all that I have commanded you. And behold, I am with you always, until the end of the age" (Mt 28:19–20).

✹ **Ascension**

Jesus' passage from humanity into divine glory in God's heavenly domain forty days after his Resurrection. It is from this domain that Jesus will come again.

It is the love of God that spurs us onward for Christ. The Holy Spirit is the fuel driving our missionary efforts. The Church always reaches out to people in all times, in all places, and in several different ways. Consider the following examples.

Did you know that *St. Patrick* was British, not Irish? In fact, Patrick was of a rather wealthy British family when a horde of Irish invaded his father's property and captured him when he was sixteen. The year was 403.

Patrick was sold to a Druid chieftain named Milchu and worked as a slave on a farm for the next six years. During that time he prayed fervently and learned the very difficult Celtic language. After six years as a slave, Patrick heard a message in a dream that told him, "Soon you will go back to your own country . . . see, your ship is ready." He escaped and trekked the 188 miles west by foot to the sea where he talked his way onto a departing ship. Eventually he was back home in England.

Under the guidance of St. Germain, Patrick studied for and was ordained a priest. His life had changed; he constantly dreamed of returning to Ireland. A short time later, the Pope appointed Patrick to return as Ireland's Apostle after others had failed in the mission, partly due to their difficulties understanding and speaking the language.

Patrick returned to Ireland in either the 430s or the 450s (many of the details of his life and missionary efforts have become shrouded in legend). He eventually traveled all over the island, bringing gifts to local chieftains and using their tribe members to act as guides.

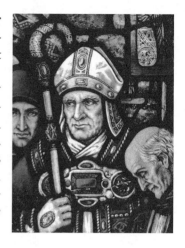

He did it all in order to bring as many souls as possible to Christ. In his *Confessions* Patrick (at right) wrote: "Among you and everywhere I traveled for your sake, amid many perils, even to remote places beyond which there was no one and where no one had ever penetrated, to baptize or ordain clergy, or to confirm the people."

Patrick died on March 17, 493.

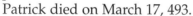

In the years between 1642 and 1649 eight Jesuit missionaries were murdered by members of the Iroquois and Mohawk tribes. These *North American Martyrs* endured years of physical and emotional discomfort while trying to bring the Catholic faith to Native Americans of the northeast.

Charles Garnier, a priest who grew up in a wealthy Paris family, often walked thirty to forty miles in dangerous territory to baptize a dying Native American.

Fr. Paul LeJeune wrote of the four worst aspects of Indian life: cold, heat, smoke, and dogs. The smoke, he said, was by far the worst as it filled the huts where women, men, and dogs slept together around the fire.

The language barrier between the French-speaking priests and the multi-language Indians had to be broken down. The Indians did not have a written language. Their words were spoken without using their lips and required several voice inflections in order to be able to be understood. Also, they did not have words to describe abstract thoughts, like faith. Besides language difficulties, each tribe practiced varying degrees of superstition, sorcery, promiscuity, and cannibalism.

The physical tortures the Jesuits suffered were severe. "We have sometimes wondered whether we could hope for the conversion of this country without the shedding of blood," missionary Gabriel Lalemant wrote. Fr. Isaac Jogues and his companions were captured by Mohawks while traveling along the St. Lawrence River. Taken to a Mohawk camp, they were forced to "run the gauntlet" between club-wielding tribal members. Jogues was then dragged unconscious up the hill where some then burnt his arms, dug fingernails into his wounds, and crunched his thumb between their teeth so that it was nearly severed.

Jogues survived this encounter and eventually prayed to return to the Mohawks to continue his evangelization. When he did in 1645, he was captured again and blamed for the deadly diseases that had plagued the tribe since he had left them. An arrow struck him in the head. His head was immediately cut off and stuck on one of the posts in the village. His body was thrown in the river.

The deaths of the other North American Martyrs were equally brutal. Fr. Jean de Brébeuf was tied to a stake. He was beaten and his fingernails were torn out. A cauldron of boiling water was poured over him in mocking imitation of Baptism. With his skin scalded, he was scalped of his skin and his heart was torn out. Some of the tribe members, marveling at his courage, came to drink his blood. Others ate his heart in hopes of being infused with this same courage.

And for what purpose did the missionaries suffer and die? To teach the faith with the hope of baptizing the Native Americans was enough of a goal. Brébeuf wrote, "We began our catechizing with the memorable truth that their souls, which are immortal, all go after death either to paradise or to hell. It is thus we approach them in public or in private. I explained that it rested with them during life to decide what their future lot was to be."

St. Katharine Drexel got a big kick as she traveled the desolate Louisiana bayous when a priest who was in her traveling party would fire off his shotgun in the air in order to call all the many black Catholics who lived in the area to Mass.

Katharine Drexel had made it one of her life's works to minister to African Americans in the years after the Civil War. She founded schools for blacks in cities from New York to Chicago to New Orleans. In 1935, she established Xavier University in New Orleans as the first Catholic college for African Americans. Today it is the only black Catholic college in the United States.

Katharine also founded schools across the country for Native Americans. When she met Red Cloud, the Sioux chieftain, she gave him a bridle and his wife a fringed shawl and a barrel of sugar. A few years later, Red Cloud protected a Drexel-founded mission from attackers during the Massacre at Wounded Knee. Late in his life Red Cloud was baptized.

Katharine Drexel's charities and missionary works are only part of her story. Born in 1858, Katharine's mother died just a month after giving birth. Her father, Francis, then married Emma Bouvier. Francis was a rich banker, and the one-time partner of J. Pierpont Morgan, one of the wealthiest men in the United States.

Katharine's father and stepmother gave her and her two sisters every advantage: tutoring, trips to Europe, the best clothes. Yet the girls were always taught that they were only stewards of their wealth, who must properly use the gifts that God had given to them. Once a week their parents opened the doors of their mansion in order to distribute food, clothing, and money directly to the poor.

Emma died in 1883, and two years later, Francis died as well. Of his estate of $15 million, he left one-tenth to charity and the rest to his daughters, with the instructions that they were to give the rest of the estate to the same charities on their passings.

Katharine's sisters followed their father's wishes. Katharine went a step farther. She spent *all* of her money on serving Native Americans and African Americans. When she asked Pope Leo XIII to send more missionaries to the United States to work with the Native Americans, the Pope responded, "Why not, my child, you yourself become a missionary?"

Katharine had been thinking all along of becoming a nun. With this encouragement, she founded a new order, the Sisters of the Blessed Sacrament for Indians and Colored People. She wrote in her order's rule that the sisters be allowed to receive daily communion, a privilege previously only allowed to monastic and contemplative orders.

At age seventy-eight, Katharine moved to her order's infirmary after suffering another in a series of heart attacks. She died in her room on March 3, 1955, about the time of the opening of the civil rights movement in the United States.

Local and Catholic

The Church in a particular area, called a *diocese* ("house"), is also truly Catholic as long as it is united to its local leader, the bishop. The sum of all the dioceses in the world are more than simply a federation in which each is a chapter; rather they are catholic through their communion with the Church of Rome, the Church where St. Peter himself was the first bishop.

Within a diocese there are parishes with given physical boundaries that include a place of worship, a church. In these local churches, where the Gospel is preached and Eucharist is celebrated, a variety of levels of income, cultures, language, and traditions exist. Yet each of these particular churches is really catholic.

Take, for example, the San Gabriel Mission parish in California, about ten miles east of Los Angeles. Originally founded by Franciscan missionaries led by Blessed Junipero Serra in 1771, the mission originally served the native Shoshone people of the area. At the time of Mexico's independence in 1833, Serra's view that the mission should be managed by the native people was disregarded. By 1852, the Franciscans had left the mission and it operated only as a small diocesan church.

New life was breathed into the Mission in 1908 with the arrival of the Claretian Missionaries. Two schools were built, and renewed outreach began to the youth of the community. Today the parish thrives and serves a parish of Anglo-, Mexican-, and Vietnamese-Americans. Ten Masses are celebrated each weekend in three languages. Amidst this great diversity is an equally great unity. As the parish's mission statement proclaims:

> The history of our Catholic tradition, the experience of our families, and the diversity of our cultures, languages, and gifts, strengthen and unite us as the Body of Christ.

Why is the Church catholic?

What was Christ's missionary mandate?

What do the stories of St. Patrick, the North American Martyrs, and St. Katharine Drexel have in common?

Describe the diversity of members of your local parish community.

Name and tell about another missionary saint. How can you emulate this saint's outreach efforts in the name of Jesus Christ?

The Church Is Apostolic

The Apostles chosen by Jesus are the foundation on which the Church began and developed. Jesus himself sent them on their mission: "Go, therefore, and make disciples of all nations" (Mt 28:19). The word *apostle* literally means "one who is sent."

Through the ministry of the Apostles, Jesus' mission on earth continued. As Jesus told the Apostles, "Whoever receives you receives me" (Mt 10:40). Through Jesus, the Apostles were united to the mission Jesus received from God the Father and given the power to carry it out. The Apostles were known among other titles in the New Testament as "servants of God" and "ambassadors of Christ."

The Church remains apostolic because it still teaches the same things the Apostles taught. And, the Church is apostolic because it is led by leaders who are successors to the Apostles and who help to guide us until Jesus returns.

The bishops are the successors to the Apostles. The Church teaches that "the bishops have by divine institution taken the place of the Apostles as pastors of the Church, in such ways that whoever listens to them is listening to Christ and whoever despises them despises Christ and him who sent Christ" (*Dogmatic Constitution on the Church*, 20). It is the bishops who confer the Sacrament of Holy Orders in three degrees—the degrees of priestly participation (bishops and priests) and the degree of service (deacons).

Yet it is not only the bishops (and priests) who are called to be apostolic. The entire Church, including religious and laity, are to take up the apostolic call to bring God's Kingdom to all the earth.

The next sections explain more how these groups work together as part of the one Body of Christ in the apostolic mission.

The Role of the Hierarchy

Simon Peter was clearly the leader of the Twelve Apostles. Jesus confided with him personally on several occasions. In fact, Peter's name is mentioned more than any other besides Jesus in the Gospels. Jesus said: "You are Peter, and upon this rock I will build my church. . . . I will give you the keys to the kingdom of heaven" (Mt 16:18–19).

Peter may have lived for more than twenty-five years after Jesus' Death and Resurrection. He traveled extensively around the Roman Empire and eventually founded, with St. Paul, the Church in Rome. Because of Peter's primacy among the Apostles, the Church at Rome came to enjoy the same primacy over other local churches. Thus, the bishop of Rome, or the Pope, is respected with authority over the universal Church in the same way that Peter once was.

All the bishops—and in a lesser way priests—share with the Pope the authority to teach in Jesus' name. This teaching office is called the **Magisterium**. The *college* or "body" of bishops

❦ **Magisterium**

The official teaching office of the Church. The Lord bestowed the right and the power to teach in his name to Peter and the other Apostles and their successors. The Magisterium is made up of the bishops in communion with the successor of Peter, the Bishop of Rome (the Pope).

has the authority to teach in union with the Pope. Magisterial teaching of the Pope and bishops can be found in their writings: council documents, papal encyclicals, pastoral letters, and sermons. The goal of these teachings is to build up the Church, administer the sacraments, and correctly proclaim the Gospel for the current age.

Infallibility is a gift of the Holy Spirit to the Church that enables the Pope and bishops to teach and proclaim a doctrine without error. This gift is based in the fact that Jesus remains with the Church for all time and that such teachings are given with the guidance of the Holy Spirit. One form of infallible teaching is when the Pope teaches "from the chair" of St. Peter. The Latin term for "from the chair" is *ex cathedra*. This type of teaching is very rare. The last time a Pope issued an *ex cathedra* teaching was in 1950 when Pope Pius XII proclaimed the Assumption, that Mary was assumed body and soul into Heaven after her death.

Another form of infallibility is found in the teaching of the entire body of bishops, in union with the Pope, especially in an Ecumenical Council. Finally, infallibility refers to the beliefs of the Church as a whole: those things that have always and everywhere been taught and believed by the Church, for example, the beliefs expressed in the Apostles' Creed.

Lay Faithful and the Consecrated Life

The term *laity* comes from the Greek word *laos*, which means "of the people." Lay people should never be viewed as second-class citizens in the Church. The laity have their own role or mission in the world to share in the priestly, prophetic, and kingly office of Christ. "Consecrated life" refers to Catholics who take vows of poverty, chastity, and obedience but are not ordained. Both committed lay people and consecrated religious have done much to strengthen the witness of Christ through the Church's two-thousand-year history as the following two examples attest:

Dorothy Day was a laywoman who by the end of her life in 1980 was known as someone who dedicated her life to help the poor. Once a communist and always influenced by its ideals, Day believed in an economy "based on human needs, rather than on the profit motive."

Dorothy's life, while always altruistic, was very confused early on. Born in New York but raised in Chicago, Day became a journalist who regularly wrote on controversial hot-button issues of the early twenti-eth century. When she protested the treatment of women political prisoners, she herself was jailed. A series of failed relationships paral-leled this part of her life. She got pregnant by one man and had an abortion. When she was twenty-nine, she found herself pregnant again. This time she married and had the baby.

The child changed her life, and she was determined to have the lit-tle girl baptized a Catholic though she herself was not Catholic and neither was the child's father. He, in fact, was an atheist. Dorothy broke up with the man one day and was baptized with her daughter the next.

The years that followed saw Day focus on the economic and social issues as she always had, but now from a Catholic perspective. She was the founder of the *Catholic Worker* newspaper, which sold—and does to this day—for one penny. The paper preached Day's economic views as well as pacifism, which she espoused during every American war that took place in her lifetime.

Besides the paper, she founded Catholic Worker Hospitality Hous-es where the homeless were sheltered and the poor fed.

She said about her life's work, "What we would like to do is change the world—make it a little simpler for people to feed, clothe, and shelter themselves as God intended them to do."

When *Alfred Bessette* arrived at the Congregation of Holy Cross novi-tiate in 1870, his pastor had sent with him a note: "I am sending a saint to your Congregation." The Congregation of the Holy Cross was a very new religious order at the time, founded in 1837 in France.

The religious brothers of the congregation did not see anything in Alfred, soon to be "Brother André," that would make them believe that they were in the presence of a saint. At age twenty-five, he could still not read or write. Plagued by a lifetime of illness, Brother André was frail and unable to do much physical work at all. The superiors of the order assigned him to be the porter at the door of their College of Notre Dame in Montreal. He stayed on the same job for the next forty years, welcoming young students and their parents. He often "moon-lighted" by giving the boys haircuts. By his barber chair he put a sim-ple sign and cup that read "Donations for St. Joseph."

Brother André's devotion to St. Joseph had developed strongly over the years. In 1904, he made a request of the archbishop of

Montreal to build a chapel to St. Joseph on the mountain near the college. The bishop agreed only if Brother André would use just the funds he collected in his dish. With only a few hundred dollars, the chapel was very small. But in time, he added roofing, walkways, heating, and the like.

In the area now known as Mount Royal, a large basilica, about 361 feet tall, sits on the spot of Brother André's first chapel. Millions of pilgrims visit it each year. It is a worthy monument to Brother André, but more to St. Joseph, whom he loved with childlike simplicity. Toward the end of his life he wrote:

> When you invoke St. Joseph, you don't have to speak much. You know your Father in Heaven knows what you need; well, so does his friend St. Joseph. Tell him, "If you were in my place, St. Joseph, what would you do?"

André Bessette died in 1936. In February 2010, Pope Benedict XVI announced that Brother André would indeed become St. André Bessette, canonized on October 17, 2010.

Why does the bishop of Rome have primacy in the Church?

Explain the meaning of *infallibility* in Church life.

Who is a lay person you admire for his or her service to the Church?

Research the location of the nearest Catholic Worker House to your area. With your sponsor, a classmate, or family member, contact the House and inquire how you might be of service.

Catholic Apologetics

Is the Catholic Church really the only true Church?

✦ The very name "catholic" means that the Church strives to reach out and include all people—this is the Church's mission. The Church teaches that "one true religion subsists in the catholic and apostolic Church" yet it recognizes that holiness can be found and God's will detected in various other Christian and non-Christian communities and in individuals who through no fault of their own have not been exposed to the Catholic Church.

Is the Church necessary for Salvation?

✤ The answer to this traditional question is "yes" simply because Jesus is necessary for Salvation and Jesus remains present in the Church, his body. Those who know and understand that the Church is the Body of Christ, yet reject it, are rejecting Salvation. However, this also means that those who never heard of Christ or the Church have not forfeited their chance for Salvation.

Do I have to believe everything the Pope says?

✤ The Church believes in the primacy of the bishop of Rome, the Pope. This means that since the time of St. Peter, Christians have been obliged to follow the teachings of the Pope in matters of faith and morals. Of course, this does not extend to matters not concerning faith (e.g., if the Pope says, "Everyone's favorite color must be blue").

What do I tell people who say to me "Catholics worship Mary"?

✤ You can tell them they are wrong. Catholics worship and adore God alone, as required by the first commandment. Worship of any other person or thing would be idolatry, honoring gods other than the one, true Lord. Catholics do venerate or respect Mary and all the saints because of their holiness and faithfulness as disciples of Christ. We revere Mary more than the other saints because she is the Mother of God, the queen of all saints.

How can a Catholic be excommunicated?

✤ To be excommunicated means that a baptized person is no longer "in communion" with the rest of the Catholic faithful. One type of excommunication is automatic and occurs when a Catholic commits a particular sinful action, defined as: desecrating the Eucharist, laying hands violently on the Pope, violating the seal of confession (for priests only), giving absolution to an accomplice in sin (for priests only), participating in an abortion, or committing the sins of apostasy, heresy, or schism. The other type of excommunication is imposed by the Church at the discretion of a local bishop for a particular action; for example, pretending to preside at Eucharist although one is not a priest.

What percentage of the world is Roman Catholic?

✚ The latest census numbered one billion Roman Catholics world-wide, about 17 percent of the world's total population. There are also an additional one billion Christians of other denominations. Islam is the second largest faith with 1.3 billion adherents (22 percent).

What is necessary for someone to become a canonized saint?

✚ The Congregation for the Causes of Saints is an office of the Pope in Rome. It examines the life of Christians who are proposed for sainthood, those who have practiced heroic virtue in their lives. The canonization process is many-tiered and may take years as the person's life, death, writings, and more are analyzed. Canonization is preceded by beatification. The person is called blessed and may be honored on a local basis. It's important to remember, though, that all Christians are called to sainthood and that anyone who is with God is, in fact, a saint.

 For **You** to **Do**

Key Events in the Church and History

The Church refers to three realities: Catholics who come together at liturgy; the local diocese, a fellowship of believers in Jesus Christ; and the universal community of believers throughout the world. The *Catechism of the Catholic Church* teaches:

> "The Church" is the People that God gathers in the whole world. She exists in local communities and is made real as a liturgical, above all a Eucharistic, assembly. She draws her life from the word and the Body of Christ and so herself becomes Christ's Body. (752)

The following timeline compares how key events in Church history correspond with those in recent Western history.

Date	Church History	Western History
1903	Pontificate of St. Pius X begins (into 1914)	
1905		Einstein publishes theory of relativity
1914–1918		World War I
1917	Apparitions of Our Lady of Fatima	
1939–1945		World War II
1962	Second Vatican Council convenes (into 1965)	
1969		Americans land on the moon
1978	Pontificate of Pope John Paul II begins (into 2005); first non-Italian pope in 400 years	
1992		Fall of Communism
1994	Vatican and state of Israel establish formal relations	
2001		United States World Trade Center destroyed in terrorist attack
2005	Joseph Ratzinger elected Pope Benedict XVI	

Assignment

Research one important event from Church history from the period above. Prepare a short report on the event. Summarize the report by explaining how it remains significant for people living today.

Prayers and **Reflections**

Word of God

As a body is one, though it has many parts, and all the parts of the body, though many, are one body, so also Christ. For in one Spirit we were all baptized into one body, whether Jews or Greeks, slaves or free persons, and we were all given to drink of one Spirit.

Now you are in Christ's body, and individually parts of it. Some people God has designated in the church to be, first, apostles; second, prophets; third, teachers; then, mighty deeds; then gifts of healing, assistance, administration, and varieties of tongues. Are all apostles? Are all prophets? Are all teachers? Do all work mighty deeds? Do all have gifts of healing? Do all speak in tongues? Do all interpret? Strive eagerly for the greatest spiritual gifts.

—1 Corinthians 12:12–13; 27–31

Conclusion of the Baptism Rite

Just as God's creature, the sun, is one and the same the world over, so also does the Church's preaching shine everywhere to enlighten all who want to come to the knowledge of truth.

—St. Irenaeus

The Apostles' Creed

I believe in God, the Father Almighty, Creator of heaven and earth; and in Jesus Christ, his only Son, our Lord: who was conceived by the Holy Spirit, born of the Virgin Mary; suffered under Pontius Pilate, was crucified, died, and was buried. He descended into hell; on the third day he rose again from the dead; he ascended into heaven, is seated at the right hand of God the Father Almighty; from thence he shall come to judge the living and the dead. I believe in the Holy Spirit, the holy catholic church, the communion of saints, the forgiveness of sins, the resurrection of the body, and life everlasting. Amen.

Prayer of St. Ignatius of Loyola

Teach us, Lord, to serve you as you deserve;
to give and not count the cost;
to fight and not heed the wounds;
to toil and not ask for rest;
to labor and not ask for any reward,
save that of knowing that we do your will through Christ our Lord.
Amen.

six

$\mathcal{M}$ORALITY

Beliefs Lead to Action

Morality involves putting your faith and religion into practice. No one appreciates someone who talks a big game then can't back it up with their actions. Living a moral life means being responsible for:

···→ what you say and do,

···→ your inaction as well your action,

···→ the motives for your behavior.

Living a moral life is only made possible by Jesus Christ, who in his Passion "delivered us from Satan and sin" and "merited for us the new life in the Holy Spirit" (CCC, 1708). Through your faith in Christ and subsequent new life in the Holy Spirit, your ability to live a moral and good life and follow Christ's example is increased and multiplied. The final fruits of the moral life are the glory of Heaven. At your Confirmation you will receive the **gifts of the Holy Spirit** to help you live a moral life.

Living a moral life as a human being also means being free. God has gifted you with the freedom "to act or not to act, to do this or that, and so to perform deliberate actions on your own responsibility" (CCC, 1731). God is not the master programmer or puppeteer high above the earth controlling your every action. You

⚘ gifts of the Holy Spirit

An outpouring of God's gifts to help us live a Christian life. The traditional seven gifts of the Holy Spirit are wisdom, understanding, knowledge, right judgment, courage, reverence, and wonder, and awe.

have been made free, a person who can initiate and control your own actions. The more you choose good, the freer you become.

Oppositely, when you choose evil, you begin a downward spin toward being a slave to sin.

This chapter explores some of the factors that go into making choices and determining what is good and what is sinful, always keeping in mind, as Pope John Paul II wrote that, "Following Christ is thus the essential and primordial foundation of Christian morality" (*Splendor of Truth*, 19). Your belief in Christ makes you a child of God, transforming you with the help of the Holy Spirit, to follow the example of Christ. You are capable of acting rightly and doing good.

Speaking of the moral life, St. Francis de Sales once put it, "One of the most excellent intentions that we can possibly have in all our actions is to do them because our Lord did them."

 Concretely, what does it mean to back up your moral beliefs with action?

The Morality of Human Acts

✔ free will

The capacity to choose among alternatives. Free will is the "power, rooted in reason and will...to perform deliberate actions on one's own responsibility" (CCC, 1731). True freedom is at the service of what is good and true.

As humans are the only creation made in God's image, through the gift of **free will** we have the opportunity to choose the good. We are able to recognize God's call, through the gift of conscience, to avoid evil and do good. When we follow the dictates of conscience, the fruit of our good decisions can be witnessed in our love for God and our love for neighbor.

Unfortunately, humans are also capable of choosing evil. Tempted by Satan, the first humans, Adam and Eve, abused the gift of free will and chose evil. This is the Original Sin. Our nature continues to carry the wound of Original Sin, and we are inclined to sin. It is only through the Passion of Christ that we are delivered from sin and the damage of sin. Christ brings us new life in the Holy Spirit.

As long as we have the gift of free will and are not bound by force to God, who is the ultimate good, there is the possibility that we can choose good over evil or evil over good. It is the gift of freedom that makes us moral. Acts that are freely chosen can be evaluated morally as good or evil. The morality of human acts depends on the object chosen, the intention, and the circumstances of the action. These elements are explained further in the following sections.

The Moral Object

The moral object is the "what" of morality; it is what we do. There are good moral actions and evil actions. There are some actions that are objectively good; for example, providing food for a poor person in the neighborhood. In summary, the object of a human act is good when it promotes the well-being and true good of others, and when it conforms to objective norms of morality like the **Ten Commandments**. Such actions lead us to God. There are some actions that are objectively bad—lying, cheating, stealing, and murder are examples.

✔ **Ten Commandments**

A source of Christian morality. God revealed them to Moses. The first three commandments have to do with love for God. The last seven refer to love for neighbor.

Sometimes there may be a difference of opinion about what is good and what is bad. In this case, we are speaking of subjective truth ("truth as it appears to me") rather than objective truth ("truth as it is in reality"). Take this example:

> A Boy Scout helps a Cub Scout work on putting together a coin collection in order to help the younger boy achieve a merit award. This is obviously a very caring act.
>
> However, what if the Boy Scout's only motivation for helping was so that he might achieve his own merit badge and further himself up the scouting ranks?
>
> Worse yet, what if the older boy only helped the younger one so that he might be able to switch one of his own less valuable coins with a coin belonging to the Cub Scout that was worth much more?

This example points out that while there are certain acts that are always wrong regardless of the intention or circumstances, with other acts the rightness or wrongness is determined by the intention and/or the circumstances.

The Intention

"The end does not justify the means." What this common saying refers to is that a good intention (like helping a friend to pass a final exam) does not make a behavior that is objectively wrong (like cheating) good or just.

A bad intention can make an act evil that is of itself good. One action can have several intentions, some of them bad and some of them good. For example:

> A high school junior, Lori, gives a freshman, Kya, a ride home from school every day. This is a nice thing to do. But Lori was only doing this in the hope that Kya's father will give her a summer job as a receptionist at his medical plaza. Additionally, when Lori is with her own friends, she gossips about Kya and describes her as being "a real pain."

Determining the intention of a specific moral situation usually involves asking a question beginning with "why." *Why am I doing this? Why do I want to do this?* Asking why determines our motives for what we do—whether good or bad. It is always important to keep our intentions good.

Circumstances

The circumstances of an action—the answers to questions beginning with *who, where, when,* and *how*—cannot make good or right an action that is evil. Rather, the circumstances contribute to the increasing or diminishing good or evil or a particular act.

For example, consider the case of the high school teen who stole bus fare from a fellow student:

> It doesn't matter if the victim of the theft was a sophomore or a freshman (the answer to the *who* question).
>
> It doesn't matter if the theft took place on the bus or off the bus (the answer to the *where* question).
>
> It doesn't matter if the money was stolen on the bus ride to school or on the bus ride home (the answer to the *when* question).
>
> It doesn't matter if theft was accompanied by a verbal threat or the victim was physically pushed to the ground (the answer to the *how* question).

None of these circumstances has any effect in making a morally wrong act—stealing—right.

How, then, can the circumstances increase or diminish the good or evil of an action?

Returning to the example of stealing, physically injuring the victim adds to the serious nature of the evil act. In another similar case, stealing five dollars from a homeless man who needs the money for food is more serious than stealing five dollars from a millionaire on his way to a Las Vegas gambling table. The evil in the first case is increased, in the second diminished.

How are humans free?

Name some specific actions that are objectively bad.

Explain the meaning of the saying "the end does not justify the means."

Jesus said: "A tree is known by its fruit." How do these words apply to moral decisions that you have made?

Undertake an action this week from purely good intentions. Share what happened with your sponsor.

Choosing Right from Wrong

Deep within us, we have a drive, or as the documents of the Second Vatican Council described, a "most secret core and sanctuary," that helps us to distinguish between good and evil. Known as *conscience*, it allows us at the appropriate times to do good and avoid evil. Conscience also

> judges particular choices, approving those that are good and denouncing those that are evil. It bears witness to the authority of truth in reference to the supreme Good to which the human person is drawn, and it welcomes the commandments. (*CCC*, 1777)

When we listen to our conscience, we can hear God speaking to us. Our conscience enables us to take responsibility for the things we do or fail to do. While the gift of conscience allows us to know and do good, we do not have an ingrained program that automatically tells us what is good and what is bad. This means we must continually form our conscience in keeping with the true good willed by God, our Creator. Catholics primarily form their conscience through learning and living the life and teachings of Jesus Christ and putting into practice the Christian virtues. More concretely, this means studying the Scriptures, praying, examining our conscience, listening to the witness and advice of others, and being guided by the authoritative teaching of the Church.

We must always follow our conscience, but we must also realize that our conscience can err if it is not informed. For example, a child raised by parents who routinely swore could not initially know that swearing is wrong. When the child grows in experience and begins to learn from others that swearing is offensive, he or she becomes more and more culpable for actions or non-actions in this area.

Simply put, our conscience helps us distinguish between sin and virtue.

Sin

When we freely choose against reason, truth, and right conscience, we sin. Sin is an offense against God. Sin turns our hearts away from God's love for us.

There are many kinds of sins. In the letter to the Galatians, St. Paul names fornication, impurity, licentiousness, idolatry, sorcery, enmity, strife, jealousy, anger, selfishness, dissension, factions, envy, drunkenness, carousing, and the like as works of the flesh that contrast with the fruit of the Spirit (Gal 5:19–21).

These kinds of acts are personal sins and can also be described by their degree of seriousness.

Mortal sin is the most serious kind of sin. When we speak of mortal sin, we use words like "destroy" and "kill." Mortal sin effectively destroys our relationship with God and kills our ability to love. It's easy to see how adultery could kill the ability of one spouse to love another as well as destroy the person's relationship with God because of a disregard for the covenant of marriage.

However, mortal sins cannot be committed by accident. For a sin to be mortal, these three conditions must exist:

1. The moral object must be of grave or serious matter. Grave matter is specified in the Ten Commandments (e.g., do not kill, do not commit adultery, do not steal, etc.).
2. The person must have full knowledge of the gravity of the sinful action.
3. The person must completely consent to the action. It must be a personal choice.

An additional and maybe obvious condition for mortal sins is that the action must be completed. Desiring to do something evil, though reflecting a serious breach in a person's relationship with God, is not of itself mortally sinful.

Let's look at an example of an action, abuse of illegal drugs, that is of itself a grave or serious matter, thus meeting the first condition of a mortal sin.

The second condition, however, could diminish a person's culpability in this area. Take the situation of a teenage boy raised in an impoverished environment who uses illegal drugs. The use of drugs is a serious sin against one's own health, a violation of the Fifth Commandment. Was the boy fully aware of the gravity of his actions? What if he witnessed his own parents using the same drugs on many occasions? Is it possible that the boy does not have the full and broad picture about the seriousness of drug use? However, if the boy pretends that he does not know the drug use is a serious sin and really does, his guilt is increased. Faked or "feigned" ignorance as the *Catechism* describes (1859) can increase the voluntary character of a sin.

What about the third condition, freedom of consent? If a person's choice is limited by things like peer or parental pressures, physical force, or extreme emotions, the degree of guilt for the sin may be lessened. This condition could apply to such sins as murder or stealing.

To be forgiven, all mortal sins must be confessed to a priest in the Sacrament of Penance as reconciliation of mortal sin "necessitates a new initiative of God's mercy and a conversion of the heart" (*CCC*, 1856).

Less serious sin is called **venial sin**. Examples of venial sins are petty jealousy, disobedience, "borrowing" a small amount of money from a parent without the intention to repay it. Venial sins, when repeated and unrepented, can lead us to commit mortal sins.

Sin is a personal action. But we also have a responsibility for sins committed by others when we cooperate with them. For example, when we protect someone we know who has vandalized school property or praise someone else ("wow, you're cool") for stealing or engaging in premarital sex.

❦ venial sin

A sin that weakens and wounds our relationship with God but does not destroy divine life in our souls.

Vices are bad habits that are linked with capital sins—pride, avarice, envy, wrath, lust, gluttony, and sloth. They are also opposed to virtues, an "habitual and firm disposition to do the good" (*CCC*, 1803).

Virtues

Virtues not only help a person to perform good acts, but also to give the best of himself or herself. A virtuous person uses all his or her bodily senses and spiritual powers to pursue the good and make good choices. As St. Gregory of Nyssa put it, "The goal of a virtuous life is to become like God." Putting virtues into practice is an effective way to avoid poor choices and sinfulness.

Virtues acquired by human effort are known as moral or human virtues. Four of these virtues form the hinge that connects all the

✔ cardinal virtues

The four hinge virtues that support moral living: prudence, or "right reason in action," concerning the best way to live morally; justice, or giving God and each person his or her due by right; fortitude, or courage to persist in living a Christian life; and temperance, or moderation in controlling our desires for physical pleasures.

others. These **cardinal virtues** are prudence, justice, fortitude, and temperance. The more you put these virtues into practice, the easier time you should have in doing what is right and good.

Prudence equates with common sense and wisdom. A prudent person seems to have a plan for his or her life, and rarely deviates from it in any given situation. You may know many prudent people or be prudent yourself. Think of anyone planning for college and career. This person has a plan. He or she will not do anything to put the plan in jeopardy, whether by doing something illegal or something immoral.

Justice consists in a person always giving their due to God or neighbor. Being just means respecting the rights of others. There are several distinctions of justice—e.g., distributive (protects common welfare), legal (governs what individuals owe society), and social (applies Gospel to structures of society). All forms of justice have to do with relationships between people and with protecting the human rights of all. As you have grown up, you have witnessed what it means to be fair and unfair. You may have seen a classmate receive an award that another person was more deserving of. You yourself may not have made a team or been given a role in a play due to favoritism on the part of a coach or teacher. You may also have witnessed teachers going out of their way to make sure a student passes a course, even after the person has already failed several times. Justice, remember, means to give each person his or her rightful due.

Fortitude is another word for courage. It enables a person to conquer fears, even the fear of death, for a just cause. The virtue of fortitude is helpful in situations that may not seem as clear-cut as life and death. A person with fortitude is able to resist the many challenges that accompany peer pressure, for example.

Temperance moderates a person's attractions to pleasures and helps to balance the way we use created goods. We can temper our desire for pleasures like food, alcohol, drugs, and sex by practicing acts of self-denial. As St. Paul's letter to Titus explains, we ought "to live temperately, justly, and devoutly in this age."

We acquire human virtues "by education, by deliberate acts and by a perseverance ever-renewed in repeated efforts are purified and elevated by divine grace" (*CCC*, 1810). In other words, together with God, we are responsible for practicing and perfecting these virtues.

The human virtues have their roots in the theological virtues, the virtues that are related directly to God. The **theological virtues**—faith, hope, and love (charity)—are the foundation of a Christian's moral life. These virtues are not gained by our efforts. They are infused into our souls by God in order to make us capable of choosing goodness over sin, right from wrong, and of meriting eternal life.

✔ **theological virtues**

Three important virtues bestowed on us at Baptism that relate us to God: faith, or belief in and personal knowledge of God; hope, or trust in God's Salvation and his bestowal of the graces needed to attain it; and charity, or love of God and love of neighbor as one loves oneself.

ALESSANDRO SERENELLI: STORY BEHIND A SAINT

Alessandro Serenelli was a convicted murderer.

The murder happened in 1902, when Serenelli was nineteen. The Serenellis shared a building with a common living area in Ferriere, Italy, with the Goretti family, whose father Luigi had died three years before of malaria. Both were farming families. Maria Goretti, the third of six children, usually stayed back at home to babysit the younger children while her mother and older siblings were working in the fields.

On July 5, 1902, Alessandro stayed at home too. He had been a constant bother to Maria and often teased her. He demanded that Maria mend his shirt but wasn't satisfied with her work. Then Alessandro began to make sexual advances on Maria. He grabbed her.

Maria called out, "No! No! It is a sin. You will go to hell!"

Angrier, Alessandro attacked Maria with a knife. He stabbed her fourteen times, reaching her heart and lungs.

Maria's screaming alerted others, and she was taken to the hospital in Nettuno where she survived for twenty hours. Asked if she forgave Serenelli, she said, "Yes, for the love of Jesus I forgive him . . . and I want him to be with me in Paradise. May God forgive him." She died kissing the crucifix.

Meanwhile, Alessandro went to his bed after the attack and pretended to be asleep. When the authorities came, he denied the killing. With the evidence overwhelmingly against him, Serenelli was hog-tied and taken to the local jail. Because he was still underage, he received a thirty-year sentence.

Imprisoned in the Regina Coeli prison in Rome, Alessandro remained unrepentant. When a priest came to see him, he lunged at the priest and howled like an animal. Soon, Alessandro refused to eat. This time of maniac behavior went on for six years.

About this time, Alessandro had a dream that changed his life. He dreamt that he was in a garden where Maria came to him and gave him lilies, the symbol of purity. Alessandro admitted his crime for the first time and lived from then on as a model prisoner.

After being released, Alessandro returned to Ferriere. He was shunned by all. Then, in hushed tones at a Christmas Eve Mass, Alessandro acknowledged his sin and asked forgiveness of God and the community. Maria's mother was there, and she publicly forgave Alessandro.

Four years later, on June 24, 1950, Pope Pius XII canonized Maria Goretti. Her mother was able to attend the ceremony in Rome.

Meanwhile, Alessandro spent the rest of his life working as a gardener at a Capuchin monastery. He died on May 6, 1970.

From Alessandro Serenelli's Testimony, May 5, 1961

I am nearly eighty years old. I'm about to depart.

Looking back on my past, I can see that in my early youth I chose a bad path which led me to ruin myself.

My behavior was influenced by print, mass-media, and bad examples which are followed by the majority of young people without even thinking. I did the same. I was not worried.

There were a lot of generous and devoted people who surrounded me, but I paid no attention to them because a violent force blinded me and pushed me toward a wrong way of life.

Little Maria was really my light, my protectress. . . .

I hope this letter that I write can teach others the happy lesson of avoiding evil and of always following the right path, like little children. I feel that religion with its precepts is not something we can live without, but rather it is the real comfort, the real strength in life, and the only safe way in every circumstance, even the most painful ones of life.

How can a person's conscience err?

Differentiate between mortal sin and venial sin.

Explain how the human virtues are connected with the theological virtues.

Write your own act of contrition.

Create a moral dilemma commonly faced by teenagers. Using the criteria for determining the morality of human acts, analyze two possible choices a person could make for this situation.

Our Moral Compass: Jesus, the Commandments, and the Church

The way Christians gauge their own personal morality is in reference to Jesus Christ who is "the way and the truth and the life" (Jn 14:6). How do you measure up to what Jesus would do and who he is? Those are questions that should never be far from your heart as you go about making everything from both very easy to quite difficult decisions.

What did Jesus do when he walked the earth? In summary, Jesus did what was pleasing to God, his Father. This meant that Jesus loved others, himself, and God. Included among the "others" that Jesus loved were his enemies, meaning, for example, the Samaritan people despised by many of his fellow Jews and even those out to put him to death. His reasoning: It is easy to love those who love us in return. It is much more difficult to love those who offer us no love and, in fact, hate us. Yet, this is what God the Father does, so we are to do the same in order to "be perfect, just as your heavenly Father is perfect" (Mt 5:48).

Just what does it take to love self, God, and others—including enemies? Consider the following examples. Answer the question, "What are some loving and moral responses?" for each. Be creative.

→ Your friend had her laptop computer stolen. It had her outline and about half of her history research paper on it.

→ You got invited to the Homecoming Dance (held after the Friday night football game). Your best friend didn't get asked.

→ Your mom has some business to attend to in the school office. On her way across the school grounds, she runs into you and some friends of yours she has never met.

→ A person who has been picking on you since grade school has just been assigned to be your lab partner for the semester.

→ You find yourself in a grocery line behind a teacher who, you believe, graded you unfairly in the previous semester.

→ The kids at your school all sit together by race in the lunchroom. A new student who is of a race different from you sits down at your lunch table.

→ You've invited some friends home after school. When you play some music, an elderly neighbor lady calls you on the phone and says, "Turn it down."

→ You are second string on your team. A friend of yours asks your opinion of the first string player who's ahead of you.

There are many God-given paths to help us be like Jesus. The Beatitudes, the Ten Commandments, and the teachings of the Church are all helps for us to be more loving, more like Christ.

The Beatitudes

The word *beatitude* means "supreme happiness." The Beatitudes, preached by Jesus in the Sermon on the Mount, respond to our natural desire for happiness. This type of happiness is not temporal or fleeting. This desire for happiness comes from God himself. It is placed in our hearts in order to draw us to God, the only One who can ever fulfill this desire.

In the New Testament, the supreme happiness is described in several ways, but most typically as "the coming of the kingdom (or reign) of God." The Beatitudes make us like God and able to share eternal life.

From the Beatitudes themselves (Mt 5:3–10), we know of Jesus' love and the kind of love to which we are called. Good enough. But, when you've read or heard the Beatitudes, you might have wondered what they could have to do with happiness. A deeper examination reveals how.

Blessed are the poor in spirit, for theirs is the Kingdom of Heaven.

In the Old Testament, the poor were described by their Hebrew name, *anawim* (ah-nah-weem). These were people without material possessions who nevertheless kept a positive attitude, realized their helplessness, and sought God for all their needs, material and spiritual. Most importantly, they trusted that God would take care of all their needs.

Blessed are they who mourn, for they will be comforted.

The ache of mourning can seem inconsolable. Imagine suffering through the death of a parent or child. But when we mourn, even in the worst of situations, we also pause to think about others who are experiencing even worse situations than ours. We empathize with them. We move deeper into the human community. And, from our deep mourning, we do receive comfort for our aching selves that only God can provide.

Blessed are the meek, for they will inherit the land.

Meekness is not considered a strength in most settings today. Aristotle thought of meekness as the midpoint between too much anger and too little anger. Anger is a natural human emotion. The gift of meekness helps us to know the most appropriate times to feel and express anger.

Blessed are they who hunger and thirst for righteousness,
for they will be satisfied.

A righteous person is one who is bothered when things are not fair or just, not only for themselves but for others. The person who seeks righteousness or justice craves that each person's every need will be met and can't be satisfied until that happens. God rewards this desire with satisfaction.

Blessed are the merciful, for they will be shown mercy.

This beatitude urges empathy. We are to think, feel, and act from another's perspective rather than our own. When we show mercy, we live the petition of the Our Father: "Forgive us our trespasses as we forgive those who trespass against us."

Blessed are the clean of heart, for they will see God.

Those who are clean of heart, are opposite from the "two-faced" people who say one thing and do another. The clean of heart do not have ulterior motives for their actions. Rather, they are honest, unselfish, and sincere.

Blessed are the peacemakers, for they will be called children of God.

We tend to think of peace as an absence of war or trouble. The Hebrew understanding of peace—shalom—means helping others enjoy all the good that life has to offer. This means that a peacemaker is active, not passive. A peacemaker looks for a variety of ways to make the local and larger community a better place to live.

Blessed are they who are persecuted for the sake of righteousness,
for theirs is the Kingdom of Heaven.

The life of a Christian on earth is not an easy one. Jesus, our model, experienced pain, suffering, abuse, and death on behalf of God's Kingdom. We must be prepared for much of the same; we may be shunned by others, even family members, for standing up for what we believe in.

The happiness promised in the Beatitudes is not all future-oriented. God's reign is happening now. Our life here on earth is the beginning of our eternal life that will culminate in paradise. Making decisions based in the Beatitudes readies us for that time.

The Ten Commandments

The Ten Commandments have also been a source for Christian morality. The Ten Commandments were revealed by God. Jesus, himself, acknowledged them. He told the rich young man, "If you wish to enter into life, keep the commandments" (Mt 19:17). Since the time of St. Augustine (fourth century), the Ten Commandments have been used as a source for teaching baptismal candidates.

The first three commandments have to do with love for God. The last seven refer to love for neighbor. As you review the commandments below, think about how each applies to decisions you make daily in your own life.

I. I, the Lord, am your God. You shall not have other gods besides me.

To worship God means we accept God as our Creator and ourselves as made in his image. To understand what it is to worship, think of some sins against the First Commandment: idolatry (false worship of many gods), atheism (denial of God's existence), agnosticism (saying no one knows for sure whether God exists). Oppositely, the First Commandment asks us to practice the virtues of faith, hope, and love. Practicing our religion also helps us to keep the first commandment.

II. You shall not take the name of the Lord, your God, in vain.

We must respect God's name and never use the name of God, Jesus, Mary, or the saints in an improper way. This means that when we take an oath or make a promise in God's name, we must be true to it. We should also respect our name and strive for holiness. God made us and knew us from the beginning of time. Our name will be with us into eternity. This commandment forbids blasphemy, a sin that involves hateful words against God, Jesus, or even the Church. Cursing is also a violation against the commandment.

III. Remember to keep holy the Sabbath day.

The Sabbath was set aside by God to remind us of the time at creation when God rested on the seventh day. It is a day intended for people to rest from their work and to praise God for his works of Salvation.

Catholics celebrate by worshiping God through attending Sunday Mass and by observing rest on Sunday, the day of Christ's Resurrection. Sunday is linked with the Paschal Mystery, the Passion, Death, and Resurrection of Jesus, commemorated in Eucharist. Catholics are required by Church law to participate in Sunday Mass or its Saturday vigil. To deliberately miss Sunday Mass is mortally sinful. We also make Sunday holy by spending time with our families, visiting our other relatives, helping the poor, or doing other charitable acts.

IV. Honor your father and your mother.

The Fourth Commandment begins the second part of the Ten Commandments having to do with love for neighbor. This is appropriate, for love truly begins at home. How can you be loving to your friends and teachers at school, when you lambasted your mom or were rude to a sibling on the ride to school? You owe your parents (and other family members) respect and obedience for as long as you live at home. When you are older, you still must respect your parents and care for them when they are old, ill, or lonely. Teachers, civil authorities, religious leaders, and other adults are also owed your respect according to this commandment.

V. You shall not kill.

All human life is of immense value. This statement applies to human life from the first moment of conception until natural death. For this reason, this commandment forbids abortion (the killing of an unborn baby) and euthanasia (mercy killing of the aged or sick).

There are times when killing is morally permissible. For example, in self-defense or when protecting the life of another. Killing in war may be morally permissible if the nation is defending itself against aggressors. Also, the traditional teaching of the Church does not exclude the use of the death penalty, if this is the only way to defend innocent lives against an unjust killer. However, the Church continues to teach that today there are very few, if any, situations in which execution of a person is necessary. Held in a secure prison, the offending person is kept away from society and has the chance to seek Redemption and conversion.

This commandment also asks us not to "kill" our own bodies, and requires us to live healthy lives of exercise, wholesome eating, rest, and to avoid harmful addictions like alcohol and drugs.

VI. You shall not commit adultery.

The sixth commandment encompasses the whole of human sexuality. In the Old Testament, the offense of this commandment primarily involved a husband having sexual intercourse with a married woman other than his wife. Jesus took the command further saying that "everyone who looks at a woman with lust" (Mt 5:28) has already committed adultery.

❦ **chastity**

The moral virtue that enables people to integrate their sexuality into their stations in life.

For people of any age or state in life, keeping this commandment involves practicing the virtue of **chastity**. Chastity involves a self-mastery over one's sexuality, rejects lust (inordinate enjoyment of sexual pleasure), masturbation (deliberate stimulation of genital organs to derive sexual pleasure), fornication (sex between unmarried persons), pornography (displaying sexual acts for a third party to see), prostitution (selling of sexual acts), rape (forcing another into sexual intimacy), and homosexual acts (sexual activity between persons of the same gender).

Rather, this commandment teaches us that sexual love must only be shared in the intimacy of a loving marriage, where sexual intercourse strengthens the unity of the marriage and results in the procreation of children.

VII. *You shall not steal.*

The Seventh Commandment forbids theft, which is the taking of another's property against his or her will. This is a matter of justice as we must respect the property rights of others.

Stealing, however, is more encompassing than just the unlawful taking of someone else's things. Stealing also includes cheating (e.g., on taxes or on a test), doing shoddy work on the job, and vandalism.

VIII. *You shall not bear false witness against your neighbor.*

We are to be truthful in our words and actions. Any misrepresentation of the truth is a violation of this commandment. This would include lying in order to prevent someone from knowing the truth and also sins called detraction (telling a person's faults for no good reason) and calumny (gossiping about another person).

IX. *You shall not covet your neighbor's wife.*

The word *covet* means to "desire something that is not one's own." In this case, like the Sixth Commandment, it is directly referring to the covenant of marriage.

Jesus restored God's original intent that marriage be indissoluble by forbidding divorce. Other sins against marriage are polygamy (having more than one spouse), incest (having sexual relations with relatives), sexual abuse of children, and living together before marriage.

X. *You shall not covet your neighbor's goods.*

Similar to the Seventh Commandment, the Tenth Commandment is opposed to greed, envy, and avarice (the seeking of riches and the power that comes with them).

The Tenth Commandment makes it clear that we desire things that give us pleasure. These desires are morally permissible as long as they do not lead us to crave things that belong to others.

In a recent billboard campaign, the message read, "What part of Thou Shalt Not don't you understand?" The point is clear: God's commandments are not merely suggestions that we can choose to follow or not according to our own whims. The commandments are rules that we are to follow if we intend to live moral and just lives.

The Church

In our own families, we are not left to move aimlessly through a maze of difficult decisions without help. Parents, older siblings, and grandparents all offer advice—and rules—for making good choices. We also belong to a family called the Church. The Church is the living Body of Christ that also nurtures our growth to holiness.

The Church gives us grace-filled moments in the sacraments. In the Liturgy of the Eucharist, we share in Christ's Paschal Mystery of Death, Resurrection, and glory and we do so in communion with those around us in faith. In the Church, we have the example of Mary and all the saints who show the way for living a moral life.

The Church is not a family limited by time or space. The Church is a living family with leaders in the Magisterium that continually call us to the moral truth of Jesus who is "the way, and the truth, and the life."

Like all families, the Church has certain rules for us to follow in order to guarantee our minimal growth in becoming good and moral people. They are known as the precepts of the Church and must be obeyed by all Catholics:

1. You shall attend Mass on Sundays and on holy days of obligation and rest from servile labor.

The "obligation" to attend Sunday Mass helps us to celebrate Christ's Resurrection. In addition, Sundays are to be days in which we relax and unwind from the week, spend time with family, and avoid unnecessary work.

Like the Sunday obligation, we are to attend Mass on specially designated holy days. In the United States, these are the feast of the Immaculate Conception (December 8), Christmas Day (December 25), the Solemnity of Mary (January 1), the feast of the Ascension (when celebrated on a Thursday, forty days after Easter), the Assumption of Mary (August 15), and All Saints' Day (November 1).

2. You shall confess your sins at least once a year.

The Sacrament of Penance ensures that we will be properly prepared to receive Eucharist. We must confess our sins any time we have sinned mortally. We can also use the sacrament to confess venial sins. Additionally, the times Advent, Lent, Easter, and the start of school are good reminders to go to confession.

*3. You shall receive the Sacrament of the Eucharist
at least during the Easter season.*

This precept is a minimal obligation to receive Jesus in the Sacrament of Eucharist. However, we should receive communion frequently whenever we are in the state of grace.

*4. You shall observe the days of fasting and abstinence
established by the Church.*

The Church has some prescribed days, such as Ash Wednesday and Good Friday, when we are to fast and abstain from certain types of food. In addition, we should practice these habits at other times in imitation of Christ and at his instruction in the Beatitudes and the Sermon on the Mount.

5. You shall help to provide for the needs of the Church.

Catholics have the duty to support the Church with gifts of their time and talents and with monetary gifts.

Remember the words of St. Francis de Sales: "One of the most excellent intentions that we can possibly have in all our actions is to do them because our Lord did them." We want to do the same things and behave in the same ways as the Lord Jesus. This means more than imitating the fashion of a current star or the jump shot of a pro basketball player. Rather, imitating Jesus is impossible until we realize that God gives us the gift of grace, a supernatural gift that can lead us to live holy and moral lives.

Practice and be able to recite the Beatitudes, Ten Commandments, and Precepts of the Church by heart.

Which Beatitude do you find most closely connected to happiness? Explain.

Share any new insight you have about the Ten Commandments.

Suggest some situations from your own life that require loving and moral responses. Act on them.

Catholic 🐟Apologetics

What is grace?

✤ Grace is God's favor to us. It is the free and undeserved help that God gives to us so that we can respond to him and share in his friendship and eternal life. Grace is a participation in the life of God.

Are Christians always obliged to obey civil law and authorities?

✤ Christians must obey their upright conscience in all matters. If civil law and authorities are opposed to the teachings of the Gospel, the fundamental rights of persons, and the moral law, then a Christian must in good conscience disobey the civil law or authorities.

How far can I go sexually?

✤ It's important to remember that God intends sexual intercourse for marriage. It is also important to note that sex is a progressive experience. Open-mouthed kissing, any type of petting, or intimate touching of another's private parts are part of the natural progression to intercourse and should be reserved for marriage. Before marriage, it is best to limit yourself to hugs, light kissing, and hand holding.

Is masturbation a sin?

✤ Again, sexual pleasure sought outside of marriage is opposed to Church teaching and is "an intrinsically and gravely distorted action." Sexual activity is meant to be relational, within the context of marriage. If a person willingly masturbates contrary to God's law, the conditions are present for it to be a mortal sin. Other factors can lessen a person's culpability: for example, immaturity, force of acquired habit, anxiety, or other psychological or social factors.

How can I tell if I made the right decision in the area of morality?

✤ If your conscience has been well formed through study of Scripture, prayer, an examination of conscience, and you have been assisted by the gifts of the Holy Spirit and the witness and advice of others, including the authoritative teaching of the Church, and you do not follow your conscience, you will often experience guilt. In this case, guilt can be productive. It reminds you of what you know to be right. Also, some rules of morality apply to every decision that you make: evil may never be done to produce a good result, the Golden Rule ("do to others as you wish done to you") always applies, and loving decisions always involve showing respect for others.

 For **You** to **Do**

The Way of Forgiveness

Penance is the sacrament that forgives our sins and renews our faith. It is the sacrament that renews, restores, and strengthens our relationship with God and the Church after it has been damaged by sin.

The **penitent** has three tasks as part of the sacrament: contrition (heartfelt sorrow and aversion for the sin committed), confession (external expression of our sorrow and our willingness to accept responsibility for our actions), and satisfaction or penance (offering recompense for injustices caused or working to rebuild what was lost).

✔ penitent

The name for a person performing penance as directed by the priest in the Sacrament of Penance.

The sacrament that the *Catechism of the Catholic Church* (1423–1424) refers to as the Sacrament of Penance is known by many names, each of which focuses on a particular dimension of the sacramental mystery.

⇢ It is called the *sacrament of conversion* because it makes Jesus' call to conversion sacramentally present.

⇢ It is called the *sacrament of penance* because it blesses the repentant sinner's efforts to change through the steps of conversion, penance, and satisfaction, and it makes those efforts effective.

⇢ It is called the *sacrament of confession* because the sinner confesses both his or her own sins and the infinite mercy and forgiveness of God.

⇢ It is called the *sacrament of forgiveness* because through this sacrament God forgives even the most serious sins.

⇢ It is called the *sacrament of reconciliation* because it fills us with God's reconciling love and restores our relationship with God and God's people.

Individual confession of grave or mortal sins followed by absolution is the only ordinary means of reconciliation between the sinner and with God and the Church. Recall that a precept of the Church teaches that we must confess our sins after we sin mortally so that we are properly prepared to receive the Eucharist.

Your Confirmation preparation involves reception of the Sacrament of Penance. The *Catechism of the Catholic Church* states: "To receive Confirmation one must be in a state of grace. One should receive the sacrament of Penance in order to be cleansed for the gift of the Holy Spirit" (1310).

Assignment

Beyond the three necessary tasks of the penitent in the Sacrament of Penance—contrition, confession, and satisfaction—is the element of forgiveness. Only God forgives sins. Yet, because he is the Son of God, Jesus said of himself that "the Son of Man has authority on earth to forgive sins" (Mk 2:10). And, through the Apostles, he gave bishops and priests the authority to forgive sins in his name.

The five Gospel passages below involve the reconciliation process. Read each passage once through slowly and reflectively. Then go back through and name how each passage represents each element of the process: contrition, confession, forgiveness, and satisfaction.

···→ Luke 15:11–32 (The Parable of the Lost Son)

···→ Luke 19:1–10 (Zacchaeus the Tax Collector)

···→ Mark 2:1–12 (The Healing of the Paralytic)

···→ John 8:1–11 (The Woman Caught in Adultery)

Bonus: Prior to confession of our sins, we must take all the necessary steps to form a good conscience. The examination of conscience is part of our contrition in seeking out the Sacrament of Penance when we pause, and with the help of the Holy Spirit, take stock of our lives and the decisions we have made or are about to make. Go back over the Gospel stories above and note how the penitent reflected on his or her sins prior to confessing them.

Prenyers and Reflections

Word of God

Jesus said, "I am the way and the truth and the life. No one comes to the Father except through me. If you know me, then you will also know my Father. From now on you do know him and have seen him."

—John 14:6–7

Act of Faith

O God,
I firmly believe all the truths that you have revealed
and that you teach us through your church,
for you are truth itself
and can neither deceive nor be deceived.
Amen.

Act of Hope

O God,
I hope with complete trust that you will give me,
through the merits of Jesus Christ,
all necessary grace in this world
and everlasting life in the world to come,
for this is what you have promised
and you always keep your promises.
Amen.

Act of Love

O my God, I love you above all things, with my whole heart and soul, because you are all good and worthy of all my love. I love my neighbor as myself for the love of you. I forgive all who have injured me, and I ask pardon of all whom I have injured. Amen.

seven

SOCIAL JUSTICE

Foundations of Social Justice

The topic of social justice is a wide ranging one. It includes the basic right to life and addresses issues like abortion, capital punishment, and euthanasia or "mercy killings," to name a few. Social justice also involves rights of everyday living like the rights of workers to a fair wage, the rights of people to food and shelter, the rights of people not to be discriminated against on the basis of race, and the rights of all people to worship God.

The United States Conference of Catholic Bishops recently highlighted seven principles that are the foundation for the Church's social teaching. The first principle is really both twofold and co-related: It calls for respect for the "life and dignity of the human person."

In this day and age, before we can even address the dignity due the human person, we must first be clear in our beliefs about the actual right for a human being to live. Yet it is only when we understand the inherent dignity of all human life—from its earliest beginnings at conception to the final breath a person takes before death—that we can really appreciate the *right* to life itself.

What is a right? A right is a claim we can make on other people and on society so that we can live a full, human life. A right is not something that has to be earned. A right is something we are due only for the fact that we, as human beings, are made in the image and likeness of God. Our right to life is something that no one can take from us because it is a right given to us by God. Unfortunately, some of society's laws do not always guarantee the right to life.

This chapter explores the first of all principles of social justice: the right to life and the inherent dignity of human life. It also explores the responsibilities that come with the rights that promote justice for all humans.

"With rights come responsibilities." How do you find that statement to be true?

The Right to Life

How did such a simple, positive statement come to be associated with a politically held or even confrontational opinion? How could anyone possibly be opposed to any person's basic right to *be alive*?

The issue of legalized abortion is one that even at your age you may be tired of hearing about. You may have, on several occasions already, debated in class or among peers the argument between the "pro-life" and "pro-choice" camps. But when in a country like the United States there are more than 1.5 million abortions each year (4,400 per day), many in the last stages of pregnancy when the child is ready to be born, the issue of abortion must stay in the forefront of our thoughts and remain as the most crucial justice issue of our time.

Why abortion is legal and so many make the "choice" to abort their babies is difficult to fathom. The Church has offered its opinion that there are two overarching reasons. First, there has been a breakdown in family life. It is the task of the family to teach fidelity, loyalty, and devotion to both the very young and to those who are sick and old. This task has been disregarded with the increase in the breakup of marriages and families due to divorce or the formation of families where the parents of children are not even married. Second, freedom—even without responsibility—is now seen as an absolute value, and the pursuit of individual happiness and personal goals in life often outweigh any concern for the consequences of this individualism on others, including an unborn child.

How can a teenager work for justice in this crucial area of opposition to abortion? Here are four ideas:

1. *Understand and act on the belief that sex is sacred.* Sex is a great gift from God. Unfortunately, this gift has been misused and abused. The media—advertisements, music, movies, instant

messaging of all kinds, and more—saturate your generation with the message that uncommitted sex is the ultimate in pleasures. You are bombarded with the view that you are unable to control your sexual urges, that everyone your age is sexually active, and if for some reason you are not, then there must be something wrong with you.

Recall the lessons you have no doubt learned from your family and years of religious education. Sexual activity should be saved for a lasting, loving, and committed relationship. This type of relationship is only present in marriage. You do have the power to control your sexual urges.

Share your belief in the sacredness of sex with your words and actions. Besides refraining from sexual behavior that can lead you on the slippery slope to sinful behavior, also refrain from gossiping about sex with your friends, or listening to jokes that are crude in their mention of sex. You may join with thousands of other teenagers and make a public commitment to refrain from sex until marriage, often called a "chastity pledge." If you choose to do this you won't be alone. Recent statistics continue to support that upwards of 60 percent of high school juniors and seniors are not sexually active. This means it's accurate to state that most teens are *not* having sex.

2. *Clearly defend the fact that life begins at conception.* One of the traditional arguments for abortion has been that somehow human life is not infused into the embryo until sometime later in pregnancy. Genetics has shown that a new human being who is distinct from both mother and father begins at conception. Believe this and take this to heart. When you do, any argument for abortion cannot be taken as anything short of the killing of human life.

3. *Work to make abortion illegal.* Abortion was legalized with the infamous *Roe v. Wade* court decision in 1973. Prior to that time, abortion was viewed as an unspeakable crime against the most innocent. It was viewed for what it was: the killing of one's own child. Researching political candidates and positions that reflect a pro-life position and supporting a vote for them is one way to effect change. Peaceful and legal protest of the legality of abortion is also a proactive effort. Supporting alternatives to abortion, especially adoption, is also effective.

4. *Pray for the life of the unborn and women considering an abortion.* Even good laws cannot change our hearts. Pray for a reversal of the "culture of death" in our society and a return to a society where life is respected, nurtured, and cared for, especially among the most vulnerable, the unborn.

Just as the right to life springs from the inherent dignity of the human person, so do other rights and responsibilities. Every person has certain basic rights, including the right to life's basic necessities: food, clothing, shelter, medical care, education, safety from war and crime, and employment. A person also has a right to security if he or she is unable to work. Every one of these rights has a corresponding responsibility or duty. To ignore the responsibilities that come with these rights is like building a house with one hand and tearing it down with the other. Practically, this means that your God-given dignity involves preserving your life through things like healthy eating and exercise. The right to education corresponds with the duty to do your best to study and learn.

The right to life extends to other areas of life and death including euthanasia, suicide, assisted suicide, and capital punishment. The Church promotes life in all of these areas and decries these crimes against life from the time of conception until natural death, from "womb to tomb." This Catholic teaching of a "consistent ethic of life" was termed a "seamless garment" by Cardinal Joseph Bernardin of Chicago. He referred to the tunic Jesus wore at his crucifixion.

Ultimately, every right a person has corresponds to duties and responsibilities to others in the family, neighborhood, and society at large. A person who claims his or her rights must respect the rights of others and work for the common good of all.

More Rights for Life

There other related basic human rights. Several of these were detailed by Pope John XXIII in his 1963 encyclical *Peace on Earth.* Listed below are a summary of some of these rights:

Right to Private Property. Related to the right to have employment, people also have the right to acquire private property and goods.

Right to Emigrate and Immigrate. Everyone has the right to move within the confines of his or her own country and, when necessary, to emigrate to another country and live there.

Right to Participate in the Political System. People have the right to take an active role in their nation's public affairs by voting and, when applicable, running for office.

Right to One's Reputation. Everyone is due respect to his or her reputation and has the right to share personal opinions freely when searching for the truth.

Right to Choose One's State in Life. People have the right to choose the vocation and career they prefer, the right to marry and have a family, or if they choose, the right to follow a vocation to priesthood or the religious life. The family itself must be considered the "first and essential cell of human society."

Right to Worship God. This, too, is an essential right. People have the right to worship God according to the direction of their conscience and to practice religion both privately and publicly.

Again, it's crucial to understand that rights do not exist without corresponding duties and responsibilities. For example, the right to owning property and goods corresponds with the duty to make sure these are owned not at the expense of others and that others in society are at least guaranteed the basic necessities for life.

 Summarize some basic human rights as detailed by Pope John XXIII.

What are some duties and responsibilities that correspond to the "right to own property and goods"?

 Why do you think so many in our society believe that an abortion is a viable choice for a woman?

 What are ways you can work to support the right to life?

"The abortion issue is the most crucial issue of our time." Agree or disagree? Cite examples to support your answer.

Human Dignity

Our guaranteed rights as human beings flow from our fundamental human dignity. As the statement of the United States Catholic bishops puts it, "Every human being is created in the image of God and redeemed by Jesus Christ, and therefore is invaluable and worthy of respect as a member of the human family" (*Sharing Catholic Social Teaching*).

This means that every person, no matter what gender, race, age, nationality, religion, or economic status, is deserving not only of all the human rights discussed in the previous section, but also of the basic respect due to their status as God's special creation. We have been given the special gift to be able to know and love God. This means that our worth comes not from what we do or what we are able to accomplish, but simply from who we are.

What does human dignity mean? Looking at how God made us gives us a clue. As the first Genesis creation story teaches:

> God created man in his image;
> in the divine image he created him;
> male and female he created them.

> —Genesis 1:27

Being created in God's image means that God's image is reflected in each person, from the richest to the poorest, youngest to the oldest, healthiest to the most ill. God's image is reflected in both genders—female and male—and in every racial composition possible. This fact makes each person worthy of profound respect.

Respect means that we will look at our neighbor as "another self," all the while bearing in mind all the human rights this person must be guaranteed so that he or she can live with dignity. There is no way rules or laws can force us to treat another with this type of respect. It is only through cultivating love in our hearts that we can look at each person as a brother or sister, as another self.

Jesus, our model for humanity, addressed the task of making ourselves a neighbor to all. Jesus increased the urgency for this task when he said that the real sign of love and respect is that whenever we love and care for the most disadvantaged ("the least ones") in our midst, we do it for him.

This duty also extends to people who think or act differently than we do. It extends to people who are our enemies. Jesus also taught,

> You have heard that it was said, "You shall love your neighbor and hate your enemy." But I say to you, love your enemies, and pray for those who persecute you, that you may be children of your heavenly Father, for he makes his sun rise on the bad and the good, and causes rain to fall on the just and unjust. (Mt 5:43–45)

The next sections review some of the challenges facing all people in loving and respecting other people and truly treating them as "other selves."

Preference for the Poor

Jesus always took the side of those most in need, both in physical need and spiritual need. We, too, as followers of Christ, are required to seek out the poor in our midst and care for them. The American bishops have called this the "preferential option for the poor" and this call is connected explicitly to the Seventh and Tenth Commandments that forbid unjustly taking from others and desiring what is due them. This duty calls us to act in several larger societal ways and in smaller personal ways.

For example, it requires working to change political and economic policies that create situations that hurt the poor. Currently the world is divided into nations that "have" and nations that "have not." A large gap exists between what have been called developed nations and third world or developing nations. It is the responsibility of the "haves" to help close the gap through plans like working to reform international economics, providing direct aid, and relieving debts that keep the developing nations mired in a spiral of despair from which they can never escape.

Individually, Christians are called to show preferential treatment to the poor. This first of all demands a change of heart, from one of selfishness and greed to one of justice. The traditional works of mercy are charitable actions that remind us how to come to the aid of our neighbor and provide for his or her bodily and spiritual necessities. The corporal (bodily) works of mercy are:

⇢ Feed the hungry.

⇢ Give drink to the thirsty.

⇢ Clothe the naked.

⇢ Visit the imprisoned.

⇢ Shelter the homeless.

⇢ Visit the sick.

⇢ Bury the dead.

The spiritual works of mercy are:

···➤ Counsel the doubtful.

···➤ Instruct the ignorant.

···➤ Admonish sinners.

···➤ Comfort the afflicted.

···➤ Forgive offenses.

···➤ Bear wrongs patiently.

···➤ Pray for the living and the dead.

Among all the works of mercy, giving to the poor is one of the chief ways we witness to love. It is one of the works of justice most pleasing to God. To do otherwise is completely contradictory to the Christian message. As the Letter of James reminds us:

> What good is it, my brothers, if someone says he has faith but does not have works? Can that faith save him? If a brother or sister has nothing to wear and has no food for the day, and one of you says to them, "Go in peace, keep warm, and eat well," but you do not give the necessities of the body, what good is it? (Jas 2:14–16)

Prejudice and Racism

Politics aside, there was a general consensus that the United States of America had crossed another barrier in 2008 with the election of the first African American president, Barack Obama. Teenagers were no exception to those who recognized the significance of the event. For example, a Harris Poll released soon after the election reported that

···➤ more than two-thirds of teens thought the election was more important than the introduction of the iPod.

···➤ a similar number thought Obama's election was as significant as the landing of the first men on the moon.

···➤ nearly one-third of teens thought the election of an African American president matched in importance the end of World War II.

Certainly the glitter of the moment gave the impression that society could move beyond long-held racist views and practices and onward to a new era of cooperation and respect. However, when reality sets in there are still plenty of incidents of racism that continue to go on in high schools across the nation. Many schools are more diverse racially than ever before, but when individuals or groups of

students prejudge others without having suffi-
cient information, **prejudice** persists.

    Racism is one of the most hateful forms of
prejudice. It is a belief that one race or ethnic
group is superior to another. Racism leads to
mistreatment of people based on skin color, national origin, religion,
and ancestry.

    Catholic social teaching is strongly opposed to prejudice and
racism. Though laws cannot change a person's attitudes and heart,
laws can and do foster justice by protecting minority groups against
others who may trample on their rights. Collectively, society must
work toward racial justice in the areas of housing, employment, education, and health care. Individually, you must work to keep your
heart and mind open to others and to create a spirit of inclusion in
your social groups, welcoming people of all kinds, including those
who at first seem so different from you.

    Human solidarity is the virtue that opposes
the problems that persist in societies held down
by not caring for the poor, by prejudice, by
racism, and by other crimes against justice. This
virtue teaches that we are all part of one human
family, that we share human dignity, and that
we are responsible for one another. Solidarity is represented when we
share both spiritual and material goods with one another, especially
with the poorest in our society.

✔ **prejudice**

An unsubstantiated or preformed judgment about
an individual or group.

✔ **human solidarity**

A Christian virtue of charity and friendship where-
by members of the human
family share material and
spiritual goods.

SR. THEA BOWMAN: FINDING HER WAY HOME

    There have been several champions among African Ameri-
cans for improved relations among all races over the past generation. One person who briefly caught the attention of the
popular culture and society in between Martin Luther King Jr.
and Barack Obama was Sr. Thea Bowman, a Franciscan Sister of
Perpetual Adoration who died of cancer in 1990 at the age of
fifty-two.

    St. Thea was born Bertha Bowman in Yazoo, Mississippi.
Baptized an Episcopalian and raised a Methodist, she was

influenced by the Franciscan sisters who taught her. When she was ten, she became a Catholic. "I had witnessed so many Catholic priests, brothers, and sisters who made a difference that was far-reaching. I wanted to be part of the effort to feed the hungry, find shelter for the homeless, and teach the children," she wrote many years later.

When she was fifteen, Sr. Thea entered the Rose Convent in La Crosse, Wisconsin. She was the only black sister. Eventually Sr. Thea would receive several college degrees, including a doctorate in English Language, Literature, and Linguistics from the Catholic University of America.

But Sr. Thea's life work was to educate black children, especially in the South, and make them aware of and appreciate their heritage as African Americans. Later, even after she became sick, she was a national spokesperson for the evangelization of African Americans. "We didn't enslave ourselves," she said. "Somebody else enslaved us. Let the people who created slavery answer to God for it, and let us thank God for the cultural and faith traditions that enabled us to overcome it."

In June 1989, just months before her death, Sr. Thea spoke to a group of United States bishops gathered at Seton Hall University. She spoke about what it meant to be black in the Church and in society. As always, she dotted her presentation with singing, even calling the bishops to join in. She sang, in part,

> Sometimes I feel like a motherless child . . .
> A long way from home . . .
> Sometimes I feel like an eagle in the air . . .
> Still I'm a long way, I'm a long way, I'm a long way . . .
> Can you hear me Church, will you help me Church? . . .
> I'm a long way from home, a long way from my home.

Sr. Thea also preached that if African Americans, Asians, Hispanics, and other races were to assimilate into the Church, the pot would really become "half gray." She once wrote:

> The heck with the melting pot. If you want to melt and fit into my mold, if you want to adopt my values and way of life, go right ahead, but don't expect me to melt to fit into yours.

Why is it necessary to show a preferential option for the poor?

Define *prejudice* and *racism*. Differentiate between the two.

 Tell about a person or group of people whom you have difficulty treating as "another self." Why is this so?

Rate from good to poor how you think various racial groups get along at your school.

 How can your life goals be adapted so that you can show a preferential love for the poor?

Other Issues of Social Justice

As mentioned before, social justice covers many issues of concern. Social justice deals with our obligation as individuals and groups to apply Jesus' teachings to the systems, structures, and institutions of society. Social justice demands that each of us be active in the life of society so that it can best meet the basic rights of all people. This section deals briefly with three areas of particular concern for teenagers: consumerism, environmental issues, and war and violence. It also offers some suggestions for fostering justice and serving others.

Consumerism

Consumerism is the uncontrolled buying and selling of goods and services, most of which are unneeded. Christians are called to turn away from the accompanying greed of consumerism and work instead for lasting gifts of God's Kingdom—in this world and the next. Christians are also asked to work for the development of other people, not just themselves. As Pope John Paul II put it:

> It is not wrong to want to live better; what is wrong is a style of life which is presumed to be better when it is directed toward "having" rather than "being" and which wants to have more, not in order to be more, but in order to spend life in enjoyment as an end in itself. (*The One Hundredth Year*, #31)

The Environment

There seem to be two main concurrent views of the environment existing today. In one, all living things—human and nonhuman—are viewed as part of the same ecology, with neither being superior to the other. Humans are not seen under this view as masters of other living things in any way. In fact, humans are more often seen as the major offenders of the environment under this view.

The Christian view comes from the first creation story in the Bible. God created the earth, the sun, moon, and stars, and all the living things on the earth including the humans. He found this creation very good. And, as God's special creature, God gave human beings dominion over creation.

Some additional Christian teachings related to the environment are that:

···→ dominion requires human care

···→ sin has led to abuse of the gifts of creation

···→ Jesus was a model of good "stewardship," that is, the care for creation that will allow the earth and its resources to flourish and be long-lasting.

There are many ways to be a good steward in regard to the environment. These include not littering, recycling paper and plastic products, saving energy by turning off electricity when possible, avoiding unnecessary car trips, consuming less in products that cause material waste, and participating in political efforts to limit pollution and other environmental hazards in your local and national area.

Violence Versus Nonviolence

Violence has been with the world since Cain killed his brother Abel. Today violence is especially prevalent. Violence is present within our families in many forms of abuse. It is also present in our neighborhoods and worldwide society taking the forms of rape, burglary, terrorism, and war. Much of this violence ends in death.

🔥 **just-war tradition**

A set of principles developed through the centuries by the Church that clearly outlines when a nation may ethically participate in a war. It also sets clear limits on armed force once a war is engaged.

The Church does not oppose all uses of violence in dealing with conflicts. However, it does teach that violence must be the last resort to solving any conflict. The Church's **just-war tradition** provides guidelines for situations in which violence can be used. For example, the war must have a "just cause" (e.g., self-defense). It also must be called by a legitimate authority, it must be fought for the right intention, the probability of success must be weighed against the loss of human life, and all ethical standards for fighting the war must be maintained.

Again, violence is always the last option. Rather, the preferred option is non-violence, that is, handing conflicts through peaceful communication, negotiation, and compromise. Violence once begun always escalates. More and more teenagers each year are killed in incidents of violence.

Being a person of peace is the first step in fostering a peaceful world. Pope Paul VI's famous words on the subject were, "If you wish peace, defend life." This means respecting and loving the lives of those around you, especially the poor in spirit described by Jesus in the Sermon on the Mount.

What Can You Do?

Many Catholic teens preparing for the Sacrament of Confirmation are asked or even required to do "Christian service" projects or tasks of some kind. Often this community service involves completing a predetermined number of hours of service prior to reception of the Sacrament of Confirmation. Usually, in such a process, the adult leaders in the parish, the Confirmation sponsors, and the parents of the candidates will help the teens choose worthwhile projects that not only fulfill a requirement, but also help them to do their part to love God and their neighbor. For example, some projects in which Confirmation candidates have recently participated include those listed below. Other projects are listed on pages 232–235.

> *World Hunger Fast.* Teens collected pledges in exchange for a one-day fast and arranged for a guest speaker to address the issue of world hunger with their peers. They donated their pledge money to an organization that provides food to the needy.

> *Peace Symposium.* A group of high school juniors prepared a "peace symposium" for an elementary school. It included dramatic presentations of peaceful solutions to everyday problems, debates and dialogue, art projects, and many suggestions for conflict resolution.

> *Racial Harmony.* Two Confirmation classes—one with predominantly white teens and the other with mostly black teens—came together for a weekend retreat as part of their sacramental preparation. The retreat theme was "Celebrate the

Differences" but by the end of the weekend the group had also found out how much they had in common.

Giving Voice for Life. Four teens (with their Confirmation sponsors) worked to support a women's shelter that cares for pregnant teens. Among their tasks: transporting school homework assignments to pregnant teens and organizing a letter-writing campaign among their peers directed to government officials to make them aware of their constituents' support for human life at all stages.

Social justice does involve a plethora of issues that can seem to be overwhelming to anyone who tries to exercise his or her Christian duty. In the final analysis, it comes down to the simple directions of Jesus to love others as we do ourselves. As the first letter to John reminds us, love for God and love for neighbor are one:

> If anyone says, "I love God," but hates his brother, he is a liar; for whoever does not love a brother whom he has seen cannot love God whom he has not seen. This is the commandment we have from him: whoever loves God must also love his brother. (1 Jn 4:20–21)

Outline the Christian view of the environment.

What is the difference between a good life based on "being" and a good life based on "having"?

How have you been affected by violence?

 Outline a social justice project you can participate in as an individual or with others.

Catholic Apologetics

Why shouldn't we have the right to choose how and when we die?

✠ Death is not a right. Death claims us; we do not claim death. Only God has absolute control over life and death. We have the responsibility to preserve and care for life. Suicide and euthanasia are contrary to this duty.

If the Bible permits justice in terms of "an eye for an eye," then why is the Church opposed to capital punishment?

✠ Jesus himself ruled out revenge as a motive for punishing those who commit crime. The Church speaks out against the death penalty because of its respect for life, even the life of a convicted criminal. Opposing the death penalty helps testify to the dignity of humanity and tells society we can break the cycle of violence. By keeping the criminal imprisoned, the person is not only kept from doing harm to others, he or she keeps the possibility of redeeming himself or herself. Finally, traditional Church teaching does not exclude recourse to the death penalty if it is the only possible way of protecting society against the criminal.

Many people say, "I am opposed to abortion except in the case of rape and incest." Why is this not an acceptable stance according to Church teaching?

✠ Crimes like rape and incest are always tragic to the women victimized. However, a child conceived in such a situation did not commit the crime and bears no guilt. Life remains a greater good in this situation than death. Committing a second wrong would not make this right. A better option in this rare but sad situation would be adoption.

Why are some people so prejudiced?

✠ Psychological studies reveal that no one is born prejudiced. They also reveal that the home is the main place for learning prejudice.

Parents pass on their own prejudices to their children. Schools, neighborhoods, and church groups can also be places where prejudices are reinforced.

What is affirmative action? Where does the Church stand on it?

✝ Affirmative action programs are set up to correct past discrimination against minorities and women by setting quotas for things like admission to college or hiring for certain jobs. The American bishops have supported the idea of affirmative action programs when the effects of past institutional discrimination persist.

Can rich people go to Heaven?

✝ Yes, Jesus came to save everyone, though he did say that it is difficult for rich people to enter the Kingdom of Heaven. The key issue is not whether or not a person is rich, but whether or not he or she is greedy. The rich person who counteracts greed by serving the poor and treating the poor as "another self" accomplishes much. Of course, it's important to remember that who is saved and who is not saved is entirely up to God.

For You to Do

Ways to Love

In Pope Benedict XVI's first encyclical *Deus Caritas Est* ("God Is Love") he wrote extensively about the importance of loving one's neighbor and service to the poor. Drawing heavily on the parable of the sheep and the goats in which Jesus describes the judgment of nations in Matthew 25:31–46, Pope Benedict equated the love we have for our neighbors, especially the most vulnerable people in our midst, with our love for the God we do not see face to face. He wrote:

> Having reflected on the nature of love and its meaning in biblical faith, we are left with two questions concerning our own attitude: Can we love God without seeing him? And can love be commanded? Against the double commandment of love these questions raise a double objection. No one has ever seen God, so how could we love him? Moreover, love cannot be commanded; it is ultimately a feeling that is either there or not, nor can it be produced by the will. Scripture seems to reinforce the first objection when it states: "If anyone says, 'I love God,' and hates his brother, he is a liar; for he who does not love his brother whom he has seen, cannot love God whom he has not seen" (1 Jn 4:20). But this text hardly excludes the

love of God as something impossible. On the contrary, the whole context of the passage quoted from the First Letter of John shows that such love is explicitly demanded. The unbreakable bond between love of God and love of neighbor is emphasized. One is so closely connected to the other that to say that we love God becomes a lie if we are closed to our neighbor or hate him altogether. Saint John's words should rather be interpreted to mean that love of neighbor is a path that leads to the encounter with God, and that closing our eyes to our neighbor also blinds us to God. (16)

Assignment

Answer the following questions based on the reading above.

1. How would you answer the Pope's questions: "Can we love God without seeing him? And can love be commanded?"

2. Recount any occasions when you have encountered someone who purports to love God yet seems to hate other people? Could you yourself ever have been accused of the same?

3. Describe the "unbreakable bond" between love of neighbor and love of God. How is this so?

4. Tell about a person in need whom you have served. Looking back on that occasion, how can you describe God's presence in it?

Bonus: Read the entire encyclical *Deus Caritas Est* at the Vatican website. Report on some other common themes between the Pope's words and Matthew 25:31–46.

Prayers and Reflections

Word of God

When the Son of Man comes in his glory, and all the angels with him, he will sit upon his glorious throne, and all the nations will be assembled before him. And he will separate them from another, as a shepherd separates the sheep from the goats. He will place the sheep on his right and the goats on his left.

—Matthew 25:31–33

Taking Action

Theirs is an endless road, a hopeless maze, who seeks for good before they seek God.

—St. Bernard of Clairvaux

Our world has enough for each person's need, but not for his greed.

—Mahatma Gandhi

Nobody who gets enough food and clothing in a world where most are hungry and cold has any business to talk about "misery."

—C. S. Lewis

World Peace Prayer

Lead us
from death to life,
from falsehood to truth,
from despair to hope,
from fear to trust.
Lead us
from hate to love,
from war to peace.
Let peace fill our hearts,
let peace fill our world,
let peace fill our universe. Amen.

Prayer of Mother Teresa

Make us worthy, Lord, to serve our fellow men and women throughout the world who live and die in poverty and hunger. Give them, through our hands, this day their daily bread, and by our understanding love, give them peace and joy. Amen.

eight

LITURGY AND SACRAMENTS

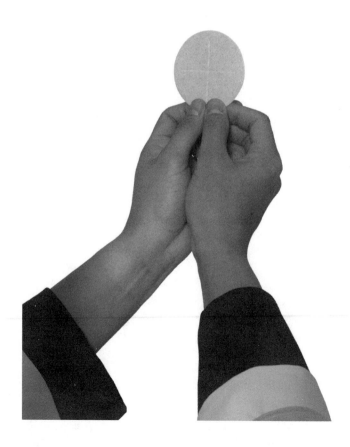

Outward Signs of God's Presence

Think of a sacrament like the old clay handprint you made for your parents when you were in kindergarten. You probably printed your name on it and your teacher added the date.

What was this object, really? Why do your parents keep this gift mounted in a prominent place, while they may have used up more expensive Christmas, Mother's Day, or Father's Day gifts you recently bought for them as soon as they had opened them?

The clay handprint was much more than a store-bought gift. It revealed something about you. When your parents hold the handprint, try to put their larger fingers in yours, marvel at your first efforts at printing your name, and remember the occasion when you gave them this gift, *you*—not just the sometimes mouthy teenager that they see every day, but the real you they have loved since the day you were born—are more present to them.

Imagine yourself moving away to college in a few years and your mom or dad taking hold of the clay handprint while you are gone. It will certainly evoke some emotion and help them to feel your presence.

Could they feel your presence if they wore the store-bought shirt you gave them just last Christmas? Sure. But the gift you created and put yourself into reveals much more about you.

God reveals himself in many, countless ways. There are unlimited people, events, and places in which we can know and feel God's presence. But God has chosen some ways to be *more* present, some ways to reveal himself more clearly, in a way that is even more real and powerful than the way you are present in a gift like the clay handprint.

These ways are the **sacraments**. A traditional definition of the sacraments reveals a great deal. It goes like this: "A sacrament is an outward sign instituted by Christ to give grace."

Christ, himself, is the prime sacrament, the gift of God the Father. This chapter looks at how Christ reveals himself through the sacraments— especially in the Paschal Mystery. It looks at the Church as sacrament. And it examines in more detail the Eucharist, the "sacrament of sacraments."

✢ **sacraments**

Outward and effective signs given by Christ to give grace. The Seven Sacraments are Baptism, Confirmation, Eucharist, Penance, Anointing of the Sick, Matrimony, and Holy Orders.

What is a gift that you have received that expresses something deep about the giver?

Make a gift (e.g., write a letter, draw a picture, assemble a photo album) of yourself and give it to someone you care about.

Jesus and the Sacraments

Sacraments are sacred and visible signs of God's loving grace active in the world. The word "sacrament" comes from two Latin words *sacramentum* ("solemn obligation") and *sacrare* ("to set apart as holy and sacred").

Though a sacrament is a sign, not all signs are sacraments. To be a sacrament, a sign must not only lead us to God, as all sacraments do, but it must come from God and be an action of God.

Jesus' "humanity appeared as a 'sacrament,' that is, the sign and instrument of his divinity and of the salvation he brings" (*CCC*, 515). Jesus is not only a sign of God the Father in our midst, he is the very presence of God.

The Scriptures support this view.

The beginning of the Letter to the Hebrews expresses it clearly:

In times past, God spoke in partial and various ways to our ancestors through the prophets; in these last days, he spoke to us through a son, whom he made heir of all things and through whom he created the universe. . . . (Heb 1:1–2)

In John's Gospel, Jesus said to his disciples:

I am the way and the truth and the life. No one comes to the Father except through me. If you know me, then you will also know my Father. From now on you do know him and have seen him. (Jn 14:6–7)

Jesus is God-in-the-flesh. His whole life, all of his words and actions reveal God the Father. It is in the Paschal Mystery—his Passion, Death, Resurrection, and Ascension—that God is most clearly revealed.

The Paschal Mystery is a unique event in history. Like other historical events, it really happened at a definite time and in a specific location. Unlike other historical events, the Paschal Mystery transcends time and place. Because through this event Jesus was able to destroy death and bring about Salvation, the Paschal Mystery is present to every generation since. Christ is truly present in these events.

Christ's presence in the Paschal Mystery is made known to us in the "liturgy," a word that means "work of the people." Christ's presence in the liturgy is a sacramental one. God the Father gave us his Son so that we might really experience what it is to be in his presence.

Pope Leo the Great explained it this way: "Whatever was visible in our Redeemer has passed over into the sacraments."

Christ Is Really Present

To be able to accomplish such a great work as our Salvation, Christ must be and always is present in the Church, especially in the sacraments. This is most clearly expressed and understood in the Eucharist. How is this so?

First, Jesus is present in the priest, the minister of the sacrament, who received a personal calling by Christ to his ministry through the Sacrament of Holy Orders. In the same way, through the Sacrament of Holy Orders, Christ is present in the minister who baptizes, hears confessions, anoints the sick, and marries. Christ, in point of fact, *is* the minister of the sacraments. The ordained minister (bishop, priest, or deacon) only acts in his name.

How is this so? Think about representatives who stand in for teachers (e.g., a substitute teacher) or parents (e.g., a babysitter). Though the original party is not physically present, through their representatives the students and children in the family are able to experience their

actual presence through things like lessons that are imparted and care that is given.

Second, Jesus is present when the Holy Scriptures are read. The Scriptures are the Word of God and are inspired by the Holy Spirit. Think of a letter—especially one that is handwritten—you have received from a close friend. You can experience the person's presence through what is written and even how it is written. This is somewhat similar to how Jesus is present in the Scriptures read at Eucharist and in the other sacraments.

Third, Jesus is present in the community that has gathered in his name. Jesus once told his disciples, "For where two or three are gathered together in my name, there am I in the midst of them" (Mt 18:20). He is present in the Church when we pray and sing. Jesus promised to be with the Church until the end of the world (Mt 28:20).

Finally, and specifically, in the Eucharist, Jesus is really present in the consecrated species of bread and wine. This presence is known as "real presence" because it is Jesus' presence in the fullest sense: "It is a *substantial* presence by which Christ, God and man, makes himself wholly and entirely present" (*CCC*, 1374). For many years, the Church has used the term **transubstantiation** to express how the reality (substance) of bread and wine changes into the reality of Jesus' risen and glorified Body and Blood.

Though any example pales by comparison, Jesus' real presence in these great gifts of bread and wine, is similar to how a child is present in the substance of a gift—maybe even a clay handprint—that he or she gives to someone else.

✤ transubstantiation

What happens at the consecration of the bread and wine at Mass, when their entire substance is turned into the substance of the Body and Blood of Christ, even though the appearances of bread and wine remain. The Eucharistic presence of Christ begins at the moment of consecration and endures as long as the Eucharistic species subsist.

Explain the following statement: "Though a sacrament is a sign, not all signs are sacraments."

What are ways that Jesus is present in the celebration of the Eucharist?

In your own words, explain how Jesus is really present in the bread and wine.

The Church as Sacrament

Like Christ, the Church is also a sacrament. The Church is a sign of our inner union with God. Because we are also in community with other people, the Church is also a sign of our union with each other. This unity is taking place now, in the diverse gathering of people of all races and cultures in the catholic, or universal, Church. At the same time, the unity is nowhere complete. The Church is also a sign of the *full* unity of people that is to come in the future.

Jesus is no longer physically present with us. Yet, as a sacrament, the Church is Christ's instrument. Christ, the head of the Church, uses the Church to dispense the graces necessary for Salvation. One way this is done is through the Seven Sacraments—"signs and instruments by which the Holy Spirit spreads the grace of Christ the head throughout the Church which is his Body" (CCC, 774).

How else does the Church fit in with our understanding of sacrament?

✔ mystery

First, like Christ, the Church is a **mystery**. A Greek word that referred to the sacraments was *mysterion*, or mystery. The Eastern churches still refer to the sacraments as "holy mysteries." The Church is the visible sign of the hidden reality of Salvation.

A reality filled with God's invisible presence. This term applies to the Blessed Trinity's plan of Salvation in Jesus Christ; the Church, which is his Body; and the sacraments.

Second, Christ loves the Church. He always has and always will. He gave up his life for the Church, and he has remained present in the Church in all the days since. The Gospels describe the faithful as a bride attached to Christ. In Mark 2:19, Jesus described himself as the bridegroom with the Church being his bride. The Church to this day is the sign of Christ's unfailing loyalty to us, his people.

❦ **efficacious symbol**

A symbol that is "capable of producing a desired effect." This means that the sacraments actually confer the grace they signify.

Third, the Church is an **efficacious symbol**. That means it is a symbol that not only points to a reality—in this case, our Salvation—but it also causes it. This is different than other symbols or signs. For example, the traditional peace sign of the 1960s was a symbol for an effort mostly by young people of that era to bring an end to the Vietnam War and violence in the streets of their own country. While some of their efforts were successful, it was their *efforts*, not the peace sign, that brought about an end to the war and violence. The Church is different. It not only points to our deeper union with God and our Salvation, it also causes this to happen. Mainly this happens through the invisible graces of the Seven Sacraments.

Seven Sacraments Instituted by Christ

Just as the Church developed the canon of the Scriptures and the other doctrines of faith, through the Holy Spirit, the Church has gradually recognized that, among its various liturgical celebrations, there are exactly Seven Sacraments that are instituted by Christ. These sacraments are Baptism, Confirmation, Eucharist, Penance, Anointing of the Sick, Holy Orders, and Matrimony.

This a common statement: *The sacraments are instituted by Christ.* What does it mean?

First of all, when the first Christians baptized (e.g., Acts 2:41), laid on hands (e.g., Acts 6:6, 8:17), healed the sick (e.g., James 5:14), and broke bread together (e.g., Acts 2:46), they were doing exactly as Jesus had commanded them to do. This is the meaning of how the sacraments were instituted by Christ.

However, for the first two centuries, there was no one term to describe the sacraments. Gradually, as the Church continued to practice these liturgical actions, they realized that they were also learning more and more about Jesus when they did so. They also came to recognize that Jesus was present with them in these actions. Moreover, they came to understand that Jesus was, in fact, the minister of these actions.

Eventually the Seven Sacraments were named by the Council of Florence in 1439. The council also explained that three things are necessary for each sacrament:

1. *Proper matter.* The essential elements used in the sacraments are determined by the Magisterium of the Church. For example, Eucharist can be celebrated only with recently made unleavened wheat-based bread and natural wine of the

grape. Ensuring proper matter helps keep the integrity of the sacraments in line with Jesus' intentions.

2. *Correct words or form.* Likewise, the order of the rites and the words spoken in the sacraments are entrusted to the Magisterium who makes sure they are observed universally in the Church. No priest, for example, may change or alter the approved liturgical texts.

3. *Designated minister.* An ordained minister—a bishop, priest, or deacon who has received the Sacrament of Holy Orders—is at the service of the community of faith in the sacraments. "The ordained minister guarantees that it really is Christ who acts in the sacraments through the Holy Spirit for the Church" (CCC, 1120).

Other Teachings about the Sacraments

More detailed information on the three Sacraments of Initiation—Baptism, Confirmation, and Eucharist—is provided elsewhere in this text. The sacraments of healing—Penance, also called Reconciliation, is mentioned in the context of Morality (Chapter 6) and Social Justice (Chapter 7). The Sacraments of the Service of Communion—Holy Orders and Matrimony—are touched on in Chapter 10. **Anointing of the Sick** is mentioned in a question concerning illness and death (page 220). You have likely had a formal study of the Seven Sacraments in your years of religious education prior to this time of Confirmation preparation. There are other teachings that are common to all of the sacraments. Some of those are detailed here.

⚘ Anointing of the Sick

A Sacrament of Healing in which the healing and loving touch of Christ is extended through the Church to those who are seriously ill or dying.

⟶ The sacraments presuppose faith. The Church's faith precedes the faith of the person who is seeking membership in the Church. There is an old saying, "The Church believes as she prays."

⟶ The sacraments act *ex opere operato* ("by the very fact of the action being performed"). It is God's power, not the worthiness of the minister or the recipient, that makes the sacraments effective. However, the fruits or benefits of the sacraments are dependent on how the person who receives them is disposed. A person who receives the sacraments with faith can accomplish great things in partnership with God.

⤳ For believers, the sacraments are necessary for Salvation. The graces of the sacraments give us a share in God's divine nature.

⤳ Three of the sacraments—Baptism, Confirmation, and Holy Orders—confer a sacramental character or seal by which the person shares in Christ's priesthood and is made a member of the Church with different responsibilities and functions. These seals are permanent; therefore these sacraments can never be repeated.

⤳ The sacraments will be celebrated to the end of time, echoing Jesus' words shared with his disciples at the Last Supper: "I have eagerly desired to eat this Passover with you . . . until there is fulfillment in the kingdom of God" (Lk 22:15, 16).

What does it mean to say that the Church is an "efficacious symbol"?

How are the sacraments "instituted by Christ"?

How does your disposition affect the fruits of the sacraments for your life?

Make an effort to celebrate the Sacrament of Penance this week. Share God's forgiveness with someone you hold a grudge against or vice versa.

Eucharist: Sacrament of Sacraments

The Vatican II document *Constitution on the Church* describes the Eucharist as the "source and summit of the Christian life" (11). All of the other sacraments and the other Church ministries are bound up in the Eucharist. To put it simply, the Eucharist is the sum and summary of our faith. St. Irenaeus wrote, "Our way of thinking is attuned to the Eucharist, and the Eucharist in turn confirms our way of thinking."

By the Eucharist, we are united with the heavenly liturgy and anticipate eternal life. At the beginning of the twentieth century, Pope Pius X was dismayed that more people did not regularly receive communion, even when they attended Mass, so he encouraged weekly and even daily communion. He lowered the age of First Communion from twelve to the age of reason (seven) so that even more people could receive the Body and Blood of Christ at the Eucharist table. Pope Pius explained:

Holy Communion is the shortest and safest way to heaven. There are others: innocence, but that is for little children; penance, but we are afraid of it; generous endurance of trials of life, but when they come we weep and ask to be spared. The surest, easiest, shortest way is the Eucharist.

The Eucharist is the sacrament that completes Christian initiation. Those who share in the priesthood of Christ through Baptism and are configured more closely to him through Confirmation, form community through their participation in the Eucharist.

Development of the Eucharist

On the night of his Last Supper, Christ instituted the Eucharist during the Passover meal. Jesus instituted the Eucharist as a memorial of his Death and Resurrection. In doing so in the context of the Passover, Jesus gave the Jewish Passover ultimate meaning. Jesus' passing over to God the Father by his Death is anticipated in the Last Supper meal and is celebrated to the end of time whenever the Eucharist is shared.

In the signs of the bread and wine, and at the recitation of Christ's words, "This is my body which will be given for you. . . . This cup is the new covenant in my blood which will be shed for you" (Lk 22:19, 20), Jesus offers an everlasting gift of himself, for he is truly present in the bread and wine. When he told the gathered Apostles, "Do this in remembrance of me," he was making them priests of the New Testament, responsible for celebrating the Eucharist until his return.

From the beginning, the Eucharist was something that kept the Church from being too rooted in the present. In the Eucharist, the participants are removed from the constraints of time so that the saving events of the past (the Last Supper and crucifixion) are made present here and now.

In the first century, Christians would gather in homes for the celebration of the Lord's Day, Sunday. Eventually some of these homes became churches. Preaching, prayer, and the breaking of the bread were essential parts of the Eucharist from the beginning. In AD 155, Justin Martyr wrote the first surviving outline of the rite of Eucharist. In these early centuries, the prayers of Eucharist varied from region to region. By the Middle Ages, however, Charlemagne attempted to unify the liturgy as a way to bring greater unity to people under his reign.

Also, by the Middle Ages, the Mass was said in Latin and the laity's role had diminished. In order to emphasize the sacrifice of the Eucharist, the altar was moved farther and farther away from the people and the priest said the Mass with his back to the people. The high point of the Mass was the elevation of the conse- crated host.

At the Council of Trent (1545–1563), the Church reaffirmed the sacrificial nature of the Eucharist. The doctrine of transubstantiation was defined. And Pope Pius V (at right) published a Roman Missal that brought uniformity to the official rite of Eucharist. This Missal was used in the Church for the next four hundred years, until the Sec- ond Vatican Council.

Today the Eucharist is most typically celebrated in the vernacular, that is, the common language of the people. Also, the Second Vatican Council worked to clarify the original meaning of the Eucharist, emphasizing the actions and elements Jesus had begun at the Last Supper: the community as a sign of the Lord's presence, the call to for- giveness and penance, the Scripture readings proclaimed and under- stood by the people, the reception of both the consecrated bread and wine by all the baptized, and the command to go forth from the Eucharist to serve others.

❦ motu propio

A term that means "of his own accord." It signifies words in papal docu- ments that were decided by the pope personally.

In 2007, Pope Benedict issued a *motu pro- pio* allowing for celebration of the Tridentine Mass in extraordinary circumstances alongside the Missal of Pope Paul VI (the ordinary form of the Mass) with the desire for "interior recon- ciliation in the heart of the Church" and to remind Catholics that there "is no contradiction between the two editions of the *Roman Missal*."

The Celebration of Eucharist

In many ways, the Mass begins before you even get to church. Think of all the things that must happen in a family on a Sunday morning before they are ever seated in a pew. The teenage daughter who likes to sleep in is cranky all the way through her shower. The middle-grade son is camped in front of the television hard to dislodge. The toddler must be dressed and given a hearty breakfast. Even Mom and Dad are slow-moving over the Sunday morning newspaper.

But, whether in the dead of winter or in a torrential thunderstorm, the family makes the effort to go to Mass. It's important that they do, for themselves, and the rest of the community. If they were absent, one part of the Body of Christ would be missing.

Many people of all ages lament that they don't want to go to Mass because "it's boring" or they "don't get anything out of it."

This attitude can only change when we begin to view liturgy as its name intends, as the "work" of the people, the work we must do in order to come to know God and to participate with God in the Salvation of the world. The work of the priest, "acting in the person of Christ the head" (*CCC*, 1348), is to preside over the assembly, proclaim the Gospel, and consecrate the bread and wine into the Body and Blood of Christ. Our work places us in an active role as well, perhaps as readers, gift bearers, or those who give communion, but always through our active participation expressed in our responses and prayer. Even more important than our presence at Mass is our understanding that God has chosen to be present there and to act through the Mass in order to give us grace.

As you probably know, the Mass is divided into two main parts, the Liturgy of the Word and the Liturgy of the Eucharist. God is present and acting in each of these parts and all of their elements. Let's examine the order of the Mass and each of its major elements:

1. *Introductory Rites.* All gather in the name of Christ. Jesus Christ himself is the high priest who presides over every Eucharist. The bishop or priest represents Christ and presides over the assembly, speaks the readings, receives the offerings, and says the Eucharistic prayer. The priest and other ministers process to the altar and bow. The priest kisses the altar out of respect. The Mass always begins with the Sign of the Cross. Just as it would be improper to join any celebration without healing divisions between you and the host or you and the other invited guests, a penitential rite follows where we ask for God's and the community's mercy and forgiveness. The ancient song of praise, the *Gloria*, comes next. The introductory rites end with an opening prayer written especially for the day or feast being celebrated.

2. *The Liturgy of the Word.* On Sundays, there are three readings from the Scriptures. The first is usually taken from the Old Testament, the second from one of the New Testament letters. In between, a psalm is sung as a response. The high point of the Liturgy of the Word is the Gospel reading, directly about the life of Jesus. There is an intended common theme between the first reading and the Gospel. The assembly stands for the

Gospel out of reverence and signs themselves three times on their forehead, lips, and heart, symbolically showing the commitment to make God's Word come alive in what we think, in what we say, and in what we do. A homily, given by the priest, helps the congregation understand more about the readings and apply them to their daily lives. The reciting of the Nicene Creed and the offering of prayers of intercession conclude the Liturgy of the Word. The prayers of the faithful are intended to be made for the needs of all people.

3. *The Liturgy of the Eucharist.* The preparation of the altar and the presentation of gifts of bread and wine as well as monetary donations begins the Liturgy of the Eucharist. The offertory has always been part of the liturgy. The *Catechism of the Catholic Church* reminds us:

> From the very beginning Christians have brought, along with the bread and wine for the Eucharist, gifts to share with those in need. The custom of the *collection*, ever appropriate, is inspired by the example of Christ who became poor to make us rich. (1351)

The Eucharistic prayer is the high point of the Liturgy of the Eucharist, and of the Mass itself. The Church has several Eucharistic prayers, but each has certain common elements. The Eucharistic prayer:

→ *offers* thanksgiving to the Father, through Christ, in the Holy Spirit for all his works;

→ *asks* the Father to send the Holy Spirit (or blessing) on the gifts of bread and wine so that they may become the Body and Blood of Christ;

→ through the words of Christ at the Last Supper, *makes* him present under the species of bread and wine;

→ *offers* his sacrifice on the cross once and for all, recalling the Passion, Resurrection, and return of Christ;

→ *offers* intercessions for the Pope, the bishops and the clergy, and the living and the dead.

Though the Eucharistic prayer seems a long recitation by the priest, it is really a dialogue with the assembly, and we respond with our agreement to all that was prayed with our resounding "Amen" or "I agree."

In the Communion Rite, the people prepare to receive Jesus in Holy Communion by reciting the Our Father and sharing a Sign of Peace. These words and actions reinforce our unity and highlight our communion with God and one another. The Lamb of God reminds us of our sinfulness and our need for God's mercy. The priest breaks the bread as another sign of our unity, that we will all share from the one loaf. Then we share in communion, eating and drinking the Body and Blood of Christ. A prayer after communion asks God to grant the effects of the mystery just celebrated.

4. *Concluding Rite.* Some visitors to a Catholic Mass once commented how "everything seems to end so quickly" after communion. Really, their observation is an accurate one. After such a climax there is really no other place the liturgy can go except to a conclusion. After the priest blesses the people, he asks them to "go in peace to love and serve the Lord." We are to carry the graces received at Eucharist out into our world.

The sacraments are tangible signs and symbolic actions by which the presence of Christ and the power of the Holy Spirit enable us to be the people of God. The sacraments are the action of Christ living through us. As Pope John Paul II put it:

What else are the sacraments (all of them), if not the action of Christ in the Holy Spirit? When the Church baptizes, it is Christ who baptizes; when the Church absolves, it is Christ who absolves; when the Church celebrates Eucharist, it is Christ who celebrates it: "This is my body." And so on. All the sacraments are an action of Christ, the action of God in Christ. (*Crossing the Threshold of Hope*)

ADORATION BEFORE THE BLESSED SACRAMENT

The world is noisy and busy. Crowded school hallways lead to hectic lunchrooms with breaks partitioned by ringing bells. Before you can even retreat to your ride for the way home, you likely have inserted your earphones for an inundation of last night's downloads. In the meantime, your fingers fly furiously to text several friends.

More than ever, you need a place to be silent. You need a place away from television, radio, music, cell phones, screaming, and shouting. You need a place to be quiet and alone with God and yourself. One of the great places the Church offers for this needed experience is Eucharistic Adoration. The Eucharist is a priceless treasure; by not only celebrating it at Mass but by praying before it outside of Mass, we have the opportunity to receive the graces that spring from it. The primary graces people who pray before the Eucharist receive are increased charity—the love of Christ—along with a greater reverence at Mass, a deeper desire for personal holiness, and a stronger connection with the parish and the entire Church. Adoration of Christ in the Blessed Sacrament also leads to devotion of service to the poor and an increase in vocations to the priesthood and consecrated life. Pope Benedict XVI wrote:

◀ **Eucharistic Adoration**

Prayer directed to Christ in the Blessed Sacrament that acknowledges his role as Savior, Sanctifier, Lord, and Master of all.

◀ **Blessed Sacrament**

A name to describe the Real Presence of Jesus in the consecrated species of bread and wine, which are his Body and Blood.

> In life today, which is often noisy and scattered, it is more important than ever to recover the capacity for interior silence and recollection: Eucharistic Adoration permits one to do this not only within one's "I" but rather in the company of that "You" full of love who is Jesus Christ, "the God who is near us."

Plan some time during your week to visit a Church and sit before the tabernacle that houses the Blessed Sacrament. Once you are there, you can pray in many different ways: You can meditate silently by gazing on the Blessed Sacrament.

You can silently speak to Jesus from the depths of your heart. You can read or recite traditional Catholic prayers and devotions such as the reading of Scripture, the reciting of the rosary, or the saying of litanies. The best way for adoration is to follow through on your commitment to do it!

The *Catechism of the Catholic Church*, quoting Pope Paul VI, teaches:

> Because Christ himself is present in the sacrament of the altar, he is to be honored with the worship of adoration. "To visit the Blessed Sacrament is . . . a proof of gratitude, and expression of love, and a duty of adoration toward Christ our Lord." (*CCC*, 1418)

How was the Eucharist celebrated in the first century?

What does it mean to say that the Eucharist is "removed from the constraints of time"?

Name the parts of the Mass.

What are the common elements of the Eucharistic prayers?

What prayer do you say to yourself after receiving communion?

Name some of your family's rituals for attending and celebrating Eucharist.

Interview your sponsor or a relative who can recall the liturgy prior to the Second Vatican Council. Ask him or her to share remembrances of the Mass and how the parish reacted to the changes in the liturgy at the time.

Catholic  Apologetics

Why are there seven Sacraments?

* While God is present everywhere and God's mystery and grace cannot be contained, there are certain places where God is "more" present. For example, it is easy to recognize God's presence in experiences of love, mercy, compassion, and justice. Over time the Church understood that not only did Jesus commission certain actions to be repeated over time, but that he was also present with them in these events. These are the Seven Sacraments. It was at the

Council of Florence in 1439 that the Church declared that there are Seven Sacraments that "both contain grace and confer it upon all who receive them worthily."

Why do you have to confess your sins to a priest in the Sacrament of Penance?

✙ The priest is both the representative of Christ and the Church. Confessing to a priest in the Sacrament of Penance is a way to experience first hand the forgiving touch and saving love of Jesus. Reconciling with the Church is important so that we can reclaim our functions within the Body of Christ.

What are the rules for receiving communion?

✙ Anyone who wishes to receive communion must be in a state of grace. If you are aware of a mortal sin you have committed, you must receive absolution for the sin in the Sacrament of Penance before going to communion. Also, you must abstain from food or drink (with the exception of water and medicines) for at least one hour before receiving communion.

Why do Catholics believe that Jesus is really present in the bread and wine and that they are not just symbolic of his presence?

✙ Jesus said, "Whoever eats my flesh and drinks my blood has eternal life. . . . For my flesh is true food, and my blood is true drink. Whoever eats my flesh and drinks my blood remains in me and I in him" (Jn 6:54–56). This is the scriptural basis for our Catholic belief. Catholics hold that at the time of the consecration (when the priest repeats Jesus' words from the Last Supper, "This is my body" and "This is my blood"), the substance of the bread and wine change into the reality of Jesus.

Why can't I receive communion in another Christian church? Why can't my friend who is Christian, but not Catholic, receive communion at my church?

✙ The very word "communion" has to do with unity, both in our beliefs about Jesus Christ and with one another. It would not be honest for a person to receive communion if he or she did not hold the same beliefs as Catholics do about Jesus; for example, that he is really present in the bread and wine. For the same reason, a Catholic cannot receive communion at a Protestant church. There are exceptions to this rule. For example, sometimes a bishop will give permission for non-Catholic parents to receive communion at the wedding of their Catholic child.

Am I really required to go to Mass every Sunday?

✛ Yes, Catholics are required to go to Mass every Sunday and holy day of obligation unless excused for a serious reason, like an illness. This is one of the Church laws, and it is broken without good reason only under the penalty of sin. There are good reasons for this rule. For one, Christ is present at the Eucharist and actively anticipating our being there. Secondly, our absence creates a void, just as missing any one part of a larger body would.

For **You** to **Do**

Contemplating the Origins of Eucharist

This passage from the Gospel of Luke recalls the events at the Last Supper when Jesus instituted the Eucharist. Read the passage slowly, pausing on the highlighted words or phrase, and then studying from the notes below how the Jews sharing the meal with Jesus would have understood their meaning.

> When the hour came, he took his place at table with the apostles. He said to them, "I have eagerly desired to eat **this Passover** with you before I suffer, for, I tell you, I shall not eat it [again] until there is fulfillment in the kingdom of God." Then he took a cup, **gave thanks**, and said, "Take this and share it among yourselves; for I tell you [that] from this time on I shall not drink of the fruit of the vine until the kingdom of God comes." Then he took the bread, said the blessing, **broke it** and gave it to them, saying, "This is my **body**, which will be given for you; **do this in memory of me.**" And likewise the cup after they had eaten, saying, "This cup is the **new covenant** in my **blood, which will be shed for you.**"
>
> —Luke 22:14–20

Notes on the Passage

"this Passover" Passover to the Jews was an occasion to celebrate freedom. Imagine Jesus saying, "I have eagerly desired to remember and celebrate our freedom with you."

"gave thanks" Jesus would have recited the *berekah*, the great prayer of the Jewish people, a thanksgiving to God for all of the gifts God had given them. The word *eucharist* itself means "thanksgiving."

"broke it [the bread]" Breaking bread was a symbol of love and friendship to the Jews. To break bread with someone was to show that you loved them like a member of your own family.

"body" This was not a biological term to the Jews, but a personal term. People *were* their bodies. When Jesus said, "This is my body" he meant: "This is me, my person."

"do this in memory of me" The Jews of Jesus' time believed that after death a person stayed alive in the nether world as long as someone on earth remembered them. That's why they recited the names of their ancestors as part of their religious feasts (see Luke 3:23–38, the genealogy of Jesus). Jesus is asking his disciples to repeat this holy meal as a way of keeping him alive in the world after his Death. Whenever we gather to "do this," Jesus promises to be present in our midst.

"new covenant" The Jews had a covenant with YHWH that held that YHWH would be their God and offer his protection and they would be his people and obey his laws. In this passage, Jesus is making a new covenant: God will love us as a parent loves a child, and we will love and serve God as sons and daughters.

"blood, which will be shed for you" Solemn agreements were sealed in blood; the blood of a lamb was sprinkled on both parties of the agreement as a sign that they were entrusting their lives to one another. (Think of the scene in *Tom Sawyer* when Tom and Huck seal an agreement with their blood.) Jesus offers his blood to seal the new contract between God and us.

Assignment

Write or share five sentences about the Eucharist. Use each of the following words in a sentence:

✤ gather
✤ forgive
✤ listen
✤ share
✤ serve

Prayers and Reflections

The Divine Praises

Blessed be God.
Blessed be his Holy Name.
Blessed be Jesus Christ, true God and true Man.
Blessed be the Name of Jesus.

Blessed be his most Sacred Heart.
Blessed be his most Precious Blood.
Blessed be Jesus in the most Holy Sacrament of the Altar.
Blessed be the Holy Spirit, the Paraclete.
Blessed be the great Mother of God, Mary most holy.
Blessed be her holy and Immaculate Conception.
Blessed be her glorious Assumption.
Blessed be the name of Mary, Virgin and Mother.
Blessed be St. Joseph, her most chaste spouse.
Blessed be God in his angels and in his saints.

Final Doxology

Through him,
with him,
in him,
in the unity of the Holy Spirit,
all glory and honor is yours,
almighty Father,
for ever and ever.

Prayer to Our Redeemer

Soul of Christ, make me holy,
Body of Christ, be my salvation.
Blood of Christ, let me drink your wine.
Water flowing from the side of Christ, wash me clean.
Passion of Christ, strengthen me.
Kind Jesus, hear my prayer;
hide me within your wounds
and keep me close to you.
Defend me from the evil enemy.
Call me at my death
to the fellowship of your saints,
that I may sing your praise with them
through all eternity.
Amen.

St. Margaret Mary Alacoque on Devotion to the Blessed Sacrament

In order to be like you, who are always alone in the Blessed Sacrament, I shall love solitude and try to converse with you as much as possible. Grant that my mind may not seek to know anything but you, that my heart may have no longings or desires but to love you.

When I am obliged to take some comfort, I shall take care to see that it be pleasing to your heart. In my conversations, O divine Word, I shall consecrate all my words to you so that you will not permit me to pronounce a single one which is not for your glory.

nine

$\mathcal{H}$OLY SPIRIT AND CONFIRMATION

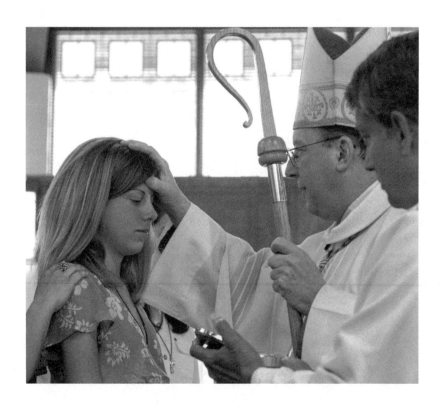

Empowered at Pentecost

Status Quo.

Have you heard or used this Latin phrase before? It literally means "the state in which." Supporting the status quo usually involves opposing any large or radical change. Sometimes it is necessary and wise to stay in the status quo.

One of those occasions was just after the events of Easter Sunday. The Risen Jesus had appeared to the Apostles and other disciples. He told them not to be afraid. The disciples responded and were skeptical for sure, but also joyful. Jesus instructed them to witness to others everything they had seen and heard. But before they were to do that, Jesus gave them one other instruction: He told them to "stay in the city until you are clothed with the power on high" (Lk 24:49). That is, they were to remain in "the state in which"—the status quo.

What could have been the reason for such a message? The disciples were enthused with the remarkable experience of just meeting the Savior who had risen from the dead. Why should they wait to get on with their lives and share this Good News?

For one, the time had to be right. There are several examples from history of people who acted exactly at the right time—and of those who did not. Consider how communism was overturned in Poland and the Soviet-dominated countries of Eastern Europe. Decades of protest, détente, and suffering had already gone before an ordinary factory worker named Lech Walesa led a worker's strike in July 1980 that eventually included ten million protesting workers. Walesa had a game plan: He encouraged the strikers to confess their sins, celebrate

Mass, and receive Holy Communion, in an open shipyard. This protest would have brought severe reprimands by the Soviet government in other years. But the action in 1980 came on the heels of a visit to Poland by the native hero Pope John Paul II. The world was watching how the Soviet government would react. This time the government buckled, and the workers were allowed to form a union. The time was right.

✤ **Paraclete**

Another name for the Holy Spirit. It means "advocate, defender, or consoler."

More importantly, as Jesus taught, the agent or power for change must be from "on high." The one Jesus was speaking of was the Holy Spirit, the **Paraclete** who proceeds from the Father and Son. The Holy Spirit, the Third Person of the Holy Trinity, came to the first disciples at Pentecost.

Pentecost is a Greek word that means "fiftieth day." Originally, Pentecost was the Jewish feast called the "Feast of the First Fruits" or the "Feast of Weeks" that happened fifty days after the Passover. Jews from all over the Roman Empire, many who spoke different languages and dialects, gathered in Jerusalem to celebrate this first harvest of summer.

Also in Jerusalem, Peter and the other disciples (including Jesus' mother Mary) were holed up in the Upper Room, fearful of being arrested and possibly murdered as Jesus was. The Acts of the Apostles describes what happened next:

> And suddenly there came from the sky a noise like a strong driving wind, and it filled the entire house in which they were. Then there appeared to them tongues as of fire, which parted and came to rest on each one of them. And they were all filled with the holy Spirit and began to speak in different tongues, as the Spirit enabled them to proclaim. (Acts 2:2–4)

Once the Spirit came to them, the disciples were no longer afraid. Peter came out of hiding and began to address the Jews gathered in the streets. He recounted for them the entire story of Salvation, concluding with Jesus the Messiah and everything that happened to him. The crowds were bewildered by what they heard. For one thing, even though they spoke several languages, each was able to understand Peter. Many thought Peter and the others were drunk, even though it was only nine in the morning!

The conclusion, however, was that about three thousand persons were baptized that day. Through the coming of the Holy Spirit, the first Christians were able to look back on and see the life of Jesus in a new light. They were able to preach confidently that "Jesus is Lord" and that Jesus was equal with the Father, true God from true God.

The disciples of Jesus were empowered at the coming of the Holy Spirit. From that point, the status quo was no longer.

Sacrament of the Holy Spirit

In the Sacrament of Confirmation, as the bishop anoints the forehead of each candidate with chrism, he says, "Be sealed with the gift of the Holy Spirit." Confirmation has been called the Sacrament of the Holy Spirit. During the rite, the bishop calls on God the Father and God the Son to send the Holy Spirit upon the candidates and empower them with seven gifts of the Spirit: wisdom, understanding, right judgment, courage, knowledge, reverence, and wonder and awe in God's presence.

Believing in God and acting on his commands is only possible by the grace and interior help of the Holy Spirit. In Baptism, God's life takes hold in us. The Holy Spirit is alive in us and offers us the gift of **sanctifying grace**, the grace which heals our human sinfulness, continues to make us holy, and gives us a share in the divine life of the Trinity. Confirmation celebrates the Holy Spirit in the life of the person being confirmed and in the community that has nurtured his or her faith.

✔ **sanctifying grace**

The grace, or gift of God's friendship, that heals fallen human nature and gives us a share in the divine life of the Blessed Trinity. A habitual, supernatural gift, it makes us perfect, holy, and Christlike (*CCC*, 1999).

What happens after Confirmation? As with the first disciples, it would be reasonable to suggest that the status quo will cease. You will be inspired by the Spirit to a new life in the Church with possibilities too large to try and mention.

In a Mass before thousands of youth and young adults, including many who were about to receive the Sacrament of Confirmation, at Randwick Racecourse in Sydney, Australia, as part of World Youth Day 2008, Pope Benedict XVI preached in his homily:

> Empowered by the Spirit, and drawing upon faith's rich vision, a new generation of Christians is being called to help build a world in which God's gift of life is welcomed, respected and cherished—not rejected, feared as a threat and destroyed. A new age in which love is not greedy or self-seeking, but pure, faithful and genuinely free, open to others, respectful of their dignity, seeking their good,

radiating joy and beauty. A new age in which hope liberates us from the shallowness, apathy and self-absorption which deaden our souls and poison our relationships. Dear young friends, the Lord is asking you to be prophets of this new age, messengers of his love, drawing people to the Father and building a future of hope for all humanity.

This chapter traces more about the Church's understanding of the Holy Spirit, delves into the application of the seven gifts of the Holy Spirit, and shares how Confirmation celebrates those gifts.

 How have you experienced the Holy Spirit's presence in your life?

 Choose a peer group that you are not a part of and find a way to collaborate with them on a worthwhile event or service project.

The Holy Spirit

The Holy Spirit is the third person of the Trinity, the last of the persons to be revealed. As St. Gregory of Nazianzus wrote:

> The Old Testament proclaimed the Father clearly, but the Son more obscurely. The New Testament revealed the Son and gave us a glimpse of the divinity of the Spirit. Now the Spirit dwells among us and grants us a clearer vision of himself. (quoted in *CCC*, 684)

How so? The story of Pentecost and even Lech Walesa are somewhat bold examples of how the Spirit dwells among us and is clearly present. What about some more common examples? Where do you witness the Spirit's presence in the following examples?

> Julie, a sophomore, feels ill and is sent home from school. When Julie's mother is called at work, she decides to take off the rest of the day to stay home with her daughter. "I know Julie's old enough to rest on the couch by herself," Mom explains. "But I also know she'll rest more comfortably if I am there."

> All the seniors enjoy taking part in their only year of an open campus at lunch. Unfortunately, Dion has a physical handicap that prevents him from driving, and no one has ever asked him out for lunch. Alexandra breaks that routine and invites Dion to be part of her regular crowd that does Thursday

lunches at a local fast-food spot. She makes sure to drive her family's mini-van on Thursdays so Dion can easily ride along.

Monday mornings are terrible for everyone in the family. Except Dad. While Mom and kids rush through the paces of showers, making lunches, and otherwise getting ready to face the week, Dad is already up and fresh. He tells his usual fare of jokes. By the time everyone is ready to leave the house, each person has smiled at least once.

Could you easily recognize Christ's presence in the actions of Julie's mom, Alexandra, and the dad of the final vignette? If so, the Spirit has done his job. The "job" of the Holy Spirit is not to speak on his own, but instead to unveil Christ to us. This explains how the world at large cannot accept the Spirit, "because it neither sees nor knows it." But, Jesus adds, "You know it, because it remains with you, and will be in you" (Jn 14:17).

It is in the Church—in people like these described above—that we come to know the Holy Spirit. As the *Catechism of the Catholic Church* teaches, we know the Holy Spirit in:

⋯→ the Scriptures he inspired

⋯→ Church Tradition

⋯→ the Magisterium, which he assists

⋯→ the sacramental liturgy

⋯→ prayer, wherein he intercedes for us

⋯→ the gifts and ministries by which the Church is built up

⋯→ the signs of apostolic and missionary life

⋯→ the witness of saints through whom he shows his holiness and continues the work of Salvation. (688)

And, as these and other stories of Spirit-filled people you know would attest, the saints may include people we meet day to day.

Tracing the Holy Spirit in Scripture

From the very beginning of creation, God's Spirit prepares the world for the time of the Messiah. The Church reads the Old Testament, searching for places where the Spirit, "who has spoken through the prophets," teaches about Christ.

The Spirit is present at the time of creation. The very first verses of the Bible tell how when creation was accomplished "a mighty wind swept over the waters" (Gn 1:2). The word "wind" is translated from the Hebrew *ruah*, which tells of God's mysterious, powerful, and life-giving presence. This breath of life is likewise present in the second creation story when God forms man out of clay "and blew into his nostrils the breath of life, and so man became a living being" (Gn 2:7).

The Holy Spirit is both revealed and concealed in mystery at the time when God makes himself present to the Hebrew fathers, especially Moses in the giving of the commandments. Although the Law was powerless to save the world from sin, it enkindled in people a stronger desire for the Holy Spirit to come.

Through the Old Testament prophets, the Holy Spirit reveals more about the Messiah and helps to prepare for his coming, especially in the "Servant Songs" of the Book of Isaiah. For example, the Good Friday reading from Isaiah tells us in part:

> He grew up like a sapling before him,
> like a shoot from the parched earth;
> There was in him no stately bearing to make us look at him,
> nor appearance that would attract us to him.
> Yet it was our infirmities that he bore,
> our sufferings that he endured,
> While we thought of him as stricken,
> as one smitten by God and afflicted.
> But he was pierced for our offenses,
> crushed for our sins;
> Upon him was the chastisement that makes us whole,
> by his stripes we were healed. (53:2, 4–5)

The Spirit's presence in the New Testament becomes even more visible. The very conception of Jesus is brought about by the overshadowing power of the Holy Spirit. The angel tells Mary at the Annunciation that "the holy Spirit will come upon you, and the power of the Most High will overshadow you. Therefore the child to be born will be called holy, the Son of God" (Lk 1:35).

The entire mission of Jesus—from the Annunciation to his Ascension—is a joint work between the Son and the Holy Spirit. Jesus doesn't reveal the Holy Spirit completely in his ministry, though he does allude to the Spirit on several occasions. For example, he tells the Samaritan woman at the well that "the hour is coming, and is now here, when true worshipers will worship the Father in Spirit and truth; and indeed the Father seeks such people to worship him. God is Spirit, and those who worship him must worship in Spirit and truth" (Jn 4:23).

It is not until it is time for his Passion, Death, and Resurrection that Jesus finally promises his disciples that he will send the Holy Spirit. "I will ask the Father, and he will give you another Advocate to be with you always, the Spirit of truth" (Jn 14:16). At Jesus' Death, he commends his Spirit into his Father's hands. After his Resurrection, he breathes on his disciples and says to them, "Receive the holy Spirit. Whose sins you forgive are forgiven them, and whose sins you retain are retained" (Jn 20:22–23). From that time on, the mission of Jesus and the Holy Spirit becomes the mission of the Church.

Jesus' promises to send the Holy Spirit were fulfilled on the feast of Pentecost. In his speech to the gathered crowds in Jerusalem, Peter was clear to them that he and the others were not drunk. Rather, quoting the Prophet Joel, Peter said:

> "It will come to pass in the last days," God says,
> "that I will pour out a portion of my spirit upon all flesh.
> Your sons and daughters shall prophesy,
> your young men shall see visions
> your old men shall dream dreams.
> Indeed, upon my servants and my handmaids
> I will pour out a portion of my spirit in those days,
> and they shall prophesy,
> And I will work wonders in the heavens above
> and signs on the earth below:
> blood, fire, and a cloud of smoke.
> The sun shall be turned to darkness,
> and the moon to blood,
> before the coming of the great and
> splendid day of the Lord,
> and it shall be that everyone shall be saved
> who calls on
> the name of the Lord." (Acts 2:17–21)

SYMBOLS OF THE HOLY SPIRIT

Besides *ruah* (wind), the Scriptures are filled with many other symbols of the Holy Spirit, including:

- *Fire.* Fire symbolizes the transforming energy of the Holy Spirit's actions. God appeared to Moses in the fire of an unconsumed burning bush. Jesus' speaking of the coming Kingdom said, "I have come to set the earth on fire, and how I wish it were already blazing!" (Lk 12:49). At Pentecost, fire in the shape of tongues rested on the disciples. The gift of tongues enabled them to speak in such a way that they were heard according to each one's own language.

- *Dove.* A dove returned to Noah with a fresh olive branch to signify the end of the Great Flood. At Jesus' baptism, the Holy Spirit in the form of a dove comes down on him and remains with him.

- *Water.* Water represents the Holy Spirit's action in Baptism. Jesus made the connection with water and the Holy Spirit when he said, "No one can enter the kingdom of God without being born of water and Spirit" (Jn 3:5).

- *Anointing.* There were several anointed ones in the Old Testament, most notably King David. The very name *Christ* means "anointed one." From the very beginning of his life, the Holy Spirit anointed Christ the Messiah.

How do we come to know the Holy Spirit in the Church?

Share an occurrence from the past twenty-four hours in which you recognize the Holy Spirit's presence.

Read and compare John 20:22 to Genesis 2:7. What is one thing you imagine that your reception of the Holy Spirit in Confirmation will inspire you to do?

The Sacrament of Confirmation

The fullness of the Holy Spirit rested on Jesus, the Messiah. This fullness was to be shared with all of the disciples. Jesus promised several times the outpouring of the Spirit. The promise was fulfilled first at Easter, and then even more dramatically at Pentecost. Those who were baptized that day received the gift of the Holy Spirit.

From the time of those Apostles, the laying on of hands on the newly baptized was understood to impart the gift of the Holy Spirit and complete the grace of Baptism. The Letter to the Hebrews (6:2) describes Baptism and the laying on of hands as one of the basic teachings of the Apostles. The Church understands this laying on of hands as the origin of the Sacrament of Confirmation and as a way to bring to Christians in all generations the fullness of grace that was present on the day of Pentecost.

Early on, an anointing with chrism (perfumed oil) was added to the laying on of hands to highlight the name Christian, which the person takes on at the time. In the Eastern churches the sacrament is called *Chrismation,* meaning "anointing with chrism." In the West, the sacrament is Confirmation, highlighting that the sacrament both confirms the promises made at Baptism and strengthens baptismal grace.

Recall from Chapter 1 that Confirmation was originally part of a single ritual that included the other Sacraments of Initiation, Baptism, and Eucharist. For those who are baptized after they have reached the age of reason (age seven or so), Confirmation is still celebrated that way today as part of the Easter vigil liturgy. However, for those Catholics who were baptized as infants, Confirmation is usually reserved for a later time, either some time in adolescence or around the time of a person's first communion. Received in either order, Confirmation is the sacrament that completes Baptism. Eucharist is the sacrament that completes both Baptism and Confirmation and brings about full initiation into the Church.

To receive the Sacrament of Confirmation, a person should be prepared. This means growing in a more intimate union with Christ and becoming more familiar with the Holy Spirit—recognizing his actions, gifts, and callings—so that once confirmed, the person can assume the responsibilities of Christian life. The candidate should also be in a state of grace. This means the person should receive the Sacrament of Penance in order to be cleansed from any serious sin. Even if one is in a state of grace, celebrating the Sacrament of Penance prepares us for reception of the gift of the Holy Spirit.

The Rite of the Sacrament

How is the Sacrament of Confirmation celebrated? The short answer is that in the Roman rite, Confirmation is typically celebrated during Mass to further strengthen its connection with Eucharist, the third Sacrament of Initiation. A more detailed answer involves examining some of the symbolic elements and actions that are a part of the rite.

First, there are several people who are an important part of the rite.

The **bishop** is the ordinary minister of the sacrament, and he fittingly celebrates the sacrament to connect our experience of the coming of the Spirit with that of the Apostles who received the Holy Spirit at Pentecost. His presence unites the candidates more deeply with the mission of the universal Church and to the mission of sharing Christ with all.

Also important at Confirmation is the candidate's **sponsor**. This person—a fully initiated Catholic—may be the candidate's godparent from Baptism, to further highlight the connection between the two sacraments. The sponsor presents the candidate to the bishop, vouches for his or her readiness, and represents the community in welcoming the candidate to a new level of mature membership in the Church. Finally, the rest of the Church—parents, relatives, friends, teachers, other parishioners—also gathers at Confirmation. They are the ones who have shared and cultivated the gift of faith in the candidate since Baptism. They *are* the Church in which the newly confirmed takes his or her place.

Second, there are words, symbols, and concrete actions that make up the rite.

After the Gospel, the pastor of the parish, or the catechist responsible for Confirmation preparation, presents the candidates to the bishop, usually by name. The bishop then gives a homily on the readings that explains the meaning of the sacrament.

The candidates then stand and renew their baptismal promises before the bishop and the community of faith.

The bishop extends his hands individually on each candidate or over the entire group of candidates—the symbolic "laying on of hands"—and prays for the outpouring of the Spirit on them.

✔ **bishop**

A successor to the Apostles. He governs the local church in a given diocese and the worldwide Church in union with the Pope and college of bishops. A bishop receives the fullness of the Sacrament of Holy Orders.

✔ **sponsor**

A guide to the Confirmation candidate who brings the candidate to receive the sacrament, presents him or her to the bishop for anointing, and will later help fulfill his or her baptismal promises faithfully under the influence of the Holy Spirit.

The essential rite of Confirmation, the anointing of the candidates with chrism, follows. Although the consecration of the chrism takes place before Confirmation, it is still an important part of the rite. This "blessing of the oils" takes place at the Chrism Mass for the diocese on Holy Thursday. The chrism is used throughout the diocese in all Confirmations over the course of the year. The word chrism has the same root as the word "Christ." As the bishop dips his right thumb in the chrism and makes the Sign of the Cross on the forehead of the candidate, he exchanges this dialogue with the candidate:

Bishop: <u>Name</u>, be sealed with the Gift of the Holy Spirit.
Candidate: Amen.
Bishop: Peace be with you.
Candidate: And also with you.

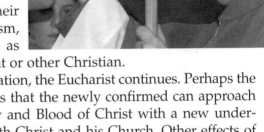

Candidates may use their own names, given at Baptism, or choose new names such as the name of an admired saint or other Christian.

After this rite of Confirmation, the Eucharist continues. Perhaps the first effect of the sacrament is that the newly confirmed can approach the altar to receive the Body and Blood of Christ with a new understanding of their oneness with Christ and his Church. Other effects of Confirmation are explained below.

Effects of the Sacrament

Confirmation brings about a special outpouring of the Holy Spirit. Because of this, the graces of Baptism are perfected at Confirmation. Like Baptism, Confirmation is given only once, for it also imprints on the person a spiritual mark or indelible character that cannot be removed. This seal of the Spirit leads the Christian to profess Christ and be his witness to the world.

Other effects of the Sacrament of Confirmation are:

⇢ It roots us more deeply in God's love, leading us to call out to God, "Abba! Father!"

⇢ It unites us more firmly with Christ.

⇢ It strengthens our bond with the Church.

⇢ It gives us the special strength of the Holy Spirit to spread and defend the faith by word and action, to confess the name of Christ boldly, and never to be ashamed of the cross.

Another effect of Confirmation is it increases the gifts of the Holy Spirit in us. The seven gifts of the Spirit are named and explained in the next section.

 | What are the requirements to receive the Sacrament of Confirmation?

 | How do you imagine the effects of Confirmation taking root in your life?

 | Find out how your sponsor will be able to speak out for your readiness to receive the Sacrament of Confirmation.

Gifts of the Spirit

As the bishop extends his hands over the Confirmation candidates, he invokes the outpouring of the Holy Spirit, praying:

> All-powerful God, Father of our Lord Jesus Christ,
> by water and the Holy Spirit
> you freed your sons and daughters from sin
> and gave them new life.
> Send your Holy Spirit upon them
> to be their helper and guide.
> Give them the spirit of wisdom and understanding,
> the spirit of right judgment and courage,
> the spirit of knowledge and reverence.
> Fill them with the spirit of wonder and awe in your presence.
> We ask this through Christ our Lord.

This traditional list of the seven gifts comes from a description of the Messiah from the Book of Isaiah (11:1–5). Think over how you would respond to these questions in relation to the seven gifts of the Holy Spirit:

⟶ What do these gifts mean to me?

⟶ How are they part of my life?

⟶ How can I share them with others?

Wisdom

Like the lyrics to a classic Johnny Nash song—"I can see clearly now, the rain is gone"—the gift of wisdom has to do with seeing reality with clarity. This means that we can look at God, others, and ourselves as God sees us.

Another way to describe the gift of wisdom might be as a "reality check." Wisdom can help us to take a long view of things at times; for example, we can see that a poor grade on one assignment won't do fatal damage to our life or our plans. Wisdom can help us take a more focused, small view, too, when needed. It can help us to put aside all the busyness of our personal lives to stop and help a young child tie a shoe or to make a Sunday evening phone call to a lonely grandparent.

Understanding

You may have caught yourself describing why a best friend is so important for you with words like the following: "Of all my friends, she is the one who *really understands* me." You may have a brother or sister who fits that description or even one of your parents. God is the friend who understands you better than any other.

The Holy Spirit gifts us with understanding so that we can understand more about God. This gift can help us with the larger mysteries of life, the questions of suffering and death, with breaking open the Scriptures and with knowing, with slightly larger depth and breadth, the God who made us.

Right Judgment

One of God's greatest gifts to us is the gift of free will. We have the freedom to choose in so many areas, including between good and bad and between life with God and life apart from God. The gift of right judgment is the Holy Spirit's help for us to make good choices in all areas of morality.

Sometimes we are only able to reap the benefits of right judgment when we realize that it is often given through another person; for example, through the advice or expertise offered by someone older, wiser, or more experienced than we are in a particular area. The gift of right judgment helps us to seek out this good advice, accept it, and apply it to a particular choice we are to make. The gift of right judgment also teaches us to learn from our past mistakes.

Courage

We all face very real fears. Fears that have to do with school: you do not think you will be able to complete a challenging course. Fears that have to do with relationships: you fear that a close friend will like somebody else more than you or that you will never find someone to share your life with as a committed partner in marriage. You may face the ultimate fear of death, both your own and that of those close to you, especially your parents.

The Latin root of *courage* is *cor*, which means "heart." With this gift of the Holy Spirit, we are able to "take heart" and be encouraged even when faced with our worst fears. Courage is also the opposite of discourage. The gift of courage is not a magical potion that makes all of our fears disappear. Rather, the gift of courage helps us to face our fears and gives us the perseverance to continue to work to overcome them.

Knowledge

Think about the wide range of knowledge you possess. Compare your knowledge in, say, the field of mathematics with what you knew about math three years ago or ten years ago. Or, look at the advances in knowledge that human beings collectively have made in the past one hundred years or even the past five years. This advance of knowledge is a gift of God, the Holy Spirit. Building on the gift of knowledge is the primary reason that you are in school.

Knowledge doesn't only have to do with amassing information about subjects or disciplines. The gift of knowledge extends to our relationships with others and theirs with us. Everyone wants to be known. We don't want to spend our lives ignored and never recognized for the unique persons we are. The gift of knowledge helps us to notice the uniqueness in our neighbor and for our uniqueness to be acknowledged as well. Finally, this gift helps us to know God and to cultivate our friendship with him.

Reverence

Most everyone is familiar with what is entailed by respect. Respect is the mutual way we honor others. Also, we can respect ourselves. This too involves doing what's best for ourselves—whether it be eating the right foods, exercising, following rules, praying, or cultivating good relationships.

The gift of reverence is a form of respect, but one to the *nth degree*. Reverence widens the circle of respect to include care, concern, and compassion for people we don't know or even see—especially the poor. We also are called to have reverence for all of God's creation—including the environment—and for God himself.

Wonder and Awe in God's Presence

This gift of the Holy Spirit has also been referred to as "fear of the Lord." How could the two descriptions be related? The similarities could be summed up in the word "Wow!" The gift of wonder and awe helps us to a more clear sense of the enormity of God, especially when seen in relation to ourselves, only one part of God's creation. The impact of such an insight could easily lead one to tremble with fear in God's presence.

Still, the gift of wonder and awe leads us to delight in God, not to live in fear of God. This is the gift that helps us experience the Almighty at the sight of a sunset over water, a snow-capped mountain, or the first steps of a small child. This gift also reminds us that in spite of God's seeming *largeness*, he loves and cares for us more than we could ever love and care for ourselves.

The fullness of these seven gifts belongs to Jesus, and he embodies them. In the Sacrament of Confirmation, these same gifts are strengthened in us. St. Ambrose reminded the Church of the importance of protecting these gifts:

> Guard what you have received. God the Father has marked you with his sign; Christ the Lord has confirmed you and has placed his pledge, the Spirit, in your hearts. (quoted in *CCC*, 1303)

 Name and write your own unique descriptions of each of the seven gifts of the Holy Spirit.

Which gift of the Spirit would you most like to possess?

 Tell why you are looking forward to receiving the Sacrament of Confirmation.

 Tell how you can use at least one gift of the Holy Spirit to help others.

Catholic 🕊️Apologetics

Is the Holy Spirit equal to the Father and Son?

✦ The Holy Spirit is equal to the Father and Son because he is God. Because of the nature of the Blessed Trinity, the Holy Spirit is entirely in the Father and the Son just as the Father is entirely in the Son and the Holy Spirit, and the Son is entirely in the Father and the Holy Spirit.

What is the sin against the Holy Spirit, spoken of in Matthew 12:31–32, that cannot be forgiven?

✠ The sin against the Holy Spirit that Jesus speaks of is attributing works of the Spirit of God to Satan, exactly what Jesus' enemies had done when they said Jesus' power over demons came from Satan. God's mercy has no limits. But anyone who deliberately rejects God's mercy, his offer of forgiveness, and the Salvation offered by the Holy Spirit by refusing to repent is guilty of the eternal sin.

Why is Pentecost sometimes called the birthday of the Church?

✠ It was on Pentecost, through the coming of the Holy Spirit, that God completed all covenants with humanity. On Pentecost, the Holy Spirit united all of Jesus' disciples into one community of faith, the Church.

Is reception of the Sacrament of Confirmation necessary for Salvation?

✠ A person who has been baptized but not confirmed can certainly be saved. But the Church teaches that Christian initiation is incomplete without reception of Confirmation and Eucharist. It follows, according to Church teaching, that all the faithful are obliged to be confirmed at an appropriate time.

At what age does the Church teach that Confirmation should be celebrated?

✠ Canon law teaches that the Sacrament of Confirmation should be conferred around the age of discretion (about seven years old) unless the bishops determine there is another more appropriate age or the person is in danger of death. In 2001, the bishops in the United States decreed that Confirmation in the Latin Rite dioceses of the United States will be between "the age of discretion and about sixteen years of age."

Why are children who are baptized at Easter also confirmed?

✠ Any child who has reached the age of discretion is considered to be sufficiently mature in the matters of faith and capable of nurturing a personal faith life and following his or her conscience. For that reason, their initiation follows the adult form in which they receive all three Sacraments of Initiation at the Easter vigil.

Can my parent be my Confirmation sponsor?

✤ No, the Church sees two distinct and important roles for parents and sponsors. In fact, it is recommended that the Confirmation sponsor be the same as the baptismal sponsor to continue to help your parents nurture your faith life.

# For **You** to **Do**

Choosing Readings for Confirmation

The *Rite of Confirmation* states that "ordinarily Confirmation takes place within Mass in order to express more clearly the fundamental connection of this sacrament with the entirety of Christian initiation" (13).

Likewise, the Liturgy of the Word for the Confirmation Mass is celebrated in the ordinary way. The readings may be taken in whole or part from the readings for the day. More commonly, special readings are chosen from the Lectionary that are especially suited to Confirmation and the Holy Spirit.

Listed below are some appropriate biblical readings for Confirmation.

Readings from the Old Testament

Isaiah 11:1–4a
🔥 On him the Spirit of the Lord rests.

Isaiah 42:1–3
🔥 I have endowed my servant with my Spirit.

Isaiah 61:1–3a, 6a, 8b–9
🔥 The Lord has anointed me and has sent me to bring Good News to the poor, to give them the oil of gladness.

Ezekiel 36:24–28
🔥 I will place a new Spirit in your midst.

Joel 2:23a, 26–30a
🔥 I will pour out my Spirit on all humankind.

Readings from the New Testament

Acts 1:3–8
🔥 You will receive the power of the Holy Spirit, and you will be my witnesses.

Acts 2:1–6, 14, 22b–23, 32–33
🕊 They were all filled with the Holy Spirit, and began to speak.

Acts 8:1, 4, 14–17
🕊 They laid hands on them, and they received the Holy Spirit.

Acts 10:1, 33–34, 37–34
🕊 The Holy Spirit came down on all those listening to the Word of God.

Acts 19:1b–61
🕊 Did you receive the Holy Spirit when you became believers?

Romans 5:1–2, 5–8
🕊 The love of God has been poured into our hearts by the Holy Spirit which has been given to us.

Romans 8:14–17
🕊 The Spirit himself and our spirit bear united witness that we are children of God.

Romans 8:26–27
🕊 The Spirit himself will express our plea in a way that could never be put into words.

1 Corinthians 12:4–13
🕊 There is one and the same Spirit giving to each as he wills.

Galatians 5:16–17, 22–23a, 24–25
🕊 If we live in the Spirit, let us be directed by the Spirit.

Ephesians 1:3a, 4a, 13–19a
🕊 You have been signed with the seal of the Holy Spirit of promise.

Ephesians 4:1–6
🕊 There is one body, one Spirit, and one Baptism.

Gospel

Matthew 5:1–12a
🕊 Theirs is the Kingdom of Heaven.

Matthew 16:24–27
🕊 If anyone wishes to follow me, let him deny himself.

Matthew 25:14–30

🔥 Because you have been faithful in small matters, come into the joy of your Master.

Mark 1:9–11

🔥 He saw the Spirit descending and remaining on him.

Luke 4:16–22a

🔥 The Spirit of the Lord is upon me.

Luke 8:4–10a, 11b–15

🔥 Some seed fell on rich soil.

Luke 10:21–24

🔥 I bless you, Father, for revealing these things to children.

John 7:37b–39

🔥 From the heart of the Lord shall flow fountains of living water.

John 14:15–17

🔥 The Spirit of truth will be with you forever.

John 14:23–26

🔥 The Holy Spirit will teach you everything.

John 15:18–21, 26–27

🔥 The Spirit of truth who issues from the Father will be my witness.

John 16:5b–7, 12–13a

🔥 The Spirit of truth will lead you to the complete truth.

Assignment

Choose one Old Testament reading, one New Testament reading, and one Gospel reading that are appropriate for the Liturgy of the Word at a Mass where the Sacrament of Confirmation is celebrated. Try to explicitly connect the theme of the Gospel with the theme of the Old Testament reading. Choose a New Testament reading that teaches a slightly different message. After you have chosen the three readings, compose a short "homily" that connects the readings with the following themes:

⟶ The coming of the Holy Spirit
⟶ The Spirit's presence in the lives of teens
⟶ The Spirit's challenge for the future

···→ The effects of the Sacrament of Confirmation

···→ The Gifts of the Holy Spirit

Share your homily either in writing or speaking with your sponsor or classmates.

Prayers and Reflections

Lou Holtz's *A Teen's Game Plan for Life*

It's great to have big dreams. But the way to make your dreams come true is through a series of smaller daily choices. This is where the WIN formula—What's Important Now"—can help.

You sure you want to be an All American? Then ask yourself twenty-five times a day "what's important now."

You wake up in the morning—"what's important now?" Get out of bed.

You're out of bed—"what's important now?" Eat breakfast. You need your strength.

What's important now? Go to class.

What's important now? Sit in the front row. Be prepared.

When you're in the weight room—"what's important now?" It's to get stronger. Not because somebody's looking. But because you know you've got to get stronger.

When you're out Saturday night and there's alcohol, and sex, and drugs—"what's important now?" If your dream is to be an All American in whatever field you've chosen, then "what's important now" is to avoid those situations.

You take any dream you want to reach and ask yourself twenty-five times a day "what's important now?" and you'll know exactly what you have to do to achieve it.

Word of God

Now when the Apostles in Jerusalem heard that Samaria had accepted the word of God, they sent them Peter and John, who went down and prayed for them, that they might receive the holy Spirit, for it had not yet fallen upon any of them; they had only been baptized in the name of the Lord Jesus. Then they laid hands on them and they received the holy Spirit.

—Acts 8:14–17

Come, Holy Spirit

Come, Holy Spirit, fill the hearts of your faithful
and kindle in them the fire of your love.
Send forth your Spirit, O Lord,
and renew the face of the earth.
O God,
on the first Pentecost
you instructed the hearts of those who believed in you
by the light of the Holy Spirit:
under the inspiration of the same Spirit,
give us a taste for what is right and true
and a continuing sense of his joy-bringing presence
and power,
through Jesus Christ our Lord.
Amen.

Opening Prayer from the Rite of Confirmation

God of power and mercy,
send your Holy Spirit
to live in our hearts
and make us temples of his glory.
We ask this through our Lord Jesus Christ, your Son,
who lives and reigns with you and the Holy Spirit,
one God, for ever and ever.
Amen.

ten

$\mathcal{Y}$OUR CHRISTIAN VOCATION

Your Maturing Faith

Can you even believe that freshmen and seniors belong to the same student body?

How different they can be!

Freshmen are intimidated, confused, without direction.

Seniors are brimming with confidence, exploring their freedom, motivated to move on to the next phase of their lives.

Or so it often seems!

What a difference a few years makes. Or, more accurately, what a difference a great deal of maturity makes.

You are maturing in many ways, including in your faith life.

The Sacrament of Confirmation, which most American Catholics still receive in their teen years, is sometimes called the "Sacrament of Christian maturity" because it brings an increase and deepening of God's grace first received at Baptism. While the sacrament itself happens only once, the effects of the sacrament continue to grow and multiply.

Some of the effects of your growing maturity in faith can be easily witnessed now. More of the effects of this maturing faith will be present as you receive the Sacrament of Confirmation, complete high school, continue your education, choose a career, and act on a vocation.

This final chapter looks at some of the specific issues and decisions you will face in your faith life over the next few years. It will also address three types of vocations Catholics are called to from the single life—marriage, priesthood, or religious life.

❧ discipleship

The life of following Jesus Christ. *Disciple* comes from a Latin word that means "learner."

Whatever career and vocational choice we decide on, as fully initiated Catholics, we share in the common vocation of **discipleship** in Jesus Christ. The chapter concludes with a reminder of how difficult—and rewarding—that call can be.

 What are three ways you have grown and changed emotionally, intellectually, and spiritually in the past year?

Discovering and Using Your Gifts

Football coach Lou Holtz (see page 204) described a simple formula for a person to determine the course for his or her life:

First, think about what it is you like to do.
Second, determine something you like to do that you are also good at.
Finally, find someone to pay you for it.

Think about the formula and apply it to things in your life that you enjoy. For example, you may love to play the guitar, but you may not be very good at it. Don't expect to go on worldwide tour yet.

Or, you may be a whiz in mathematics and not as good in English. Still, reading good literature is a real pleasure for you. Even though your aptitude test may suggest that you become an accountant, your lack of enthusiasm for working with numbers would suggest that you find a career more to your liking.

The third criteria—finding someone to pay you—is certainly an important one. We live in a free-market economy where each person is responsible to support him- or herself, as well as his or her dependent family members.

On the other hand, we must ask ourselves what standard of living we expect for our family and ourselves. How much money do we really need? This is one time we must keep in mind the cardinal virtue of temperance, that is, our moderation of pleasures and our balance in the way we use created goods.

In these last years of high school, and through the next four to ten years after graduation, you will be making some of the most important choices of your life, choices that will determine your career and vocation. In each of these areas you will find it necessary to recognize your talents and gifts and understand the best ways to use them. You will also need to rely on a **discernment** process of prayer to help you determine God's will for your life.

Self-Esteem and Your Gifts

In your years in school you have probably already learned a great deal about the importance of **self-esteem** and its related term self-concept. Put simply, your self-concept is how you think of yourself. If you look honestly at yourself and feel good about yourself, then your self-esteem will be high. Looking honestly means naming your gifts—be they in the areas of academics, athletics, fine arts—and balancing them between feelings of narcissism and worthlessness.

Narcissism, a word that means "unhealthy self-love," rears itself in people who brag or are otherwise full of themselves. These people may in fact be talented in particular areas. However, by calling undue attention to themselves, these talents are obscured. Also, people who are narcissistic find it difficult to recognize the talents in others. Narcissists rarely make good "team" players; instead, the focus is always on themselves.

On the other end of the spectrum are people who think of themselves as worthless. Nothing they do is good or right for them, or so they say.

To achieve healthy self-esteem, you must find a balance between narcissism and worthlessness. At times, everyone is going to brag about his or her accomplishments. Sometimes this is just a way to hide some perceived or real deficiencies or feelings of worthlessness. At other times, particularly after some defeat or failure, we all struggle with feelings of doubt about our self-worth.

To be able to honestly name your personal God-given talents and gifts, you must have healthy self-esteem. There are several things you can do to help in this task. For example:

> *Pay attention to your "self-talk."* This is the running conversation you carry on with yourself over the course of a day. Is the tone of this conversation more negative than positive? Do you catch yourself thinking, "I can't do that," or "I'll fail at that for sure"? If so, replace this negative self-talk with positive messages in which you praise yourself for some of good things— both big and little—you do during the course of a day.

✔ discernment

A decision-making process that involves praying over a decision, asking for the guidance of the Holy Spirit, making the decision, and then evaluating it.

✔ self-esteem

A way to describe the value we place on ourselves.

Don't focus on things over which you have no control. If the coach tells you that you will play outfield, don't focus your thoughts on how you might do as a pitcher. For now, your concern should be on being the best outfielder you can be. Also, don't sulk about past mistakes. Learn from them, but then move on. Finally, ignore the hurtful comments of others. For example, ignore the comments of a jealous teammate who says, "You are not a good outfielder. I should be playing in that position."

Be with people who support you and can help improve your self-esteem. Again, this step involves honesty. You don't want to focus on people who falsely build up your talents ("You are the best dancer in the entire city"). On the other hand, you do want to listen to trusted friends and acquaintances who give you an honest assessment ("You aren't a bad dancer. In fact, you're better than most").

When your self-esteem is at a healthy level, you can make a more honest personal assessment of your talents and gifts. You can take a look at what you like to do, what you are good at, and think about several possibilities for applying these interests to career, ministry, and vocation.

Discerning Choices and Making Them Happen

Discernment is the name for our ability to make a concrete choice for our lives. Put in religious terms, discernment is our way of discovering what God intends for our lives. It is our way of determining God's will for us. Discernment involves looking at all sides of a decision, considering many alternatives. Discernment mainly involves praying over a decision. Finally, discernment means making a decision, acting on it, and evaluating it.

Beginning right now, you have several important decisions you must make leading to high school graduation and beyond. One of these involves your vocation—a choice that involves God's calling to marriage, religious life, committed single life, or to priesthood. Another decision involves choosing a career. A career is a job that expresses a person's gifts and talents. Consider how the following discernment process applies to these important choices:

1. *Dream.* To dream is one of the privileges of freedom that God provides. You are also fortunate to live in a nation that for the most part respects your freedom. At your age, it's perfectly fine to dream big dreams. You can dream about being the president

of the United States, a Navy seal, a Broadway actor, or the scientist who discovers a cure for cancer. The only limit to your dream is that it must be humanly possible.

2. *Realism.* Temper your dreams with realism. These are the dreams that have the best chance at succeeding. For example, if you are afraid of heights, it's best not to dream of being an astronaut who will orbit the earth.

3. *Plan.* Once you've identified your talents and interests, think about how these might work into a career. Remember, a career is different than a job. A job may only be a way to earn a wage. A career is a job with an extra dimension: it is an opportunity to express what you like and what you are good at. Planning for a career should begin now. First, do research for the career you are interested in. For example, if you have aptitude and interest in chemistry, you may consider a career in pharmacy. What does it take to be a pharmacist? What are the college requirements? What is it that attracts you to this career?

4. *Seek advice.* Talk over your career ideas with parents, teachers, counselors, and anyone you know who already is active in your potential career. Don't expect these people to simply validate your opinions. Ask them to play "devil's advocate" and present to you a real list of pros and cons that can help you in making a decision.

5. *Pray.* Involve God in all of your decisions, especially these larger ones that may impact your life for years to come. Ask yourself: How does this career support your life as a Christian? Is there anything contradictory about this career and the Gospel of Jesus Christ? How will this career give you satisfaction? Continue to talk to God about this choice. Pay attention to God's answers (maybe through the words of a person you trust).

6. *Act on your decision.* If you choose to go ahead with this career, take the next step. This may mean applying to a college well known for the major you are considering, or apprenticing at a trade school or with an employer in this field.

7. *Evaluate.* There is no need to look back and "second guess" your decision on a regular basis. However, it is important to choose regular checkpoints to evaluate how your career process is going. If, you are uncomfortable with your choice, begin the process again at Step 4.

As much as you envision your future and plan for a career, it is likely that you will make three to five career changes in the course of your lifetime. You may end up in a career you have never considered. For example, one recent college graduate who hoped to land a career as a film editor, ended up teaching high-school math instead. As a teacher, he discovered he liked working with computers, so he went back to college and got a second degree in computer science. He ended up with a job as a computer programmer. "If I hadn't gone into teaching, I wouldn't have known how much I liked computers," he said.

Define *self-esteem.*

What are the seven steps for discernment?

Use Lou Holtz's formula to determine a potential course for your life.

Where do you find yourself on the self-esteem spectrum from narcissistic to worthless?

Apply the seven discernment steps to a career you are considering.

A Call to Love

Just as a career is more than a job, a vocation involves much more than a career. *Vocation* is a word that means "call." For Christians, the primary call is a call to be a disciple of Christ. This call, given at Baptism, requires Christians to bring God's love to others, and to share the Good News of Redemption offered by Jesus Christ to all.

The perfection of love is holiness. We carry out this basic Christian call in the context of a particular state of life, which is also known as vocation. Taken in this context, a vocation is to the ordained, consecrated, or lay states of life. An ordained man may also be consecrated or religious (a member of a religious community). A more specific

vocation within the lay state of life is to marriage. Some **lay people** also have a specific
vocation to the single life.

In years past, high school graduates were
more likely to commit to one of the specific
vocations like marriage, priesthood, or religious life within a few years after high school
or college graduations. Today, the average age
for marriage is rising (approximately twenty-
seven years for men, twenty-five years for
women). It is also more typical for men in their thirties to be ordained.
In any case, now is the appropriate time to consider how the specific
vocations within your primary Christian vocation fit with your
dreams and goals for life.

❦ **lay people**

All members of the
Church who have been
initiated into the Church
through Baptism and are
not ordained (the clergy)
or in consecrated life. The
laity participates in Jesus'
prophetic, priestly, and
kingly ministries.

Vocation of Marriage

Even at your age, you've probably thought about marriage and
what it would like to be married.
Most people do. In fact, a majority
of adults eventually are married. In
that regard, marriage is the "most
popular" Christian vocation.

Marriage is a sacrament administered by the couple to one another. The priest or deacon who
officiates serves as a witness on
behalf of the Church. The sacrament is based on the mutual consent of the man and woman to give
themselves to one another until
death, in order that they might
make their relationship one of faithful and fruitful love.

Why might you want to eventually marry? People marry for many
different reasons. Some people marry because they are "in love,"
though they may not have a clear understanding of what being in love
means. Others marry to escape a situation at home or to get a "new
start." Some marry because there is a pregnancy involved.

The decision to enter into marriage should never be taken lightly. The intimate bond of marriage is intended to represent the same bond that Jesus formed with his Church. It is an unbreakable bond; that is the reason the Church does not recognize divorce. It is a bond in which the couple is expected to bring forth new life and to raise their children in the Christian faith. The Church, "on the side of life," teaches that every act of sexual intercourse in marriage must remain open to the procreation of human life.

Besides just thinking about what it would be *like* to be married, there are several things you can do right now to prepare for your future marriage. Marriage is based on respect and honor between spouses. You can practice these skills in the ways you treat friends of both sexes. Marriage also includes many opportunities for "give-and-take" and for truly listening to the needs and concerns of the other. For now, you may be the person who compromises more frequently in your current relationships as a way to practice for a time when you are married. Marriage demands faithful and unbroken commitment. You can practice these skills through your commitment to your own family and friends, to a job, and to your schoolwork. Finally, in marriage, the wife and husband are faithful to each other physically. This gift of chastity is one you should keep in your current state of life. Saving sex for marriage is the best gift you can give to your future spouse on your wedding night and beyond.

Vocation of Priesthood and Religious Life

The term *vocation* is traditionally used to describe callings to the ordained ministry of a priest or the religious life of a sister or brother. Certainly neither priesthood nor religious or consecrated life is typical in the sense that planning and training for these vocations takes place in logical, sequential steps.

🕊 **ministerial priesthood**

The priesthood of bishops and priests that confers on them a sacred power for the service of the faithful.

The **ministerial priesthood** is different from the **common priesthood** of the baptized in that it confers a sacred power for the service of the faithful. Ordained ministers—in three degrees of bishop, priest, and deacon—serve the Church by teaching, by leading worship, and by their governance.

🕊 **common priesthood**

The priesthood of all the baptized in which we share in Christ's work of Salvation.

The Sacrament of Holy Orders is only conferred on baptized men, following the example of Jesus and the early Church who only called men to be Apostles and bishops. In the Roman

Catholic Church, priests are men who live celibate lives and who promise to remain celibate "for the sake of the kingdom of heaven" (see *CCC*, 1619). Ordination is conferred in silence through the laying on of hands by the bishop and the bishop's solemn prayer of consecration, followed by a Mass with concelebrating priests.

A man doesn't just become a priest; he is called to that vocation by God. The vocation of most priests began with a "nagging feeling"— often present from grade school on—that this is the life that God wants for them. Other signs that men are being called to priesthood include:

⤑ other people telling them they would make a good priest

⤑ a desire to pray

⤑ going to Mass more than usual and imagining themselves as presider

⤑ trying out some ministries associated with priesthood (e.g., teaching, caring for the sick, counseling others)

The term *religious life* does not mean the same thing as the ordained priesthood. Religious are not a separate classification of people in the Church "in between" priests and lay people. In fact, religious can be from either state of life, ordained or lay. Religious can also be women or men. Women religious are called sisters, men religious are called brothers. Some men religious are also priests. Religious live in communities usually founded by a charismatic leader to serve a specific purpose in the Church.

Religious take vows to live out the **evangelical counsels** of poverty, chastity, and obedience. Prior to their profession of vows, they live a period of religious formation that helps them and the community decide if they are right for each other.

> **✔ evangelical counsels**
>
> Vows of personal poverty, chastity understood as life-long celibacy, and obedience to the demands of the community being joined that those entering the consecrated life profess.

As with marriage, your late teen and early adult years are a time to think about a possible call to priesthood or consecrated life. If you feel a call to serve Christ in a radical way, if you want to use your talents to serve others, and if you are capable of making a commitment, you may want to explore a vocation to priesthood or consecrated life.

Fr. Vincent Coppola, C.S.C., offered this suggestion for someone considering the priesthood or consecrated life:

> Act on faith—take the leap into the unknown. Go with what is in your heart. If your honest discernment leads you to conclude that

this isn't the life for you, then you will be a better person for going through the discernment process. God's grace works in such mysterious ways, you may discover something you would have never dreamed of considering previously. Either way, it is a "win-win" situation.

Until you choose a vocation of marriage, priesthood, or consecrated life, you fall naturally into the single state of life. For some people, however, the single life is not a transitional state; rather, it is a permanent vocation, though one not marked by a Church rite. Examples of people who choose a single life vocation are adult children who care for their invalid parents and lay people who choose to be missionaries either in their own country or another country. People with a **homosexual orientation** who try to live the Church's call to chastity also take up the vocation to the single life in many cases.

 homosexual orientation

Sexual attraction or orientation toward persons of the same sex. This is differentiated from homosexual acts that are morally wrong because they violate the purpose of sexual activity.

 How is a vocation "much more" than a career?

 What are some things a person your age can do now to prepare for a future marriage?

Name some things that appeal to you about the radical lifestyle of a priest or religious.

Investigate the Church requirements for anyone seeking out the vocations of priesthood, consecrated life, and married life.

Life in the Trinity

On a summer day a few years ago, a sixteen-year-old honor student named Helen Marie left her house to do some rollerblading on a bike path near her home in Palmetto, Florida. Within the hour, she was dead. Carla, an eighteen-year-old senior from a local Catholic school, was speeding down the adjoining two-lane road trying to get home to see her parents before they left on a trip. On the way, she reached down for her phone, lost control of her car, and jumped the bike path, striking Helen Marie.

Helen Marie died instantly.

At her trial, Carla was convicted of DUI manslaughter. She had been drinking tequila and smoking marijuana before the accident. She was sentenced to six years in a juvenile prison and four years of probation.

Carla wept bitterly at the sentencing and was deeply apologetic. As her attorney pointed out, "Her emotions cannot be expressed."

Meanwhile, Helen Marie's parents called the sentencing "merciful," saying they were not out for revenge.

Her father added, "Our daughter was the very sort of person our communities seek. Our loss is everybody's loss."

Many, many lives were changed in a heartbeat on that summer day when Helen Marie died.

When Helen Marie left to go rollerblading, she expected to return home. She certainly did not expect to die that afternoon.

Thousands of teens are killed each year in accidents involving drunk drivers. Other teens die from acts of crime and violence. And, even though it is rare, many more teens are stricken with fatal illnesses, including cancer. The fact is that our lives on earth are fragile and uncertain. Speaking of the end of the world, but also applicable to our own death, Jesus said, "But of that day and hour no one knows, neither the angels of heaven, nor the Son, but the Father alone" (Mt 24:36).

A reminder of your own mortality is a necessary way to end this chapter and this period of your life when you prepare for and receive the Sacrament of Confirmation. When we live each day aware of the possibility that it could be our last, our focus on what is really important becomes much clearer.

Death brings a sense of urgency to our lives. Remaining aware of our mortality reminds us that we are given only a limited amount of time to bring our lives to fulfillment.

We should prepare for the hour of our death. An ancient litany of the saints asks us to be spared from a "sudden and unforeseen death" so that we might, along with many of the saints, experience a desire for death so that we can finally return to God himself. It is our final communion with the Blessed Trinity, with Mary, the angels, and all the saints that is **Heaven**.

Heaven

Our final communion with the Blessed Trinity, Mary, the angels, and all the saints.

STRAINING FORWARD

The *Catechism of the Catholic Church* teaches, "Creation has its own goodness and proper perfection, but it did not spring forth complete from the hands of the Creator" (CCC, 302). Instead, the universe, including each person, is created by God "in a state of journeying" toward an ultimate perfection that hasn't yet been reached. The ways that God guides his creation toward perfection is known as divine providence.

It is comforting to know that God loves and cares for us so much that he has a special plan for our lives and guides us to it. As the book of Proverbs teaches:

Many are the plans in a man's heart,
but it is the decision of the Lord that endures. (Prv 19:21)

The Fathers of the Church, in particular Gregory of Nyssa, spoke of the soul's journey toward Christ and heavenly perfection as something in which we must consistently engage.

They referred to this process as *epektasis*—an unending "straining forward," as St. Paul calls it in the Letter to the Philippians:

Forgetting what lies behind and straining forward to what lies ahead, I press on toward the goal for the prize of the heavenly call of God in Christ Jesus. (Phil 3:13)

Epektasis is going forward, exercising spiritual muscles, reaching out to God and others, and straining with hope. Epektasis begins in this life and extends to the next, for eternity. Thus, even eternal life is part of—not the end of—our journey.

We Believe in Life Everlasting

Read that faith statement again: "We believe in life everlasting." Isn't this what it's all about? Isn't this the reason for *why* you believe?

Let that statement sink in. We believe that we will live forever. What could this mean in practical terms? For one, time and space will never have control of us. What else? Will we be reunited with our family members and friends who have died before us? Yes, we expect to. Will we never be burdened with sickness, disease, pain, and suffering again? True again.

The Gospels were formed out of one sentence: Jesus is risen! All of the rest of the Scriptures are somewhat of an exercise in filling in the details. In fact, if we do not believe this essential *kerygma*, or message, our faith is useless. As St. Paul put it,

> If Christ has not been raised, then empty too is our preaching; empty, too, your faith. . . . If Christ has not been raised, your faith is vain; you are still in your sins. Then those who have fallen asleep in Christ have perished. If for this life only we have hoped in Christ, we are the most pitiable people of all. (1 Cor 15:14, 17–18)

Because of Jesus Christ, Christian death has a positive meaning. Christ's Death was his final act of self-giving. With his Death, we are saved. In Baptism, we have already "died with Christ;" our physical death merely completes our incorporation into his act of Redemption. In death, we are called back to God. With faith, a Christian can legitimately long for death. St. Teresa of Avila wrote, "I want to see God, and in order to see him, I must die." Or, as in the words of St. Thérèse of Lisieux, "I am not dying; I am entering life." Only through death can we pass into the fullness of God's Kingdom.

Amen!

Both the Bible and our Creed end with the same word: **Amen**.

Amen is a Hebrew word that means "believe."

To believe means to say Amen to God's Words, his promises and commandments, and completely to God himself in Three Persons—Father, Son, and Holy Spirit.

Your everyday life as a Christian should be both a talking and walking Amen. This is the way to live out the faith professed at your Baptism and confirmed in the Sacrament of Confirmation.

♥ Amen

A Hebrew word for "truly" or "it is so," thus signifying agreement with what has been said. New Testament and liturgical prayers, creeds, and other Christian prayers end with Amen to show belief in what has just been said.

Jesus himself is the definitive Amen. All of the promises of God find their completion in Jesus. That is why the "Great Amen" of our liturgy is made through Jesus to the glory of God:

> Through him, with him, in him,
> in the unity of the Holy Spirit,
> all glory and honor is yours,
> almighty Father,
> God, for ever and ever.
> Amen!

What is the essential kerygma of our faith?

Describe an incident that caused you to be aware of the fragile nature of life.

Do you really believe that you will live forever?

Describe what kind of Catholic you will be in ten years? In thirty years? At the end of your life?

Reach out to an organization at your school or in your community that encourages teenagers to refrain from drinking and driving.

Catholic Apologetics

Does everyone have a vocation?

✛ A Christian's primary vocation, given at Baptism, is to bring God's love to others. Everyone also has a unique vocation because God has a plan for everyone. A vocation involves understanding God's will for our lives. It involves understanding who we are now and who we will become in the future.

How many years of training does it take to become a priest?

✛ Training for the diocesan priesthood usually involves four years of graduate study after college. Many dioceses also require an extra year of "internship" so that the seminarian (candidate for priesthood) can live and minister at a parish. Finally, the candidate is ordained a deacon for a period of time before being ordained a priest. This period may last anywhere from a few months to a few years.

Does the Church have rules for who you can marry?

✛ Yes. A person cannot marry while married to someone else. Religious, permanent deacons, or priests cannot marry unless they have received a dispensation from their vow of celibacy. Blood brothers and sisters cannot marry, nor can first cousins. Family members who have established legal ties (e.g., step-brothers to step-sisters) cannot marry either. Also, a license from a civil court is necessary for marriage. Some states also require a couple to have a medical examination before marriage.

How does the Church care for the sick and dying?

✛ All the faithful are obliged to care for the sick and dying, through their prayers and visits. Also, the Sacrament of Anointing of the

Sick is a sacrament of healing in which the healing and loving touch of Christ is extended through the Christian community to those who are seriously ill or dying.

Why does God allow death?

✢ Death was not part of God's original plan for humans. Death was the consequence of the first sin of Adam. However, "Just as in Adam all die, so too in Christ shall all be brought to life" (1 Cor 15:22).

What is meant by "rising from the dead"?

✢ At death, the body and soul are separated. The body decays, and the soul goes on to meet God. Through the power of Jesus' Resurrection, God will grant incorruptible life to our bodies by uniting them with our souls at the end of time.

Do we know when the world will end?

✢ Many religious groups today make predictions about when the end of the world will occur. Several claim the end is imminent. Recall Jesus' words when asked this question by the Apostles. He told them, "but of that day or hour, no one knows . . . only the Father" (Mk 13:32). Rather, Jesus expects that we will live every day as if it were our last.

 For **You** to **Do**

Your Call to Discipleship

In Baptism, you were initiated to a life in Christ. As you mature in faith, you, too, are challenged to put aside your own desires to follow God's will, to accept your suffering as a way to share in the suffering of Christ, and to serve others.

In Baptism, you were also initiated into the Church, a community of people who travel the road of discipleship with you. Your Christian vocation to holiness and whatever particular vocation you ultimately accept is intimately bound up with others. The *Catechism of the Catholic Church* highlights the communal character of the human vocation:

> The human person needs to live in society. Society is not for him an extraneous addition but a requirement of his nature. Through the exchange with others, mutual service and dialogue with his brethren, man develops his potential; he thus responds to his vocation. (CCC, 1879)

Whereas your last years of high school are the time to *begin* to discern in more detail the particular Christian vocations like marriage, holy orders, consecrated life, and the committed single life, there is no time like the present to deepen your commitment to Christian discipleship. Try out these suggestions for growing in your relationship with Jesus Christ:

✛ Spend more time in prayer. Pray, "not mine, but your will be done."

✛ Don't seek out suffering, but accept disappointments, setbacks, and pain that do come your way as an opportunity to share in the cross of Christ.

✛ Do something helpful for another person. Keep this act of service off your college application! Rather, take it back to God in prayer.

In God's due time, his plan for the rest of your life will be known to you. While the challenges of Christian discipleship will never be diminished, you will be at peace in your God-given vocation.

Assignment

Take some time to complete the following sentences. Refer to the completed sentences whenever you take time to discern a career and vocation.

✛ I would like to be a person who . . .
✛ Right after high school I plan to . . .
✛ If I could achieve one dream for the future it would be . . .
✛ I am happiest when . . .
✛ I see myself as the kind of Catholic who . . .
✛ I would describe my faith as . . .
✛ I would consider a religious vocation if . . .
✛ My idea of a "perfect" marriage is . . .

Prayers and Reflections

Party Poem

I went to a party, Mom, I remembered what you said,
You told me not to drink, Mom, so I drank soda instead,
I felt really proud inside, Mom, the way you said I would,
I didn't drink and drive, Mom, even though others said I should.
I know I did the right thing, Mom, I knew you're always right,

Now the party is finally ending, Mom, as everyone drives out of
   sight,
As I got into my car, Mom, I know I'll get home in one piece,
Because of the way you raised me, Mom, as responsible and sweet.
I started to drive away, Mom, but as I pulled onto the road
The other car didn't see me, Mom, and it hit me like a load.
As I lie here on the pavement, Mom, I hear the policeman say
The other guy is drunk, Mom, and I'm the one who'll pay.
I'm lying here dying, Mom, I wish you'd get here soon,
How come this happened to me, Mom, my life burst like a balloon?
There is blood all around me, Mom, most of it is mine,
I hear the paramedic say, Mom, I'll be dead in a short time.
I just wanted to tell you, Mom, I swear I didn't drink,
It was the others, Mom, the others didn't think.
He didn't know where he was going, Mom, he was probably at the
   same party as I,
The only difference is, Mom, he drank and I will die.
Why do people drink, Mom? It can ruin your whole life.
I'm feeling sharp pains now, Mom, pains just like a knife.
The guy who hit me is walking, Mom, I don't think it's fair,
I'm lying here dying, Mom, while all he can do is stare.
Tell my brothers not to cry, Mom, tell Daddy to be brave,
And when I get to heaven, Mom, write "Daddy's Girl" on my
   grave.
Someone should have told him, Mom, not to drink and drive,
If only they had talked to him, Mom, I would still be alive.
My breath is getting shorter, Mom, I'm becoming very scared,
Please don't cry for me, Mom, because when I needed you, you
   were always there.
I have one last question, Mom, before I say good-bye,
I didn't ever drink, Mom, so why am I to die?
This is the end, Mom, I wish I could look you in the eye,
To say these final words, Mom, I love you and good-bye.

—Author Unknown

Two Choices

There are only two kinds of people in the end: those who say to
God, "Thy will be done," and those to whom God says, in the end,
"Thy will be done." All that are in Hell chose it.

—C. S. Lewis

Imitation of Christ

Every action of yours, every thought, should be those of one who expects to die before the day is out. Death would have no great terrors for you if you had a quiet conscience. . . . Then why not keep clear of sin instead of running away from death? If you aren't fit to face death today, it's very unlikely you will be tomorrow. . . .

—From *The Imitation of Christ*

Glory Be

Glory be to the Father, and to the Son, and to the Holy Spirit: as it was in the beginning, is now, and ever shall be, world without end. Amen.

Prayer of Blessed Elizabeth of the Trinity

O my God, Trinity whom I adore, help me forget myself entirely so to establish myself in you, unmovable and peaceful as if my soul were already in eternity. May nothing be able to trouble my peace or make me leave you, O my unchanging God, but may each minute bring me more deeply into your mystery! Grant my soul peace. Make it your heaven, your beloved dwelling and the place of your rest. May I never abandon you there, but may I be there, whole and entire, completely vigilant in my faith, entirely adoring, and wholly given over to your creative action. Amen.

appendix

CATHOLIC HANDBOOK FOR FAITH

Origins of the Sacrament of Confirmation

From the time of Pentecost, the Apostles imparted on the newly baptized the gift of the Spirit by the laying on of hands. This completed the grace of Baptism and is "rightly recognized by the Catholic tradition as the origin of the sacrament of Confirmation, which in a certain way perpetuates the grace of Pentecost in the Church" (CCC 1288, quoting Pope Paul VI).

The *laying on of hands* is an ancient ritual gesture used in Confirmation that symbolizes the giving of the Father's own Spirit to the recipient. When the bishop extends his hands over or imposes his hands on candidates for Confirmation, many similar events from Scripture are recalled. For example, Jacob blessed his grandsons Ephraim and Manasseh and gave them two portions of the Promised Land (see Genesis 48:14). Moses blessed Joshua as he commissioned him to lead the people into the Promised Land (see Numbers 27:18, 23). And, in similar fashion, Jesus offered blessings through a laying on of hands. For example:

> And people were bringing children to [Jesus] that he might touch them, but the disciples rebuked them. When Jesus saw this he became indignant and said to them, "Let the children come to me; do not prevent them, for the kingdom of God belongs to such as these. Amen, I say to you, whoever does not accept the kingdom of God like a child will not enter it." Then he embraced them and blessed them, placing his hands on them. (Mk 10:13–16)

The Letter to the Hebrews (see Hebrews 6:2) describes the laying on of hands as one of the basic teachings of the Apostles. When the Apostles laid their hands on the newly baptized, they were giving a divine blessing and imparting the gift of the Holy Spirit. The same thing happens to us in Confirmation today. We receive the bishop's confirmation that the Holy Spirit resides in us and acts within us.

Very early on, an anointing with perfumed oil called chrism was added to the laying on of hands. The Old Testament often mentions the use of oil. Among the ancient Israelites (as well as peoples of other cultures), olive oil was a sign of abundance and joy. Besides being used in cooking and in providing light, oil had many other uses as well. It cleansed the body (as in anointings before and after a bath). It limbered muscles (as in anointings of wrestlers and other athletes). It helped with healing (as in anointings used to soothe bruises, wounds, and dry skin). And it beautified (as in anointings that gave radiance to the skin).

In religious uses, anointing with oil had the purpose of consecration. Among the objects anointed in the Old Testament were the Ark of the Covenant, the tent of meeting, and the furniture of the tent (see Exodus 30:22–33). Among the people anointed were priests and kings. For example, when God selected David to be king of Israel, the prophet Samuel anointed him. "Then Samuel, with the horn of oil in hand, anointed [David] in the midst of his brothers; and from that day on, the spirit of the Lord rushed upon David" (1 Sm 16:13).

To be chosen by God for a particular mission was to be God's "anointed one." The Messiah, in particular, is God's "anointed one." The name *Christ* means "anointed one" and is used to show that Jesus is the Messiah.

Sacred Chrism, the oil used in Confirmation, takes its name from Christ. Chrism is a mixture of olive oil (which by its rich and abundant nature symbolizes the Spirit's overflowing outpouring of grace) and balsam (a fragrant perfume—sometimes referred to as "the balm of Gilead"—used in healing and preservation from corruption). The balsam symbolizes the sweet "odor" of Christianity, found in virtuous living and imitating Christ (see 2 Corinthians 2:15). Those who are anointed with Sacred Chrism have a new identity—that of Christians. All anointed followers of Jesus share in his mission and have the special duty of proclaiming his Gospel to the world. *Chrismation* is the name the Eastern Church uses for the Sacrament of Confirmation (cf. CCC 1289).

Two Traditions of the Sacrament Emerge

In the first centuries, Confirmation was generally part of one single celebration with Baptism. St. Cyprian called it a "double sacrament." Because the original minister of the sacrament is a bishop, logistics was among several issues that led to the separate celebrations of Baptism and Confirmation. The growing number of infant Baptisms, the increase in rural parishes, and the growth of dioceses prevented bishops from being at each celebration of the sacrament. Because the dioceses covered vast geographic areas and transportation was primitive, it was impossible for a bishop to attend all the Baptisms in his diocese. He began to limit his visits to parishes either annually or biannually. It was at this time two traditions for celebrating the Sacrament of Confirmation emerged, one in the East and one in the West.

In the Roman Church (the West), there was a desire to maintain the bishop's explicit connection with the sacrament. A bishop sustains and serves the Church's unity, catholicity, and connection with the Apostles. His presence at Confirmation expresses the unity of the new Christian with the bishop and those elements.

To maintain the connection with the bishop, double anointing with Sacred Chrism was begun. The priest at Baptism gives the first anointing with Sacred Chrism. As explained in Chapter 3, it signifies that the person baptized participates in the prophetic, priestly, and kingly offices of Christ. The bishop at Confirmation confers the second anointing. However, if an adult is baptized, only one postbaptismal anointing is administered, and it is done by the priest.

The Eastern Churches, following their ancient practices, continue to give greater emphasis to the unity of the Sacraments of Initiation rather than separating Baptism and Confirmation by several years. In the East, Baptism and Confirmation are celebrated together, with the priest doing the anointing. To maintain connection with the bishop, the priest anoints only with *myron* (chrism) consecrated by the bishop.

Teachings about Confirmation

While the sacrament was celebrated from the beginning of the Church after being modeled and instituted by Christ's laying on of hands and sending of the Spirit, it was the Church Councils of Riez (439) and Orange (441) that first used the name *Confirmation* for postbaptismal anointings. These councils required bishops to visit rural parts of their dioceses regularly to confirm the newly baptized. The Second Council of Lyons (1274) used the name *Confirmation* on an official list of the Seven Sacraments.

In the sixteenth century, the Council of Trent defended the sacramental character of Confirmation, which had been challenged by Protestant reformers who felt that Baptism had been weakened by overemphasizing the laying on of hands and anointing. The Council of Trent specified the age for Confirmation—sometime between the age of discretion and about age fourteen. In those years, reception of First Communion took place after Confirmation, meaning the traditional order of the three Sacraments of Initiation was preserved.

In 1910, Pope St. Pius X permitted children to receive First Communion at the age of seven. He desired to increase devotion to the Eucharist and encourage the faithful to receive Communion on Sundays, feast days, and even daily if possible. Before that, Catholics had often felt unworthy to frequently receive Holy Communion. Because of this change, Confirmation was celebrated later, after First Communion, and the traditional order of the sacraments was not followed. Today this is the order for receiving the sacraments for most Catholics who are baptized as infants.

The revised *Rite of Confirmation* allows for the bishops of individual nations to name the appropriate age for Confirmation. In the United States, the age of Confirmation varies from diocese to diocese; it can be designated by the local bishop anywhere from the age of discretion through around sixteen years old. Adults who are baptized receive all three Sacraments of Initiation at one time.

Confirmation, whether it is celebrated with Baptism or some years later, recalls a person's Baptism. The *Rite of Confirmation* approved in 1971 after the Second Vatican Council included several changes that help people see the intimate connection between Confirmation and Baptism. For example:

1. The Rite of Christian Initiation of Adults calls for all adult converts to celebrate Baptism, Confirmation, and Eucharist at the same time at the Easter Vigil.

2. The *confirmandi* (plural of *confirmand*) are encouraged to use their baptismal name as their Confirmation name. This name usually is that of a canonized saint or Christian hero who inspires the person to be a good Christian. In the past, the confirmandi were required to choose a name other than their baptismal name, to show that they were being given a new identity, a new mission, in Confirmation.

3. Previously, Confirmation sponsors were usually different from the person's godparents. Today, the Church encourages baptismal godparents also to act as Confirmation sponsors (see *Code of Canon Law* 893 §2 and *CCC*, 1311). It is the sponsor's duty "to see that the

confirmed person acts as a true witness of Christ and faithfully fulfills the obligations connected with this sacrament" (*Code of Canon Law*, 892).

4. The ritual of Confirmation, if celebrated separately from Baptism, includes a public renewal of baptismal promises and a Profession of Faith by the confirmandi.

In Confirmation, we remember who we are—Christ's own possessions. We also remember how the Spirit has been working in us since Baptism to make us stronger and more committed Christians.

Rite of Confirmation within Mass

Liturgy of the Word

The readings may be taken in whole or in part from the Mass of the day or from the texts for Confirmation (see pages 201–203).

Presentation of the Candidates

After the Gospel, the pastor, priest, deacon, or catechist presents the candidates for Confirmation, sometimes calling them by name.

Homily or Instruction

The bishop gives the homily, offering an explanation of the readings and a deeper understanding of the mystery of Confirmation.

Renewal of Baptismal Promises

After the homily, the candidates stand and the bishop questions them. The candidates respond "I do" to the following questions:

Do you reject Satan and all his works and all his empty promises?

Do you believe in God the Father almighty, creator of heaven and earth?

Do you believe in Jesus Christ, his only Son, our Lord, who was born of the Virgin Mary, was crucified, died, and was buried, rose from the dead, and is now seated at the right hand of the Father?

Do you believe in the Holy Spirit, the Lord, the giver of life, who came upon the Apostles at Pentecost and today is given to you sacramentally in Confirmation?

Do you believe in the holy catholic Church, the communion of saints, the forgiveness of sins, the resurrection of the body, and life everlasting?

The Laying on of Hands

The bishop and all the priests who will minister the sacrament with him lay hands upon all the candidates.

The Anointing with Chrism

The bishop dips his right thumb in the chrism and makes the Sign of the Cross on the forehead of the one to be confirmed saying: "N., be sealed with the Gift of the Holy Spirit." The newly confirmed responds: "Amen." The bishop says: "Peace be with you." The newly confirmed also responds: "And also with you."

General Intercessions

The general intercessions include specific intentions for the confirmed, their parents and sponsors, the Church, and for all people.

Liturgy of the Eucharist

After the general intercessions, the Liturgy of the Eucharist is celebrated according to the *Order of the Mass*, with these exceptions: the Profession of Faith is omitted since it has already been made; some of the newly confirmed may join those who bring the gifts to the altar; when Eucharistic Prayer I is used, the special form of "Father, accept this offering" is said.

Sample Service Project Ideas

Service projects are often a part of Confirmation preparation and the time immediately after the reception of the Sacrament of Confirmation. The general ideas following are meant to encourage you to explore specific projects in these areas within the parish, local, and larger world community.

Parish

Parish Council. Inquire about being an adjunct member of the parish council or a full member of a parish committee. For example, some councils or committees work on parish bazaars, auctions, or golf tournaments, which you could help organize or staff. Councils are also involved in parish census taking and surveys. In any case, you can attend a series of council meetings and report on its topics to your peers and share issues and concerns of your peers with the council members.

Liturgical Minister. Confirmed Catholics are able to serve as lectors and Eucharistic ministers. Most parishes sponsor ongoing training for these ministries. Plan to enroll in a session either before or after Confirmation.

Homebound Ministry. Contact the minister responsible for visits and pastoral care to those who are homebound. Most of these people are infirm or elderly and can always use an extra hand in running errands to the grocery store or pharmacy and doing cleaning chores outdoors and in the house.

Religious Education. You've probably spent many years in parish religious education classes and programs. What insights can you offer to the Director of Religious Education? How can you help? Inquire about being a catechist's aide or even undergoing training to be a catechist yourself. You may also be needed to help organize and staff a vacation bible school for young children.

Free Babysitting. Parents of young children always appreciate an occasional afternoon or evening of uninterrupted time with their spouse or on their own. With a group of peers, provide a safe room with plenty of activities (crafts, games, videos) for children up to the age of ten. Arrange with a parish representative to provide the necessary parental permission slips.

Evangelization. To *evangelize* means "to bring the Good News to others." Concentrate on members of your peer group who are absent from parish activities. Organize into competitive "teams." Award points to teams that are able to bring new teens to parish-sponsored events, more points for those teams whose sponsored teens return again and again. The team with the most points after a given time "wins"—maybe a free dinner or ticket to an amusement park.

Bereavement Ministry. Focus your ministry on consoling your peers on any losses they have experienced—from the death of a relative to the death of a pet to a divorce in the family. Write notes, visit the bereaved, help with any day-to-day tasks that may have been put aside.

Local Community

Recreation Helper. Contact your local recreation department for programs in which you can volunteer. There may be a need for coaches, referees, tutors, or arts and craft teachers. You may also be able to provide input for additions to teen programming you see a need for.

Hospital Helper. Most hospitals provide several volunteer opportunities. You may be assigned to deliver flowers to the rooms of patients or to monitor visiting hours. Or, on your own, you may collect items for gift packages suitable for children (coloring books, crayons, videos) and bring them to the hospital for distribution.

Museums. Local and regional museums are in need of volunteers to provide directions to guests, do clerical work, or help with special promotions. A children's museum often uses volunteers to help with programming and field trips.

Against Teenage Drinking. Schools and communities sponsor organizations like Students Against Drunk Driving that promote intolerance of drinking and driving, and drinking before the age of twenty-one in general. Members meet and promote the message to teenagers.

Thanksgiving Dinner. Arrange to sponsor a free dinner for the poor. Thanksgiving is the usual time for such an event, but you may consider another holiday so as not to duplicate the efforts of other community agencies. Ask parishioners to donate the food items for the menu. You and your group advertise and prepare the dinner, host and wait on tables, provide entertainment, arrange transportation, and staff clean-up efforts. You might also wish to distribute blankets to the poor as part of this event.

Animal Shelters. Publicly supported animal shelters or local zoos need volunteers to help with certain tasks. Most of these tasks involve cleaning and caring for the facility. If you have an interest in animals, you may consider this type of work.

Public Library. Consider working at the library. Most public libraries have many volunteer opportunities. You may be asked to shelve books, work at a resource desk, or redo bulletin board displays.

Larger Justice Issues

World Hunger Fast. Thousands of people in the world today continue to starve due to inequitable distribution of food. Organize a hunger fast among your peers. Collect pledges in exchange for a one-day fast. Donate the proceeds to a world hunger agency.

Right to Life. Supporting the right to life of all—from the unborn to the elderly, from the sick to those condemned to death row—is a crucial service issue. Ways to volunteer your efforts include participating in letter-writing campaigns to government officials, peacefully demonstrating in support of these issues, and praying with others who support these issues. Other more direct service may include gathering and transporting school homework assignments for pregnant teens, assisting at shelters for women, and helping to organize a blood drive for the Red Cross.

Peace Symposium. Achieving peace begins in the hearts and actions of all people, young and old. Think about some ways elementary-age students can learn to deal with life situations in a peaceful way. Prepare peace symposium for elementary schools that include things like dramatic presentations of peaceful solutions to everyday problems, debates and dialogue, art projects and journal writing, and many suggestions for conflict resolution.

Special Missions. There are many areas of this and neighboring countries in dire need of help in repairing housing. One national group—Catholic Heart Workcamp—sponsors one-week outings where teens assist in these areas. Another possibility is taking a pilgrimage to Mexico after collecting supplies for those in need—especially at an orphanage.

Homeless Shelters. The temporary residences for people with no place to go usually have many needs. One idea is to sponsor a series of Sunday night suppers at a homeless shelter. Vary the menu themes. If possible arrange for entertainment and a prayer service to go along with the serving of meals.

Interracial Harmony. Sponsor a series of social events between members of your peer or youth group and those teens of a different race and peer or social group. Consider having a volleyball game, cook-out, or retreat with the other group. Include opportunities to dialogue about solutions for interracial harmony.

Care for the Environment. Participate in a sponsored clean-up day for the environment or in maintenance for a local roadway. Confer with a local agency that supports an environmental issue (e.g., "Heal the Bay" or "Save the Forest"). Find out how you can participate.

50 Questions

Write your answers to each of the following questions. Some of the answers can be found in this book. Others you will need to research from other resources, including by asking help from people in your parish.

1. Define *catechumenate*.
2. What are some differences between the Rite of Christian Initiation for Adults (RCIA) and the Rite of Baptism of Children (RBC)?
3. Name the elements of the basic rite of Baptism.
4. How many adults were baptized at your parish at the last Easter vigil?
5. How many children were baptized in the last calendar year at your parish?

6. What are the central beliefs about God espoused in our Catholic creeds?

7. Name at least four attributes of God.

8. Name and explain three dogmas about the Holy Trinity.

9. Where is the tabernacle placed in your parish? Why is it placed where it is?

10. When is the Feast of the Holy Trinity?

11. How did the early Church answer Arius's claim that Jesus only took the "appearance" of a man?

12. Define *Incarnation*.

13. What did Jesus tell his disciples would happen to him in Jerusalem?

14. How can you come to know Jesus?

15. How do you think you would respond if someone held a gun to your head and asked, "Do you believe in Jesus Christ?"

16. Name and explain three kinds of writing in the Bible.

17. What are the three stages of the composition of the Gospel?

18. How did the Second Vatican Council encourage a renewed interest in the Scriptures for Catholics?

19. What is meant by the term *Septuagint*? *Vulgate*?

20. Which of the following translations of the Bible are accepted by Catholics? Protestants? Both?

King James	*New Jerusalem*	*New Revised Standard*
New American	*The Way*	*Good News*

21. What were the causes of the schism between the churches of East and West and of the Protestant Reformation?

22. How does the Church answer the criticism that "Catholics pray to saints"?

23. Define *infallibility* related to Church teaching.

24. Who is the bishop of your diocese? What do you know about him?

25. Define and tell the function of each of these Church structures:

archdiocese	college of cardinals	parish
diocese	deanery	parish council

26. How does the morality of human acts depend on the object chosen, the intention, and the circumstances of the action?

27. Write the Beatitudes.

28. Write the Ten Commandments.

29. Write the precepts of the Church.

30. How can the Sacrament of Penance help you to live a moral life?

31. How is the Paschal Mystery like other historical events? How is it different from other historical events?

32. Define *transubstantiation*.

33. According to the Council of Florence, what three things are necessary for a sacrament to be valid?

34. Name the two main parts of the Mass. What takes place in each part?

35. Put these parts of the Mass in sequential order:

Penitential Rite	Gospel	Consecration
First Reading	Our Father	Communion
Homily	Sign of Peace	Holy, Holy, Holy
Eucharistic Prayer	Offertory	Concluding Rite

36. Name and explain three basic human rights.

37. What is meant by the phrase "preferential option for the poor"?

38. List the corporal works of mercy.

39. List the spiritual works of mercy.

40. Outline the Church's basic positions on the justice issues of consumerism, the environment, and war and violence.

41. Write at least four ways Catholics are able to know the Holy Spirit.

42. What is the essential rite of Confirmation?

43. Name four effects of the Sacrament of Confirmation.

44. List the seven Gifts of the Holy Spirit.

45. How many candidates will be confirmed at the next Confirmation at your parish?

46. How is self-concept related to self-esteem?

47. Who administers the Sacrament of Matrimony?

48. What does the Church teach about sex outside of marriage?

49. What is meant by the term *consecrated life*?

50. How is the ministerial priesthood different from the common priesthood?

GLOSSARY

Abba—The Aramaic word for "Daddy." This was the way Jesus addressed God, his Father.

Abortion—The direct and deliberate ending of a pregnancy by killing an unborn child. Direct abortion, willed as either a means or an end, gravely contradicts moral law.

Absolution—The statement by the priest in the Sacrament of Penance whereby a person's sins are forgiven.

Agnosticism—The opinion that no one knows for sure whether God exists.

Amen—A Hebrew word for "truly" or "it is so," thus signifying agreement with what has been said. New Testament and liturgical prayers, creeds, and other Christian prayers end with Amen to show belief in what has just been said.

Anointing of the Sick—A Sacrament of Healing in which the healing and loving touch of Christ is extended through the Church to those who are seriously ill or dying.

apocalyptic literature—The word *apocalypse* means "revelation" or "unveiling." Apocalyptic literature, usually written in times of crisis, uses highly symbolic language to bolster faith by reassuring believers that the current age, subject to the forces of evil, will end when God intervenes and establishes a divine rule of goodness and peace.

Apostasy—The abandonment or denial of one's faith.

Apostles—The Apostles are those who are "sent" to be Christ's ambassadors, to continue his work. In its widest sense, the term refers to all of Christ's disciples whose mission is to preach his Gospel in word and deed. It also refers to the Twelve whom Jesus chose to help him in his earthly ministry. The successors of the Twelve Apostles are the bishops.

Ascension—Jesus' passage from humanity into divine glory in God's heavenly domain forty days after his Resurrection. It is from this domain that Jesus will come again.

Assumption—The Church dogma that teaches that the Blessed Mother, because of her unique role in her Son's Resurrection, was taken directly to Heaven when her earthly life was over. The Feast of the Assumption on August 15 is a holy day of obligation.

Atheism—The denial of God's existence.

baptism of blood—A martyr for the Christian faith who died before he or she could receive the sacrament receives a baptism of blood. The effects are the complete remission of sin and immediate entrance into Heaven.

Baptism—The first Sacrament of Initiation. It is "the basis of the whole Christian life, the gateway to life in the Spirit, and the door which gives access to the other sacraments" (*CCC*, 1213).

Beatitudes—*Beatitude* means "supreme happiness." The eight Beatitudes preached by Jesus in the Sermon on the Mount respond to our natural desire for happiness.

Bible—The inspired Word of God. The word *bible* means book. The Bible is made up of seventy-three books and is divided into the Old and New Testaments.

bishop—A successor to the Apostles. He governs the local church in a given diocese and the worldwide Church in union with the Pope and college of bishops. A bishop receives the fullness of the Sacrament of Holy Orders.

blasphemy—Any thought, word, or act that expresses hatred or contempt for God, Christ, the Church, saints, or holy things.

Blessed Sacrament—A name to describe the Real Presence of Jesus in the consecrated species of bread and wine, which are his Body and Blood.

Book of Elect—In the second of the three stages of RCIA, the catechumens write their names in a "Book of the Elect" as a sign of their willingness to prepare themselves for full incorporation into the Church.

Canonization—A process that recognizes the particular example of a Christian who has led a good and holy life and died a death faithful to Jesus and that declares the person to be a saint.

Canon—The official list of inspired books of the Bible. Catholics list forty-six Old Testament books and twenty-seven New Testament books in the canon.

Capital Sins—Vices that are opposed to the virtues. They are pride, avarice, envy, wrath, lust, gluttony, and sloth.

cardinal virtues—The four hinge virtues that support moral living: prudence, or "right reason in action," concerning the best way to live morally; justice, or giving God and each person his or her due by right; fortitude, or courage to persist in living a Christian life; and temperance, or moderation in controlling our desires for physical pleasures.

catechetical—Having to do with a process of "education in the faith" for young people and adults with the goal of making them disciples of Jesus Christ.

catechumenate—The process of study, prayer, and participation in community for the purpose of preparing for the Sacraments of Initiation.

Catholic—A mark of the Church that means "universal" or "for everyone."

chastity—The moral virtue that enables people to integrate their sexuality into their stations in life.

Christ—The Greek term for "Messiah." It means "the anointed one."

Church—The Body of Christ on earth. The Church is the community of people who profess faith in Jesus Christ and who are guided by the Holy Spirit. The Roman Catholic Church is guided by the Pope and his bishops.

common priesthood—The priesthood of all the baptized in which we share in Christ's work of Salvation.

Communion of Saints—The term refers to the unity of all those living on earth (the pilgrim Church), those being purified in purgatory (the Church suffering), and those enjoying the blessings of Heaven (the Church in glory).

Confirmation—A Sacrament of Initiation, it is sometimes known as the Sacrament of the Holy Spirit. It completes Baptism and seals the recipient with the Holy Spirit and confers the seven gifts of the Holy Spirit.

Conscience—A person's "most secret core and sanctuary" that helps them to determine between good and evil.

Consecrated—A word that describes a life dedicated to living by the evangelical counsels of poverty, chastity, and obedience. Besides religious life, other styles of consecrated life include an eremitic lifestyle as a hermit, taking a vow as a consecrated virgin or widow (in the Eastern Churches), or participating in a secular institute of consecrated life or a society of apostolic life.

Consumerism—The uncontrolled buying and selling of goods and services, most of which are unneeded.

covenant—A sacred and unbreakable agreement that God made first with the Israelites and renewed in Jesus with the Church.

creed—A statement of our beliefs, a summary of our faith. Catholics recite the Nicene Creed at Mass. The Apostles' Creed is another summary of our faith.

Diocese—The Church in a particular local area. It is united to its local leader, the bishop.

discernment—A decision-making process that involves praying over a decision, asking for the guidance of the Holy Spirit, making the decision, and then evaluating it.

discipleship—The life of following Jesus Christ. *Disciple* comes from a Latin word that means "learner."

Divine Providence—God's leading and guiding us to our final end, Salvation and union with him.

Divine Revelation—The way God communicates knowledge of himself to humankind, a self-communication realized by his actions and words over time, most fully by his sending us his divine Son, Jesus Christ.

Ecumenical Councils—Worldwide, official assemblies of the bishops under the direction of the Pope. There have been twenty-one Ecumenical Councils, the most recent being the Second Vatican Council (1962–1965).

Ecumenism—The movement, inspired and led by the Holy Spirit, that seeks full visible unity of all Christians.

efficacious symbol—A symbol that is "capable of producing a desired effect." This means that the sacraments actually confer the grace they signify.

Encyclical—A letter written by the Pope about some important issue and circulated through the entire Church.

Epiphany—The name for the feast that celebrates the mystery of Christ's manifestation as Savior of the world.

Eucharistic Adoration—Prayer directed to Christ in the Blessed Sacrament that acknowledges his role as Savior, Sanctifier, Lord, and Master of all.

Eucharist—The source and summit of Christian life, the Eucharist is one of the Sacraments of Initiation. The word *Eucharist* means "thanksgiving." The Eucharist commemorates the Last Supper, at which Jesus gave his Apostles his Body and Blood in the form of bread

and wine and the Lord's sacrificial Death on the cross.

evangelical counsels—Vows of personal poverty, chastity understood as lifelong celibacy, and obedience to the demands of the community being joined that those entering the consecrated life profess.

evangelization—A period in the catechumenate when a person hears God's Word and responds to it.

Excommunication—To be excommunicated means that a baptized person is no longer "in communion" with the Church. Some excommunications are automatic, including the sins of apostasy, heresy, or schism.

Exegesis—A Greek word meaning "leading out." It is the study or explanation of a biblical book or passage.

faith—One of the theological virtues. Faith is an acknowledgment and allegiance to God.

free will—The capacity to choose among alternatives. Free will is the "power, rooted in reason and will . . . to perform deliberate actions on one's own responsibility" (*CCC*, 1731). True freedom is at the service of what is good and true.

Gentiles—The name for anyone not of the Jewish faith; a Christian.

gifts of the Holy Spirit—An outpouring of God's gifts to help us live a Christian life. The traditional seven gifts of the Holy Spirit are wisdom, understanding, knowledge, right judgment, courage, reverence, and wonder and awe.

godparent—The sponsor of one who is baptized. The person takes on the role of helping the newly baptized child or adult in the Christian life.

Gospels—The heart of the Scriptures, "Gospel" refers to the Good News preached by Jesus. The four Gospels in the New Testament are the Gospels of Matthew, Mark, Luke, and John.

grace—The supernatural gift of God's friendship and life. Grace allows us to respond to God and share in his nature and eternal life.

Heaven—Our final communion with the Blessed Trinity, Mary, the angels, and all the saints.

Heresy—The denial of essential truths of the Church.

Holy Trinity—The central mystery of the Christian faith. It teaches that there are Three Persons in one God: Father, Son, and Holy Spirit.

Homily—A reflection given by a bishop, priest, or deacon that reflects on the Scripture readings during Mass or the sacraments. The homily helps us hear God's Word and apply it to our lives today.

homosexual orientation—Sexual attraction or orientation toward persons of the same sex. This is differentiated from homosexual acts that are morally wrong because they violate the purpose of sexual activity.

human solidarity—A Christian virtue of charity and friendship whereby members of the human family share material and spiritual goods.

Idolatry—The false worship of many gods.

Immaculate Conception—The belief that Mary was conceived without Original Sin. The Feast of the Immaculate Conception is on December 8.

Incarnation—The dogma that God's eternal son assumed a human nature and became man in Jesus Christ to save us from our sins. The term literally means "taking on human flesh."

Infallibility—A gift of the Spirit whereby the Pope and the bishops are preserved from error when proclaiming a doctrine related to Christian faith or morals.

inspiration—The guidance given to the human authors of the Sacred Scripture so that they wrote what God wanted written for our benefit.

just-war tradition—A set of principles developed through the centuries by the Church that clearly outlines when a nation may ethically participate in a war. It also sets clear limits on armed force once a war is engaged.

Kerygma—The essential message of our faith that Jesus Christ is Lord and that he is risen.

Kingdom of God— The rule of God over all people; it is established in stages, beginning with Jesus' public ministry and ending, finally, at the end of time when he comes again.

lay people—All members of the Church who have been initiated into the Church through Baptism and are not ordained (the clergy) or in consecrated life. The laity participates in Jesus' prophetic, priestly, and kingly ministries.

lectio divina—Literally, "divine reading." This is a prayerful way to read the Bible or any other sacred writings.

Lectionary—A book containing all Scripture references that are used in liturgy.

Liturgy—The official public worship of the Church. It is a word that means "work of the people."

Lord—When referring to Jesus, the title "Lord" proclaims his divinity. The Greek translation of the Old Testament used the word *Kyrios* ("Lord") to render the most sacred name YHWH ("I am"), which God revealed to Moses.

Magisterium—The official teaching office of the Church. The Lord bestowed the right and the power to teach in his name to Peter and the other Apostles and their successors. The Magisterium is the bishops in communion with the successor of Peter, the Bishop of Rome (Pope).

Marks of the Church—The four traditional marks of the Church are one, holy, catholic, and apostolic.

martyrdom—The state of choosing to suffer and give up one's life for faith rather than renouncing it.

ministerial priesthood—The priesthood of bishops and priests that confers on them a sacred power for the service of the faithful.

Miracles—Powerful signs of God's Kingdom worked by Jesus.

monotheism—Describes religions that believe there is only one God. Christianity, Judaism, and Islam are three great monotheistic religions.

Morality—Putting your faith and religion into practice through making good decisions in word and action.

Mortal Sin—A serious violation of God's law of love that results in the loss of God's life (sanctifying grace) in the soul of the sinner. To commit mortal sin, there must be grave matter, full knowledge of the evil done, and full consent of will.

motu propio—A term that means "of his own accord." It signifies words in papal documents that were decided by the pope personally.

mystagogia—A period of intense prayer in which neophytes can gradually assume their role in the Church.

mystery—A reality filled with God's invisible presence. This term applies to the Blessed Trinity's plan of Salvation in Jesus Christ; the Church, which is his Body; and the sacraments.

neophytes—Those newly received into the Church through the Sacraments of Initiation at the Easter Vigil.

Omnipotence—An attribute of God that he is everywhere, unlimited, and all-powerful.

Original Sin—The fallen state of human nature into which all generations of people are born. Jesus Christ came to save us from Original Sin.

Pantheism—The belief, in opposition to Christian doctrine, that God and nature are one and the same.

Paraclete—Another name for the Holy Spirit. It means "advocate, defender, or consoler."

Paschal Mystery—The way our Salvation is made known through the life, Death, Resurrection, and Ascension of Jesus. The Paschal Mystery is made present in the sacraments, especially the Eucharist.

Passover—The most important Jewish feast; it celebrates the Exodus, YHWH's deliverance of the Chosen People from Egypt.

Penitent—The name for a person performing penance as directed by the priest in the Sacrament of Penance.

Pentecost—The day when the Holy Spirit descended on the Apostles and gave them the power to preach with conviction the message that Jesus is risen and is Lord of the universe.

Polytheism—The belief, in opposition to Christian doctrine, that there are many gods.

Precepts of the Church—Rules Catholics follow to help them in becoming good and moral people. They include attending Mass on Sundays, confessing your sins at least once a year, receiving communion during the Easter season, keeping the holy days of obligation, and observing days of fasting and abstinence.

prejudice—An unsubstantiated or preformed judgment about an individual or group.

Protestant Reformation—An effort to reform the Catholic Church in the sixteenth century that led to the separation of large numbers of Christians from the communion with Rome and with each other.

providence—God's leading and guiding us to our final end, Salvation and union with him.

Purgatory—Purification after death for those who die in God's friendship but still need to be purified because of past sins before entering Heaven. It is also called "the Church suffering."

Racism—One of the most hateful forms of prejudice; the belief that one race is superior to another.

RCIA—Acronym for Rite of Christian Initiation for Adults. The process by which anyone of catechetical age is initiated into the Catholic Church.

Resurrection—Three days after Jesus was buried in a tomb, he rose from the dead. Belief in the Resurrection is central to our Christian faith.

Rite of Acceptance—A celebration marking the beginning of the catechumenate where the unbaptized inquirers publicly declare to the Church their intentions to continue their faith journey.

Sacrament of Holy Orders—A Sacrament of vocation in which the Church ordains baptized men to the orders of deacon, priest, and bishop.

Sacrament of Matrimony (Marriage)—A Sacrament of vocation administered by the couple themselves. It is based on the mutual consent of the man and woman to give themselves to one another until death.

Sacrament of Reconciliation—Another term for the Sacrament of Penance in which Christ extends his forgiveness to sinners through the absolution conferred by a priest.

Sacrament of Penance—The name for the sacrament that allows a sinner to return to communion with Christ and the Church.

sacraments—Outward and effective signs given by Christ to give grace. The Seven Sacraments are Baptism, Confirmation, Eucharist, Penance, Anointing of the Sick, Matrimony, and Holy Orders.

Sacred Scripture—The inspired Word of God; the written record of God's Revelation.

Sacred Tradition—The living transmission of the Church's Gospel message found in the Church's teaching, life, and worship. It is faithfully preserved, handed on, and interpreted by the Church's Magisterium.

Salvation—The extension of God's forgiveness, grace, and healing to the world through Jesus Christ in the Holy Spirit.

Salvific Trinity or Economic Trinity—The active and inseparable work of the Triune God—Father, Son—and Holy Spirit—in Salvation History.

sanctifying grace—The grace, or gift of God's friendship, that heals fallen human nature and gives us a share in the divine life of the Blessed Trinity. A habitual, supernatural gift, it makes us perfect, holy, and Christ-like (*CCC*, 1999).

schism—A break in Church unity that takes place when a group of Christians separates itself from the Church. This happens historically when the group breaks in union with the Pope, for example, when the Eastern Orthodox Church broke from the Roman Catholic Church in 1054.

self-esteem—A way to describe the value we place on ourselves.

Sign of the Cross—A clear profession of faith in the Blessed Trinity: "In the name of the Father and of the Son and of the Holy Spirit." The Sign of the Cross is a formula that begins many Catholic prayers and worship.

Social Justice—The Church's teaching on the way the Gospel and Tradition are applicable in our society. Includes basic life and death rights. It also involves rights of everyday living like the rights of workers to a fair wage, the rights of people to food and shelter, the rights of people not to be discriminated against on the basis of race, and the rights of all people to worship God.

Son of God—A title that refers to Jesus. He is the unique Son of God the Father, the Second Person of the Holy Trinity. Jesus Christ is the natural son of the Father who shares God's very nature.

Soul—The innermost or spiritual part of a person. The soul is eternal.

sponsor—A guide to the Confirmation candidate who brings the candidate to receive the sacrament, presents him to the bishop for anointing, and will later help fulfill his or her baptismal promises faithfully under the influence of the Holy Spirit.

Stewards—Those who properly use the gifts that God has given to them, in particular the care for creation that will allow the earth and its resources to flourish and be long lasting.

Synoptic Gospels—The Gospels of Matthew, Mark, and Luke. They are so much alike that it appears they were created with "one-eye," which is the meaning of the word *synoptic* in Greek.

Temperance—The cardinal virtue that helps to control our appetites, especially in the areas of food, drink, sex, and possessions.

Ten Commandments—A source of Christian morality. God revealed them to Moses. The first three commandments have to do with love for God. The last seven refer to love for neighbor.

theological virtues—Three important virtues bestowed on us at Baptism that relate us to God: faith, or belief in and personal knowledge of God; hope, or trust in God's Salvation and his bestowal of the graces needed to attain it; and charity, or love of God and love of neighbor as one loves oneself.

transfiguration—An occasion when Jesus revealed his divine glory before Peter, James, and John on a high mountain, where his face "shone like the sun and his clothes became white as light" (Mt 17:2).

transubstantiation—What happens at the consecration of the bread and wine at Mass, when their entire substance is turned into the substance of the Body and Blood of Christ, even though the appearances of bread and wine remain. The Eucharistic presence of Christ begins at the moment of consecration and endures as long as the Eucharistic species subsist.

venial sin—A sin that weakens and wounds our relationship with God but does not destroy divine life in our souls.

Vices—Bad habits linked to capital sins (pride, covetousness, envy, anger, gluttony, lust, and sloth).

Virtues—Good habits that help us to live a moral life.

Vocation—The calling or destiny we have in this life and in the hereafter.

Works of Mercy—Charitable actions that remind us how to come to the aid of a neighbor and his or her bodily and spiritual necessities.

YHWH—The name for God used in the Old Testament. It means "I am who I am."

IN THE
SACRAMENT OF CONFIRMATION

_____

NAME

received the Gift of the Holy Spirit and will send out the Spirit to the world

on this _____ day of _____

in the year _____ .

_____

Parish

_____

Bishop

_____

Pastor

_____

Sponsor